STUDY GUIDE WITH READINGS TO ACCOMPANY PAPALIA/OLDS

A Child's World

INFANCY THROUGH ADOLESCENCE

SEVENTH EDITION

Ruth Duskin Feldman

THE McGRAW-HILL COMPANIES, INC.

NEW YORK   ST. LOUIS   SAN FRANCISCO   AUCKLAND   BOGOTÁ   CARACAS
LISBON   LONDON   MADRID   MEXICO CITY   MILAN   MONTREAL   NEW DELHI   SAN JUAN
SINGAPORE   SYDNEY   TOKYO   TORONTO

McGraw-Hill

A Division of The McGraw·Hill Companies

Study Guide with Readings to Accompany Papalia/Olds
A Child's World INFANCY THROUGH ADOLESCENCE

1 2 3 4 5 6 7 8 9 0   SEM SEM 9 0 9 8 7 6 5

ISBN 0-07-048769-3

This book was designed and set by Steven J. Feldman.
The editors were Beth Kaufman and David Damstra;
the production supervisor was Paula Keller.
Quebecor-Semline was printer and binder.

Acknowledgments Chapter 1 "Becoming Human" by Nancy Maries Brown. Reprinted with permission from the Penn State magazine *Health & Human Development Research*. Chapter 2 "Genetic Testing: Kids' Latest Rite of Passage" by Terence Monmaney. Reprinted from *Health,* © 1995.   Chapter 3 "Partners in Pregnancy" by Trisha Thompson. First appeared in the June/July 1992 issue of *Child* magazine. © 1992 Trisha Thompson. Chapter 4 Excerpts from *The Blue Jay's Dance* by Louise Erdrich. Copyright © 1995 by Louise Erdrich. Reprinted by permission of HarperCollins Publishers, Inc. Chapter 5 Excerpt from *Diary of a Baby* by Daniel N. Stern. Copyright © 1990 by Daniel N. Stern, M.D. Reprinted by permission of BasicBooks, a division of HarperCollins Publishers, Inc. Chapter 6 "Read Me a Story" by James Trelease, author of *Read-Aloud Handbook* (Penguin, 1995). Chapter 7 "Are the Two's So Terrible?" by Rita Rooney. Reprinted with permission from the Penn State magazine *Health & Human Development Research*. Chapter 8 "Why Parents Kill" by J. McCormick with S. Miller and D. Woodruff. From *Newsweek*, 11/14 © 1994, Newsweek, Inc. All rights reserved. Reprinted by permission. Chapter 9 "Charles" by Shirley Jackson. "Charles" from *The Lottery* by Shirley Jackson. Copyright © 1948, 1949 by Shirley Jackson. Copyright renewed 1976, 1977 by Laurence Hyman, Barry Hyman, Mrs. Sarah Webster, and Mrs. Joanne Schnurer. Reprinted by permission of Farrar, Straus and Giroux, Inc. Chapter 10 "Getting Out of the Way" by Naomi Aldort. Copyright © 1994 Naomi Aldort. For reprint permission write to N. Aldort, Eastsound, WA, 98248-1719. Originally printed in *Mothering*, Sub. $18.95 (505) 984-8116. Chapter 11 Excerpt from *Reading Between the Lips* by Lew Golan. Reprinted with permission from *Reading Between the Lips* by Lew Golan, published in 1995 by Bonus Books, Inc., 160 East Illinois Street, Chicago, IL 60611. Chapter 12 "On Teaching for Understanding: A Conversation with Howard Gardner" by Ron Brandt. Reprinted with permission of the Association for Supervision and Curriculum Development. Copyright © 1993 by ASCD. All rights reserved. Chapter 13 "The Legacy of Rejection" by Don Oldenburg. © 1993 The Washington Post. Reprinted with Permission. Chapter 14 "Suicide & Intolerance" by Judith Maloney. Reprinted with permission from Penn State magazine *Health & Human Development Research*. Chapter 15 "Becoming Navajo" by Roland A. Lee. *Native Peoples Magazine*, Summer 1989 issue. Chapter 16 Excerpt from *I Know Why the Caged Bird Sings* by Maya Angelou. Copyright © 1969 Maya Angelou Reprinted by permission of Random House, Inc.

CONTENTS

LIST OF READINGS

PREFACE:
TO THE STUDENT

This *Study Guide with Readings* has been designed to help you get the most out of *A Child's World*, Seventh Edition, by Diane E. Papalia and Sally Wendkos Olds. It is not intended as a a substitute for *A Child's World*; rather, it is just what its title implies—a guide to help you absorb and interpret the material in the text. Although some of the material in your textbook will be familiar to you (since you once inhabited the world of childhood), much of it will be new; and you must now see all of it from a new perspective, as an adult and a student of child development. Using this Study Guide will increase your understanding of the material and improve your ability to remember it, to apply it, and to build on it throughout this course, in related courses, and in your own life.

The Study Guide will help you to:

- Organize and focus your learning

- Check your mastery of the material in the text

- Practice dealing with typical examination formats

- Think analytically about the subject matter

- Broaden your perspective on child development

How the Study Guide Is Organized

The Study Guide's sixteen chapters correspond to Chapters 1 to 16 of *A Child's World*. Each chapter of the Study Guide begins with a brief "Overview" of the text chapter and has the following five major parts:

> Chapter Review
> Chapter Quiz
> Topics for Thought and Discussion
> Chapter Reading
> Answer Key

Let's take a look at each of these, to give you an understanding of how the Study Guide works and how you'll be using it.

CHAPTER REVIEW

The Chapter Review is a way to organize and focus your learning. It will help you identify and reexamine important material in the text chapter and also help you decide which material will need further study.

The Review is divided into sections that correspond to the major headings in the text chapter. This format lets you break your study into manageable "chunks" and makes it easier for you to locate information in the text, check answers, and concentrate on areas where you need to do more work.

Typically, each section of the Review has three elements: Framework, Important Terms, and Learning Objectives.

Framework: The Framework is an outline of all the subheadings in the text section. (When there are no subheadings within a section, this element is omitted.) The Framework shows you the section at a glance and indicates the relationship among different topics taken up in the section. You might think of it as a road map. You can use it to preview the section; you should refer to it frequently as you read, to get your bearings;

and later, you can use it to remind yourself where you have been.

You can also use the Framework to guide your reading by using the "questioning" approach. You'll notice that some of the text headings are in the form of questions; others can be rephrased as questions, which you can keep in mind as you read. For example, in Chapter 1, you'll find the heading, "Influences on Children's Development." You might ask yourself, "What are the influences on children's development? When do these influences occur?" If you can give a tentative answer, jot it down. Then, when you find the answer in the text, check to see if you were on the right track.

Important Terms: Important Terms is a fill-in-the-blanks exercise which covers all the "key terms" in the text section. It checks your knowledge of terms and meanings; it gives you practice with completion-type test items; and, when you have filled it in, it will serve as a glossary for the section, to be used for reference and review. (For text sections without key terms, the Important Terms exercise is omitted.)

Can you fill in the blanks without referring to the text? If you do need to consult the text, can you go directly to the passage you need? If you must turn to the text often, or if you have trouble finding the information you want, you'll know that you need additional study.

Check your work against the Answer Key. Your wrong answers will let you know where more work is needed.

Learning Objectives: The Learning Objectives are a list of tasks you should be able to accomplish when you have studied the section. To check your understanding of the text material, see if you can accomplish each objective without recourse to the text. If you need to look at the text, note how readily you can locate the necessary information.

You can use the space provided below each objective to make brief notes. But the Learning Objectives can also serve another purpose, since they resemble essay-type test items. Writing out complete, formal answers to some or all of them—on separate paper—will give you needed practice in the essay format.

The Answer Key provides text page references for the Learning Objectives, but it's up to you to write the actual answers.

CHAPTER QUIZ

The Chapter Quiz will check your mastery of the text material. It also gives you practice with three types of questions often found on tests:

> Matching
> Multiple choice
> True-or-false

Take the quiz when you are reasonably confident about your mastery of the entire chapter. This is a closed-book test. Put the textbook away—far away, if you are easily tempted—and allow about as much time to take the quiz as you would have for a classroom examination.

As you take the quiz, pay attention to your "comfort level." Are you uncertain or uneasy about many items? Do you find that you must skip many items? Do you find that you are often just guessing? If so, stop and review the text again.

If your comfort level is high—that is, if you're confident about most of the questions—complete the quiz and then check the Answer Key. You should not be satisfied unless you've gotten almost all the answers right. Remember that this quiz is easier than an actual classroom examination because you take it when you decide you're ready, you are not under so much tension, and you can pace yourself. If you miss more than a few (very few) questions, restudy the material.

TOPICS FOR THOUGHT AND DISCUSSION

The Topics for Thought and Discussion are designed to help you think analytically about the subject matter. They call not only on your grasp of the material in the text but also on your ability to interpret it and apply it. Therefore, you should

work on them only after you are satisfied with your performance on the Review and the Quiz.

These questions are like essay items on examinations, topics for writing assignments, and topics presented for group or class discussions. They are open-ended and thus do not have definite "right" or "wrong" answers. But this does not mean that all answers are equally good. The value of your answers depends on how clearly and logically you make and support your points.

The material in your textbook should give you *ideas*. If you are without ideas when you consider any of the Topics for Thought and Discussion, then you are not getting all you should from the text. But, equally important, your ideas must be supported by *facts*. If you have ideas but cannot state facts to back them up, you have not really mastered the material.

To help yourself think through these questions, sketch out your answers in written form. Your sketch need not be a full, formal answer but it *should* always include your main point or points and specific supporting details. Do not be discouraged if you have to refer back to the text. Many of these questions are quite challenging and require careful consideration, not quick recall.

For practice in dealing with essay examinations—and to improve your writing in general—develop as many of your sketches as possible into full, formal, polished answers. Examine your answers carefully. Have you stated your point clearly and organized your supporting material logically? Have you expressed yourself grammatically?

You'll also find the Topics for Thought and Discussion useful for group study, and as ideas for writing assignments when you can choose your own topic.

CHAPTER READING

The Chapter Readings have been chosen to help you broaden your perspective on child development. Each reading selection supplements an important subject treated in the text chapter. A few of the selections are classics; most are recent. They have been taken from newspapers, journals, magazines, and books—autobiography, fiction, and nonfiction. They may provide additional information, present different viewpoints, demonstrate practical applications of principles or theories, report on new research, or humanize an issue. They represent a sampling of the rich material you can encounter by reading widely, and they should challenge you to read carefully and critically.

A brief Introduction sets the scene for each selection by providing background information about the author, the subject, or both.

Each selection is followed by Questions About the Reading. Like the Topics for Thought and Discussion, these questions resemble essay items on examinations, issues for group discussions, and subjects for written assignments. You should sketch out written answers—always being sure to state your point and back it up with specific evidence drawn from the selection, from your textbook, and from your own experience. Then, write complete, formal answers for some or all of the questions, to sharpen your writing skills.

ANSWER KEY

The Answer Key for each chapter gives answers, with text page references, for the Important Terms exercise and for the entire Chapter Quiz. It also gives text page references for the Learning Objectives.

Use the Answer Key wisely, to check your work. Don't use it as a crutch; don't "peek" when you should be testing your recall. If you misuse the answers, you'll be cheating no one but yourself.

Before You Begin: Learning Aids in Your Textbook

The Seventh Edition of *A Child's World* itself contains several important study aids. You should take advantage of these features as you read each chapter of the text.

Chapter Contents: On the opening page of each chapter you'll see a listing of major headings. This is your first view of the chapter; take a few minutes to examine it, asking yourself, "What topics does this chapter cover, and how are they organized?"

Preview Questions: Following a brief overview, you will find some questions designed to direct your attention to significant material covered in the chapter. A good way to make use of this learning aid is to check off each Preview Question as you find the answer in the text, making a brief note of the answer and the page where it appears. When you've finished the chapter, turn back to the Preview Questions. Can you answer each one fully without referring to the text?

Key Terms: In each chapter, the authors identify certain "key terms." These are printed in *bold italic* in the running text, defined in the margins, and then listed at the end of the chapter (in order of their appearance in the text, with page references). Whenever you encounter a key term, stop and read its definition. Is the definition clear to you? (If not, reread the explanation in the text.) Can you think of a specific example? When you've finished a chapter, use the list at the end to review the vocabulary and check your mastery of it.

Boxes: The boxes (which are listed in the chapter contents) illuminate many topics covered in the text. Read them as carefully as the text itself and ask yourself questions about them: "How does this box relate to the subject matter in the text?" "Why was this topic chosen for highlighting?" If a box takes up a controversial issue, what is your opinion?

Tables and Illustrations: Pay close attention to tables, figures, and photographs. They illustrate, summarize, or crystallize material in the text, making it easier to understand and remember.

"What do you think?" Inserts: These thought-provoking questions following some sections of the text are meant to stimulate your thinking about controversial issues and to help you see the relevance of theory and research to real life situations and problems.

Summary: The summary at the end of each chapter, in the form of a numbered list, gives a quick review of the main points and is a good way for you to check your learning when you've completed the chapter. Is each of the numbered items familiar to you? Can you expand on each?

Suggested Readings: Also at the end of each chapter is a list of recommended readings. These interesting, informative books can be used for research or writing assignments, or simply to learn more about topics introduced in the chapter.

Glossary: The glossary at the end of the book brings together all the key terms from every chapter, in alphabetical order, with their definitions and with page references to the text. It is useful for reference and review.

Bibliography: You may not have thought of the bibliography as a study aid, but it can be: it is an excellent guide to books and articles for further research.

People who teach and write about study skills will tell you that a crucial part of learning effectively is being an "active reader"—being alert, perceptive, and involved as you read. You'll find that using these special features in *A Child's World* will help you become an active reader and thus a more efficient learner.

Acknowledgments

The author would like to thank her daughters, Laurie Feldman and Heidi Feldman, who contributed their considerable skills as teachers and writers and their insights and experience as adult learners in drafting sections of this Study Guide, and her son, Steven J. Feldman, who designed and typeset this revised edition. Special appreciation goes to the editor, Beth Kaufman, who kept production on track; to Katrina Redmond, who obtained permission for use of the readings; and to Susan Gamer, editor of the first edition, who helped develop the format.

Ruth Duskin Feldman

About the Author of This Study Guide...

Ruth Duskin Feldman received her bachelor's degree from Northwestern University, where she graduated with highest distinction and was elected to Phi Beta Kappa. A former teacher, she has developed educational materials for all levels from elementary school through college. She is the award-winning author of two books and a coauthor of several others—including the Fourth Edition of Diane E. Papalia and Sally Wendkos Olds's widely used textbook Human Development *and, with Diane E. Papalia and Cameron Camp, the forthcoming textbook* Adult Development and Aging. *She prepared the test banks to accompany the Fifth Edition of* Human Development *and the Sixth Edition of* A Child's World.

A CHILD'S WORLD: THEORIES, ISSUES, AND METHODS FOR STUDYING IT

OVERVIEW

Chapter 1 introduces you to the study of child development. In this chapter, the authors:

• Define child development and explain why its study is important

• Outline the periods into which the text divides childhood and the aspects of development to be studied for each period

• Point out several types of influences on how children develop and the contextual levels within which influences occur

• Discuss several important theoretical perspectives from which child development has been viewed

• Describe the major types of methods for studying child development and discuss advantages and disadvantages of each

• Discuss ethical issues regarding research on children

CHAPTER 1 REVIEW

Section I A Child's World: Concepts and Issues

FRAMEWORK FOR SECTION I

A.   What Is Development, and Why Should We Study It?
B.   The Whole Child: Aspects of Development
C.   Periods of Childhood
D.   Influences on Children's Development
E.   Contexts of Development
    1.   An Ecological Approach

IMPORTANT TERMS FOR SECTION I

Completion: Fill in the blanks to complete the definitions of key terms for this section of Chapter 1.

1.   **development:** Change and _____ over time.

2.   **child development:** Scientific study of changes and _____ throughout childhood.

3.   _____ **change:** Change in amount, such as in height, weight, or size of vocabulary.

4.   _____ **change:** Change in kind, as in the nature of intelligence.

5.   **physical development:** Changes over time in body, brain, sensory capacity, and _____ skills.

6.   _____ **development:** Changes over time in mental abilities, activities, and organization.

7.   _____ **development:** Changes in a person's unique style of behaving, feeling, and reacting.

8.   **cohort:** People _____ at the same time and in the same place.

9.   _____ **approach:** Bronfenbrenner's system of understanding development, which identifies five levels of environmental influence, from intimate to global.

LEARNING OBJECTIVES FOR SECTION I

After reading and reviewing this section of Chapter 1, you should be able to do the following. (Note: Here and throughout this study guide, when you are asked to give examples, try to think of examples other than those given in the text.)

1.   Explain the difference between quantitative and qualitative change and give at least one example of each.

2.   Identify four goals of child development as a scientific discipline.

3.   Distinguish the three aspects of development and give an example of how each interacts with one of the other two.

4.   List the five periods into which your text divides childhood and identify the approximate age range and major developments of each.

5. Identify three types of noninherited influences on children's development, and give an example of each.

6. Identify five levels of environmental influence that, according to Bronfenbrenner, provide the context for understanding development.

Section II A Child's World: Perspectives on Child Development

FRAMEWORK FOR SECTION II

A. Early Approaches
B. Today's Approaches
  1. Psychoanalytic Perspective
    a. Sigmund Freud: Psychosexual Theory
      (1) Stages of Psychosexual Development
      (2) Id, Ego, and Superego
      (3) Defense Mechanisms
    b. Erik Erikson: Psychosocial Theory
      (1) Erikson's Approach
      (2) Erikson's Eight Crises of Personality Development
    c. Jean Baker Miller: Relational Theory
    d. Evaluation of Psychoanalytic Perspective

  2. Learning Perspective: Behaviorism and Social-Learning (Social-Cognitive) Theory
    a. Behaviorism
      (1) Classical Conditioning
      (2) Operant Conditioning
      (3) Reinforcement and Punishment
      (4) Shaping New Responses
    b. Social-Learning (Social-Cognitive) Theory
    c. Evaluation of Learning Perspective
  3. Cognitive Perspective
    a. The Cognitive-Stage Theory of Jean Piaget
      (1) Cognitive Structures
      (2) Principles of Cognitive Development
    b. Evaluation of Piaget's Theory
    c. Information-Processing Approach
  4. Ethological Perspective
    a. Evaluation of Ethological Perspective
  5. Contextual Perspective: Vygotsky's Sociocultural Theory
    a. Evaluation of Contextual Perspective

IMPORTANT TERMS FOR SECTION II

Completion: Fill in the blanks to complete the definitions of key terms for this section of Chapter 1.

1. **theory:** Set of related statements about data, designed to integrate the data, _____ behavior, and predict behavior.

2. **data:** Information obtained through _____.

3. **hypothesis:** Possible _____ for an observation; used to predict the outcome of an experiment.

4. _____ **perspective:** View of humanity that is concerned with the unconscious forces motivating behavior.

5. **psychosexual development:** In Freudian theory, the different stages of development in which _____ shifts from one body zone to another.

6. **psychosocial development:** _____'s theory of personality development through the life span, stressing societal and cultural influences on the ego at eight stages.

7. _____: School of psychology that emphasizes the study of observable behaviors and events and the role of the environment in causing behavior.

8. **classical conditioning:** _____ in which a previously neutral stimulus (conditioned stimulus) acquires the power to elicit a response (conditioned response) by association with an unconditioned stimulus that ordinarily elicits a particular response (unconditioned response).

9. **operant conditioning:** Learning in which a response continues to be made because it has been reinforced; also called _____ *conditioning.*

10. **reinforcement:** Stimulus that follows a response and _____ the likelihood that the response will be repeated.

11. **punishment:** Stimulus that follows a behavior and _____ the likelihood that the behavior will be repeated.

12. **social-learning theory:** Theory proposed by Bandura that behaviors are learned by observing and imitating _____. Also called *social-cognitive theory.*

13. _____ **learning:** Learning by watching others.

14. **cognitive perspective:** View of humanity that sees people as active, not reactive, and emphasizes _____ , rather than _____ , change.

15. **cognitive development:** Changes in mental powers and qualities that permit _____.

16. **scheme:** In _____'s terminology, the basic cognitive unit; an organized pattern of _____ generally named after the _____ involved.

17. **organization:** In _____'s terminology, the tendency to create _____ that bring together all of a person's knowledge of the environment.

18. **adaptation:** In _____'s terminology, the _____ processes of assimilation and accommodation.

19. **assimilation:** In _____'s terminology, the incorporation of a new object, experience, or concept into existing _____ structures.

20. **accommodation:** In _____'s terminology, changes in existing _____ structures to include new _____.

21. **equilibration:** In _____'s terminology, striving for _____ balance.

22. **information-processing approach:** Method based on analyzing the _____ processes underlying intelligent behavior.

23. **ethological perspective:** Scientific view that focuses on the biological and _____ basis of behavior.

24. **contextual perspective:** View of humanity that sees the person as developing in a _____ context.

25. **sociocultural theory:** _____'s theory, which analyzes how specific cultural practices affect development.

26. **zone of _____ development (_____):** Vygotsky's term for the level at which children can almost perform a task on their own and, with appropriate teaching, can perform it.

27. **scaffolding:** _____ support given to a child who is mastering a task.

LEARNING OBJECTIVES FOR SECTION II

After reading and reviewing this section of Chapter 1, you should be able to do the following. (Remember: When you are asked to give examples, try to think of examples other than those given in the text.)

1. Briefly describe five trends that led to the scientific study of child development.

2. Identify five major perspectives on child development and their main distinguishing features.

3. Name the five stages of psychosexual development, according to Freud's theory, and identify the approximate age range and chief characteristics of each stage.

4. Name the three major components of personality according to Freud's theory, and explain each term in your own words.

5. Define and give examples of five common defense mechanisms, according to Freud's theory.

6. Explain how Erikson's theory of psychosocial development modifies and expands upon Freud's psychosexual theory, particularly with regard to the development of the ego.

7. Explain what Erikson meant by a crisis in personality, and discuss the implications of the way in which the crisis at each stage of development is resolved.

8. Summarize the main differences between male and female development, according to Miller's relational theory.

9. Briefly evaluate Freud's, Erikson's and Miller's theories.

10. State two basic assumptions of the learning perspective.

11. Name the two major theories that take the learning perspective, and explain the similarities and differences between them.

12. Name and describe the two types of conditioning and give at least one example of each.

13. Explain the difference between negative reinforcement and punishment.

14. Describe how shaping can be used in behavior modification and give an example.

15. Briefly evaluate behaviorism and social learning theory.

16. State two basic assumptions of the cognitive perspective.

17. Explain the processes by which cognitive growth occurs, according to Piaget's theory, and summarize Piaget's stages of cognitive development.

18. Briefly evaluate Piaget's cognitive-stage theory.

19. State the basic assumptions, goals, and methods that distinguish the information-processing approach.

20. State the basic assumptions, goals, and methods that distinguish the ethological perspective, and discuss the relationship between imprinting and attachment.

21. State the basic assumptions, goals, and methods that distinguish Vygotsky's sociocultural theory and discuss its relevance to teaching and learning.

Section III A Child's World: How We Discover It

FRAMEWORK FOR SECTION III

A. Methods for Studying Child Development
   1. Nonexperimental Methods
      a. Case Studies
      b. Observation
         (1) Naturalistic Observation
         (2) Laboratory Observation
      c. Interviews and Questionnaires
      d. Clinical Method
   2. Experimental Methods
      a. Variables and Groups
      b. Sampling and Assignment
         (1) Selecting the Sample
         (2) Assigning Subjects
      c. Types of Experiments
      d. How the Types of Experiments Differ
   3. Comparing Experimental and Nonexperimental Methods
   4. Developmental Data-Collection Techniques
      a. Longitudinal Studies
      b. Cross-Sectional Studies
      c. Comparing Longitudinal and Cross-Sectional Studies
      d. Sequential Strategies
B. Ethics of Research
   1. Rights of Participants
      a. Right to Privacy
      b. Right to Informed Consent
      c. Right to Self-Esteem
   2. Social Decisions

IMPORTANT TERMS FOR SECTION III

Completion: Fill in the blanks to complete the definitions of key terms for this section of Chapter 1.

1. **scientific method:** System of established principles of scientific inquiry involving the systematic and _____ study of development.

2. **correlation:** _____ relationship between variables.

3. **case studies:** Studies of a single case, or individual _____.

4. _____**observation:** Research method in which behavior is studied in natural settings, with no attempt to manipulate behavior.

5. _____ **observation:** Research method in which people are observed in a controlled setting with no attempt to manipulate behavior.

6. _____: Research technique in which people are asked, either face to face or on the telephone, to state their attitudes, opinions, or histories.

7. _____: Research technique in which people are asked to fill out a form that explores their attitudes, opinions, or behaviors.

8. **clinical method:** Type of nonexperimental research method developed by Piaget that combines observation with careful, individualized _____.

9. **experiment:** Highly controlled, _____ (repeatable) procedure in which a researcher assesses the effect of manipulating variables; provides information about cause and effect.

10. _____ **variable:** In an experiment, the variable that is directly controlled and manipulated by the experimenter.

11. _____ **variable:** In an experiment, the variable that may or may not change as a result of changes in the _____ variable.

12. **experimental group:** In an experiment, people who receive the treatment under study; changes in these people are compared with changes in a(n) _____ group.

13. _____ **group:** In an experiment, people who are similar to people in the experimental group but who do not receive the treatment whose effects are to be measured; the results obtained with this group are compared with the results

obtained with the experimental group to assess _____.

14. **sample:** In an experiment, a group of people chosen to _____ the total population.

15. **random sample:** Sampling technique in which each member of the _____ has an equal chance of being selected for study.

16. _____**study:** Research that follows the same person or people over a period of time.

17. _____ **study:** Research that assesses different people of different ages at the same time.

LEARNING OBJECTIVES FOR SECTION III

After reading and reviewing this section of Chapter 1, you should be able to do the following. (Remember: When you are asked to give examples, try to think of examples other than those given in the text.)

1. Name five nonexperimental methods of studying child development, give at least one example for the use of each method, and state at least one advantage and disadvantage of each.

2. Explain the uses and limitations of correlational studies, and give examples of positive and negative correlations.

3. Explain how and why experimenters select a random sample.

6. Compare advantages and disadvantages of experimental and nonexperimental methods.

4. Explain and compare two ways of assigning subjects of an experiment to experimental and control groups.

7. Name and describe three techniques of data collection, give at least one example of the use of each technique, and briefly discuss advantages and disadvantages of each.

5. Name three types of experiments, give at least one example of each, and state the two major ways they differ from each other.

8. Explain three important ethical concerns about the rights of participants in research on child development.

CHAPTER 1 QUIZ

Matching—Who's Who: Match each person at the left with the appropriate description on the right.

1. Albert Bandura ___
2. Sigmund Freud ___
3. Erik Erikson ___
4. Urie Bronfenbrenner ___
5. Ivan Pavlov ___
6. John B. Watson ___
7. G. Stanley Hall ___
8. Jean Piaget ___
9. B. F. Skinner ___
10. Mary Ainsworth ___
11. Konrad Lorenz ___
12. Jean Baker Miller ___
13. Lem Semenovich Vygotsky ___
14. Bärbel Inhelder ___

a. American psychologist who formulated basic principles of operant conditioning

b. psychologist who expanded on Freud's theory to emphasize the role of society in personality development

c. Russian physiologist who studied classical conditioning

d. leading advocate of social-learning theory

e. originator of ecological approach for understanding influences on development

f. first psychologist to formulate a theory of adolescence

g. originator of the "strange situation" for studying attachment

h. Swiss scholar, famous for his observations of children and his theory of cognitive stages of development

i. originator of psychoanalytic perspective

j. behavioral psychologist who applied stimulus-response theories of learning to child development

k. ethologist who studied imprinting

l. Russian psychologist who originated contextual perspective

m. psychiatrist who proposed a theory emphasizing development within relationships

n. child psychologist who collaborated with Piaget

Multiple-Choice: Circle the choice that best completes or answers each item.

1. Qualitative change involves change in
   a. amount
   b. kind
   c. both amount and kind
   d. either amount or kind, depending on the specific situation

2. The goals of child development as a discipline include *all but which* of the following?
   a. description
   b. explanation
   c. prediction
   d. compensation

3. The prenatal stage is defined as lasting until
   a. the pregnant woman "feels life"
   b. the fetus's basic body structures and organs are formed
   c. the fetus's brain develops
   d. birth

4. Which of the following is an example of an influence on development that affects a particular cohort?
   a. puberty
   b. a disabling accident
   c. the end of the Cold War
   d. retirement

5. In Bronfenbrenner's terminology, the interlocking systems that contain the developing person compose the
    a. microsystem
    b. mesosystem
    c. exosystem
    d. macrosystem

6. Culture appears to exert a strong influence on
    a. the age at which babies learn to walk
    b. the sequence of learning to talk
    c. sentence structure
    d. none of the above

7. Apparently, professional involvement in children's lives began
    a. in the sixteenth century with books of advice on child rearing
    b. in the nineteenth century with the passage of child labor laws
    c. in 1904, when G. Stanley Hall published *Adolescence*
    d. as a result of Freud's development of the psychoanalytic perspective

8. According to Freud's theory, the chief source of pleasure during the phallic period is the
    a. mouth
    b. anus
    c. genitals
    d. superego

9. In Freud's theory, the id is
    a. present at birth
    b. not developed until infants recognize that they are separate beings
    c. replaced by the ego when infants recognize that they are separate beings
    d. a source of gratification

10. Which of the following is *not* a Freudian defense mechanism?
    a. regression
    b. repression
    c. reinforcement
    d. reaction formation

11. In Erikson's theory, the "virtue" developed during infancy is
    a. trust
    b. hope
    c. attachment
    d. obedience

12. Which theorists have been criticized as having an antifemale bias?
    a. Freud and Erikson
    b. Erikson and Miller
    c. Freud and Miller
    d. Freud, Erikson, and Miller

13. The learning perspective includes
    a. cognitive-stage theory
    b. sociocultural theory
    c. behaviorism
    d. information-processing approach

14. Which of the following is an example of classical conditioning?
    a. Vicky is so used to having her picture taken with a flashbulb that she no longer blinks at the flash.
    b. Pavlov's dogs salivate when given food.
    c. Jason will suck on a nipple more if it activates a recording of his mother's voice than if it activates a recording of a strange voice.
    d. "Little Albert" learns to pat furry objects.

15. In operant conditioning, negative reinforcement is
    a. withdrawal of a privilege
    b. withdrawal of an aversive event
    c. another term for punishment
    d. generally ineffective

16. Social-learning theory is an outgrowth of
    a. behaviorism
    b. the contextual perspective
    c. sociocultural theory
    d. the ecological approach

17. Learning theories stress
    a. cognitive stages
    b. developmental changes
    c. hereditary influences
    d. environmental influences

18. The term *scheme* is associated with
    a. Freud
    b. Erikson
    c. Piaget
    d. Lorenz

19. Imprinting results from
    a. a predisposition toward learning during a critical period
    b. placing an infant in the "strange situation"
    c. an adult's directing and organizing a child's learning
    d. a child's mental manipulation of incoming sensory information

20. Vicky, age 8, has almost mastered the multiplication tables but is having trouble with some combinations. According to Vygotsky's theory, her parents should:
    a. insist on daily practice, and test her until she gets a perfect score
    b. leave her alone, since she will learn on her own when she is ready
    c. give plenty of praise to build her self-esteem
    d. give hints and ask leading questions to help her get the answers she can't get by herself

21. Which of the following can be used to establish a causal relationship?
    a. case study
    b. laboratory observation
    c. experiment
    d. any of the above

22. A correlation describes
    a. cause and effect
    b. direction and magnitude of a relationship between variables
    c. practical implications of a relationship between variables
    d. which variable in an experiment is dependent and which is independent

23. Observer bias can be a problem in all but which of the following research methods?
    a. case study
    b. naturalistic observation
    c. laboratory observation
    d. questionnaire

24. Which kind of experiment is used to study environmental effects on identical twins?
    a. laboratory experiment
    b. field experiment
    c. natural experiment
    d. none of the above; experimentation on human beings is unethical

25. The longitudinal, cross-sectional, and cross-sequential methods are ways of
    a. selecting a sample
    b. collecting data
    c. calculating correlations
    d. establishing ethical criteria for research

True or False? In the blank following each item, write T (for *true*) or F (for *false*). In the space below each item, if the statement is false, rewrite it to make it true.

1. Early childhood is the years from 6 to 12.

    ____

2. Cross-cultural research is valuable because the importance of certain influences on children varies in different societies. ____

3. According to Bronfenbrenner's ecological approach, the effect upon a child of the parents' divorce is part of the child's exosystem. ____

4. A theory is information obtained through research. ____

5. A hypothesis is a prediction that can be tested by research. ____

6. In Freud's theory, psychosexual development is a series of stages in which gratification shifts from one part of the body to another. ____

7. In Freud's theory, the superego represents the reality principle. ____

8. Erikson's theory is essentially based on Piaget's. ____

9. According to Erikson, successful resolution of each crisis requires discarding a negative trait entirely in order to acquire the corresponding positive trait. ____

10. According to Miller's theory, healthy personality development primarily involves autonomy and individuation. ____

11. Most of Freud's patients in Vienna were children and adolescents. ___

12. The learning perspective sees change as qualitative. ___

13. Learning theorists see development as occurring in clearly defined stages. ___

14. In classical conditioning, an unconditioned stimulus automatically elicits an unlearned response. ___

15. *Instrumental conditioning* is another term for classical conditioning. ___

16. Reinforcement is a crucial element in classical conditioning. ___

17. According to social-learning theory, children develop abilities through observing and imitating models. ___

18. According to Piaget, cognitive growth results from accommodation and assimilation. ___

19. Information-processing research includes the monitoring of infants' eye movements. ___

20. John Bowlby's convictions about the importance of the mother-baby bond were based on studies of animals and clinically disturbed children. ___

21. Tests based on Vygotsky's concept of the zone of proximal development generally pose problems up to 2 years above a child's current level of actual development. ___

22. The clinical method combines observation with standardized, structured questioning. ___

23. Random sampling is the best way to assign subjects to groups in an experiment. ___

24. The experiments that are most generalizable are those that are the most rigidly controlled. ___

25. According to the principle of the *self-fulfilling prophecy*, a prediction may bring about the hypothesized result. ___

TOPICS FOR THOUGHT AND DISCUSSION

1. The authors of your text say that modification of behavior to promote optimal development is one of the goals of the scientific discipline of child development, and they give an example of a situation in which such treatment may be desirable. On what basis should decisions be made to modify a child's behavior? Can such decisions be called scientific, or are they bound to be subjective? Do you see any ethical issues arising out of such decisions?

2. The authors of your text treat infancy and toddlerhood as one period of development. What reasons, if any, might there be to view them as separate periods?

3. According to the authors, Bronfenbrenner's ecological approach, which identifies five levels of environmental influence on the individual, is helpful in understanding development. Do you agree? Can you think of an example (not given in your text) in which an ecological analysis would be revealing?

4. Cross-cultural research can tell researchers which aspects of development are universal and which are culturally determined. How, specifically, might such information be useful?

5. According to the authors, psychoanalytic theories are hard to test. Why might this be so? Can you suggest methods to assess these theories?

6. According to behaviorists, people of all ages learn in the same way—basically, by classical or operant conditioning. Is the idea that children and adults learn in the same way consistent with your experience, or can you think of aspects or types of learning that seem to be different at different ages?

7. Unlike behaviorism, social-learning theory sees people as playing an active role in their own learning, and it recognizes cognitive influences on behavior. Why, then, is social-learning theory not considered part of the cognitive perspective?

8. Many of Piaget's ideas about cognitive development were based on observations of his own children. Can such personal observations be as scientific as clinical observations, a method Piaget also used? Why or why not?

9. The ethological concept of the mother-baby bond originally was based on findings of animal research. What might a psychoanalytic theorist say about how such bonding comes about? A behaviorist? A social-learning theorist? A cognitive theorist? A contextual theorist?

10. According to your textbook, several important theories, such as those of Freud, Erikson, and Vygotsky, were influenced by their originators' personal experiences or by the historical and cultural milieu in which they lived. Do such influences make such theories less scientific? Is it possible for a scientist studying children to divorce his or her thinking from personal experience? Should scientists try to do so?

11. Of the three types of experiments, the one that is most controlled—laboratory experiments—has the least generalizability to real life. Can you think of ways in which researchers might deal with this problem?

12. The section on ethical considerations of research with children lists three rights of participants: privacy, informed consent, and self-esteem. Is research that cannot be designed without interfering with one or more of these rights ever justified?

CHAPTER 1 READING

INTRODUCTION

Can scientists gain more accurate information about children by studying them in the laboratory or at home? Judith Dunn, whose research methods are described in this article, comes down strongly on the latter side of this argument. One of the subjects she touches on is the variability of the family environment siblings experience—a topic covered in more detail in Chapter 2 of your text. Among Dunn's writings are *The Beginnings of Social Understanding* and *From One Child to Two*. The article is condensed from *Health and Human Development Research*, Volume I, published by Pennsylvania State University in 1990.

BECOMING HUMAN: THE BEGINNINGS OF A CHILD'S SOCIAL UNDERSTANDING

by Nancy Marie Brown

An ordinary day in Cambridge, England: A mother gives in to the incessant demands of her little girl. Her firstborn, a son, watches—as does a visitor, an outsider wielding note pad and tape recorder who will later describe the two children to a lecture hall full of curious scientists as Andy, "a rather sensitive, anxious, concerned little boy of two and a half," and Susie, "only 14 months, a boisterous, extroverted, ebullient, and persistent little girl who rather tyrannized poor Andy."

What happens after Susie's mother capitulates challenges standard theories of how children develop:

"You are a determined little devil," the mother says to Susie, in a warm, affectionate tone.

At this, Andy chimes in sadly, even mournfully, "I'm not a determined little devil."

And his mother turns to him, laughing, and says, "No, you're not! What are you? A poor old boy."

Judith Dunn, the observer of this scene, is professor of human development [at Pennsylvania State University]. The recipient of a 1989 Outstanding Research Achievement Award, she told of Susie and Andy in her award lecture, highlighting three points: First, Andy and Susie show how different children from the same family can be. Second, Andy is interrupting a conversation between his mother and his sister, which proves he has been monitoring the exchange between the two. Third, Andy's remark is a judgment of himself. "Those of you who are developmental psychologists will know that it's all wrong," Dunn said in her lecture, "for a child of two-and-a-half to be saying that kind of thing, to be reflecting on himself and making a comment about what kind of person he is. According to the textbooks, it's not until children are six, seven, or even eight that they should be able to reflect on themselves."

Is Andy exceptional? No, but Dunn's research methods are. She does not bring Andy into the clinic and assign him standardized tasks; she watches him in his natural environment, where he behaves as a family member, a witness and respondent to the exchanges between the other people in his world. "Within this family world of familiar others," she writes, "children . . . are clearly not blinkered. They monitor with interest the relations between others, comment on and intervene in the interactions of others, cooperate with others in conflict against a third, and are able to use one family member against another."

It is as a member of the family that a child develops what Dunn calls "social knowledge," the understanding that "other people have feelings and minds like his or her own, yet also different." Social knowledge, Dunn believes, is "the crucial development of becoming human."

In 1963, while beginning to study animal behavior at Cambridge University, Dunn gave birth to a daughter. Eighteen months later, she had twin boys. The twins, especially, intrigued her: "They were so different, one from the other," she remembers, "and I knew I behaved so differently to each of them." When the children went off to nursery school, Dunn returned to Cambridge for her Ph.D., becoming involved in a study of 80 mothers and children from pregnancy to birth and through five years. Two-thirds of the children were not their mothers' firstborn. "All sorts of interesting things happened between the baby and the older sibling—things which weren't supposed to happen at all," Dunn remembers: unexpected because no one had ever done a scientific study of siblings.

After 47 articles and five books, Dunn left England to become a professor at Penn State in 1986; her experience had taught her "to study kids in situations that are important to them," which meant she must become a neighbor—a rigorous, systematic, and scientific neighbor—whose regular visits caused a little excitement but no great disruption of family life.

She is now such a neighbor to 50 Pennsylvania second-born children from 33 months to four years old, investigating what they know of other people's motivations and feelings. She also is analyzing the continuing observations of 45 families in Cambridge, whose children are now between 6 and 10; studying the biographies and autobiographies of writers and their often less-famous brothers; and collaborating with Penn State behavioral geneticist Robert Plomin, Dunn's husband, on a study of the siblings in the Colorado Adoption Project.

"Behavioral geneticists," says Dunn, "found that siblings who shared more than 50 percent of their genes and who grew up in the same family were almost as different as totally unrelated people. The ways in which these children were similar, that was genetic. The ways they were unlike each other . . . well, that presented a huge challenge.

"Whatever your source of information about a sibling relationship, less than a third of the siblings are reported to be experiencing similar things within that relationship. The way families influence children is not the way psychologists have usually assumed."

* * *

There is a new baby in Fay's house. She pats the baby in her mother's arms. "Baby. Baby," she says. "Monster. Monster."

There is a new baby in Marvin's house, too. He is standing on the edge of the pram, rocking it. "Don't stand on there, there's a good boy," says his mother, "or you'll tip her out."

"I want her out."

These examples from Dunn's book *Sisters and Brothers* ring true for any parent of siblings, but Dunn's analyses of how these children grow as a result of the competition brings several surprises. Dunn has found, for instance, that the more affection the mother shows to the baby in relation to the older child, the better the older one, three years later, is able to judge other people's feelings and intentions. "People broadly suppose that how secure you feel with your mother is likely to be important for all aspects of development. We really don't know that."

* * *

Annie is building a tower of blocks and quarreling with her little brother, John, who snatches some away. Mother steps in. "Hey, hey, no fighting!" she says, and gives half the blocks to John and half to Annie.

"Not Annie. Not that," says John, and throws his blocks away.

"You don't want that?" asks his mother. "Can Annie have all of them?"

"No."

"Annie can't have them, but you don't want them?"

"No! No!"

Parents of two-year-olds have seen enough similar events to guess John's age easily; Dunn includes this story in her book *The Beginnings of Social Understanding* to explain that temper tantrums are not necessarily bad, not necessarily things to be squelched willy-nilly. "The power of those emotional experiences and the complexity of that family world," she says,

"play a crucial part in the development of social understanding. The emotion experienced in these exchanges may well influence what the child *learns*."

The Cambridge two-year-olds had tantrums when their wills met rules. But the transgressions that produced tantrums at two resulted, in the same child at three, in sophisticated reasoning—as, for instance, in an example of a three-year-old girl and her five-year-old brother, which Dunn included in her award lecture: "It's a dispute over a toy vacuum cleaner," Dunn told her audience, "which of course belongs to the little girl in the family—who would ever give a little boy a toy vacuum cleaner? The little boy has mended it, and he uses these claims to having it: He wants it, he fixed it, and he made it work. The mother tries to get the little girl to give it back by saying, 'Are you going to let Shawn have a turn?'

"The little girl is furious, desperate to keep her toy. Under the stress of this drive to get her way, purple with fury, she says, 'I have to do it. *Ladies* do it.' She's making a claim about the gender appropriateness of using a vacuum cleaner—much to the embarrassment of her mother, who says, 'Yes, ladies do it. And men do it sometimes. Daddy sometimes does the hoovering, doesn't he?' My point is that under the emotional stress, this child is behaving in a very sophisticated way. She's making a normative claim, a claim that's not simply something idiosyncratic about that family, but something much more general about cultural life in England."

"Psychiatrists have always taken the view," Dunn continues later, "that when people are upset they fall apart at the seams and don't function effectively. That may be true for the real extremes of distress, but we found that, as long as the children were not completely out of control with anger, it seemed that certain sorts of learning happened best in the context in which the mother and child were arguing." It is because of the strong emotion, she explains, that the children paid attention, remembered, reflected on, and learned from the experience. It is also clear that when the child is upset, the mother is more inclined to explain, to offer reasons.

In clinical experiments, such as when a child is asked to explain the actions and motivations of storybook characters, very young children are not so facile with the concepts of rules and transgressions. The difference, Dunn finds, is the context: In the clinic, the children are perhaps curious, but the puzzles are not puzzles they want solved. The Cambridge children, Dunn saw, understood such things as authority, justice, and others' feelings, and argued with the most sophistication, only when their own self-interest was threatened.

Past research on children has been "relentlessly serious," focusing on anxiety, guilt, and fear, says Dunn. "This bleak emphasis misses one very striking feature of children's social knowledge—the use they make of it, that interesting moral issue. Even before they can use many words, they find the rules and the roles of their world a source of humor and jokes. From the moment they begin to understand what behavior can be disapproved of and what is the naughty thing to do, this is a source of huge humor.

"If you look at what children find funny, it's a window on their understanding of the rules, because what's funny is a violation of what's usually done."

A child wants to understand the social world, Dunn argues, because of his or her role in the family. "It is the motivation to express himself within the relationship," she writes, "to cooperate, to get his way or to share amusement, that leads the child to discover the ways of the family world."

Her observations show that children as young as 18 months know how to tease and comfort, they understand something of what is allowed and what is not, they can anticipate the consequences of their hurtful actions and the responses of adults to their misdeeds, and they are curious about the causes of other people's actions and feelings.

By two-and-a-half to three, they have a "practical" understanding of responsibility, know how rules apply to different family members and how those rules can be questioned, can summon up excuses of intent ("I didn't mean it") and incapacity ("I don't feel good"), and have a grasp of the authority relations within the family.

"Moral understanding," says Dunn, "depends in part upon a child's general knowledge about the social world. What our observations show is that children have a far subtler comprehension of their social world than we have given them credit for."

QUESTIONS ABOUT THE READING

1. What research method, discussed in your text, does Judith Dunn employ in studying young children? Does she make a good case for the advantages of this method? Does the method seem well-suited to the study of sibling relationships? What limitations, if any, do you see in it? Can you suggest ways to overcome any such limitations, perhaps by combining more than one method of study?

2. Dunn's approach to child study grew out of her experience with her own babies. Were any of the major theorists and researchers mentioned in Chapter 1 of your text influenced by personal experience? Can such influences enhance or endanger scientific study?

3. Do you see similarities between Dunn's methodology and the methods used by Piaget to study children?

4. Dunn reports several findings that challenge common beliefs about children's development. Do these "surprises" tend to convince you of the value of her findings and methods or to make you skeptical about them?

5. Do you agree with Dunn's comment that social knowledge is crucial to becoming human? If so, at what point does a child become fully human? Does Dunn's emphasis on the development of social understanding fit in with any of the theoretical perspectives described in your text?

6. Does Dunn appear to place more emphasis on either qualitative or quantitative change?

7. On which of Bronfenbrenner's levels of environmental influence is Dunn's work focused? Do any of her findings reflect other levels of influence?

8. Dunn's work was done both in Cambridge, England, and in Pennsylvania. Do her findings exemplify any of the values of cross-cultural research mentioned in your text?

ANSWER KEY FOR CHAPTER 1

Note: Numbers in parentheses refer to pages in the textbook where answers can be found.

CHAPTER 1 REVIEW

Important Terms for Section I

1. continuity (page 14)
2. continuity (14)
3. quantitative (14)
4. qualitative (14)
5. motor (15)
6. cognitive (15)
7. personality and social (16)
8. growing up (17)
9. ecological (18)

Learning Objectives for Section I

1. (page 14)
2. (14)
3. (15-16)
4. (16, 17)
5. (16-18)
6. (18-20)

Important Terms for Section II

1. explain (page 23)
2. research (23)
3. explanation (23)
4. psychoanalytic (24)
5. gratification (24)
6. Erikson (29)
7. behaviorism (31)
8. learning (31)
9. instrumental (33)
10. increases (33)
11. decreases (34)
12. models (34)
13. observational (35)
14. qualitative, quantitative (36)
15. understanding (37)
16. Piaget, behavior, behavior (38)
17. Piaget, systems (38)
18. Piaget, complementary (38)
19. Piaget, cognitive (38)
20. Piaget, cognitive, experiences (38)
21. Piaget, cognitive (39)
22. mental (39)
23. evolutionary (40)
24. social (41)
25. Vygotsky (41)
26. proximal, ZPD (42)
27. temporary (42)

Learning Objectives for Section II

1. (page 22)
2. (23, 25)
3. (26, 27)
4. (26-28)
5. (28)
6. (28-29)
7. (27, 29)
8. (29-30)
9. (30-31)
10. (31)
11. (31-36)
12. (31-34)
13. (33-34)
14. (34)
15. (36)
16. (36)
17. (27, 37-39)
18. (39)
19. (39-40)
20. (40-41)
21. (41-42)

Important Terms for Section III

1. controlled (page 43)
2. statistical (43)
3. life (43)
4. naturalistic (45)
5. laboratory (46)
6. interview (47)
7. questionnaire (47)
8. questioning (47)
9. replicable (48)
10. independent (49)
11. dependent, independent (49)
12. control (49)

13. control, cause and effect (49)
14. represent (49)
15. population (49)
16. longitudinal (52)
17. cross-sectional (52)

Learning Objectives for Section III

1. (pages 43-48)
2. (45)
3. (49)
4. (49)
5. (50-51)
6. (44, 51)
7. (51-54)
8. (54-55)

CHAPTER 1 QUIZ

Matching—Who's Who

1. d (page 34)
2. i (24)
3. b (28-29)
4. e (18)
5. c (31)
6. j (32)
7. f (23)
8. h (37-38)
9. a (33)
10. g (41)
11. k (40-41)
12. m (29)
13. l (41)
14. n (37, 38)

Multiple-Choice

1. b (page 14)
2. d (14)
3. d (17)
4. c (16-18)
5. b (18)
6. a (20)
7. a (22)
8. c (26, 27)
9. a (26)
10. c (28)
11. b (27, 29)
12. a (30)
13. c (31)

14. c (31-32)
15. b (33-34)
16. a (34)
17. d (36)
18. c (38)
19. a (40-41)
20. d (42)
21. c (44, 48, 51)
22. b (45)
23. d (44, 45, 46)
24. c (50)
25. b (51-54)

True or False?

1. F—Early childhood is the years from 3 to 6. (page 17)
2. T (20)
3. F—The effect of the parents' divorce is part of the child's microsystem. (18)
4. F—A theory is an attempt to organize and explain information obtained through research. (23)
5. T (23)
6. T (24, 26, 27)
7. F—The superego represents socially approved values. (28)
8. F—Erikson's theory is a modification of Freud's. (28)
9. F—Successful resolution requires a balance between a positive trait and a negative one. (29)
10. F—According to Miller's theory, healthy personality development occurs within relationships. (29-30)
11. F—Most of Freud's patients were adults. (30)
12. F—The learning perspective sees change as quantitative. (31)
13. F—Learning theorists do not describe stages of development. (31)
14. T (31-32)
15. F—*Instrumental conditioning* is another name for operant conditioning. (33)
16. F—Reinforcement is an element of operant conditioning. (33-34)
17. T (35)
18. T (38)
19. T (40)
20. T (41)

21. T (42)
22. F—The clinical method combines observation with individualized questioning. (47)
23. F—Random sampling is the best way to ensure that a sample is representative. (49)
24. F—Laboratory experiments, which are the most rigidly controlled, typically are the least generalizable. (50-51)
25. T (54)

HEREDITY AND ENVIRONMENT

OVERVIEW

Chapter 2 traces the earliest development of a child, beginning with the parents' decision to conceive. In this chapter, the authors:

- Discuss why and when people choose to have children

- Describe human reproduction and explain how a new human life is created

- Explain the genetic mechanisms through which offspring inherit characteristics from parents

- Explain genetic transmission of various types of birth defects and discuss how genetic counseling and prenatal diagnosis can help parents who are worried about bearing a child with such a defect

- Discuss the relative influence of heredity and environment and how these factors interact

CHAPTER 2 REVIEW

Introduction and Section I Choosing Parenthood

FRAMEWORK FOR SECTION I

A. Why People Have Children
B. When People Have Children

IMPORTANT TERMS FOR INTRODUCTION AND SECTION I

Completion: Fill in the blanks to complete the definitions of key terms for this section of Chapter 2.

1. _____ : Inborn influences on development carried on the genes, that is, inherited from the parents.

2. **environment:** Combination of _____ influences, such as family, community, and personal experience, that affect development.

3. _____-versus-_____ **controversy:** Debate over the the relative importance of hereditary and environmental factors in influencing human development.

LEARNING OBJECTIVES FOR SECTION I

After reading and reviewing this section of Chapter 2, you should be able to do the following.

1. Explain why deciding whether or not to have children is more complicated today than it was in preindustrial times.

2. State reasons for the trend toward having children later in life.

Section II The Beginning of Pregnancy

FRAMEWORK FOR SECTION II

A. How Does Fertilization Take Place?
B. What Causes Multiple Births?

IMPORTANT TERMS FOR SECTION II

Completion: Fill in the blanks to complete the definitions of key terms for this section of Chapter 2.

1. _____ : Process by which sperm and ovum fuse to form a single new cell; also called *conception*.

2. **zygote:** Single cell formed through _____ .

3. **fraternal, or _____ twins:** Two people who are conceived and born at approximately the same time as a result of the fertilization of two ova.

4. **identical, or _____ twins:** Two people with identical genes, arising from the formation of one zygote that divided.

LEARNING OBJECTIVES FOR SECTION II

After reading and reviewing this section of Chapter 2, you should be able to do the following.

1. Explain what happens during ovulation and fertilization.

2. Explain the difference between fraternal and identical twins and cite factors affecting the incidence of each.

Section III   Influences of Heredity and Environment

FRAMEWORK FOR SECTION III

A. The Mechanisms of Heredity: Genes and Chromosomes
B. What Determines Sex?
   1. Sex Selection
   2. Sex Differences
C. Patterns of Genetic Transmission
   1. Dominant and Recessive Inheritance
   2. Genotypes and Phenotypes
   3. Other Forms of Hereditary Transmission
      a. Sex-Linked Inheritance
      b. Incomplete Dominance
      c. Polygenic Inheritance
      d. Multifactorial Transmission
D. Genetic and Chromosomal Abnormalities
   1. Defects Transmitted by Dominant Inheritance
   2. Defects Transmitted by Recessive Inheritance
   3. Defects Transmitted by Sex-Linked Inheritance
   4. Chromosomal Abnormalities
E. Genetic Counseling
   1. How Genetic Counseling Works

F. The Importance of Environment
G. How Heredity and Environment Interact
   1. "Nature Versus Nurture": Hereditary and Environmental Factors
      a. Reaction Range
      b. Canalization
      c. Maturation
      d. Interplay between Heredity and Environment
H. Effects of Heredity and Environment
   1. Ways to Study the Relative Effects of Heredity and Environment
      a. Family (Kinship) Studies
      b. Adoption Studies
      c. Studies of Twins
   2. Some Characteristics Influenced by Heredity and Environment
      a. Physical Traits and Conditions
      b. Intelligence
      c. Personality
      d. Temperament
      e. Personality Disorders

IMPORTANT TERMS FOR SECTION III

Completion: Fill in the blanks to complete the definitions of key terms for this section of Chapter 2.

1. _____: Rod-shaped particle found in every living cell; carries the genes.

2. _____: Functional unit of heredity; determines the traits that are passed from one generation to the next.

3. **DNA (deoxyribonucleic acid):** Chemical carrying the instructions that tell all the cells in the body how to make the _____ that enable them to carry out their various functions.

4. _____: One of a pair of genes affecting a trait; the genes may be identical or different.

5. **homozygous:** Possessing _____ alleles for a trait.

6. **heterozygous:** Possessing _____ alleles for a trait.

7. _____: Principle that when an offspring receives genes for contradictory traits, only one of the traits—the dominant trait—will be expressed.

8. **recessive inheritance:** Expression of a recessive trait, which occurs only if a person (or an animal or a plant) is _____ for the trait (has two alleles carrying it).

9. **genotype:** Pattern of _____ carried by a person.

10. **phenotype:** _____ characteristics of a person.

11. **sex-linked inheritance:** Process by which certain _____ genes are transmitted differently to male and female children.

12. **carrier:** In genetics, a person with an allele which is not _____ but which can be passed on to future generations.

13. _____ **inheritance:** Interaction of a number of different genes to produce certain traits.

14. _____ **transmission:** Interaction of both genetic and environmental factors to produce certain traits.

15. **Down syndrome:** Disorder caused by a(n) _____ twenty-first chromosome; characterized by mental retardation and various physical abnormalities.

16. _____ **counseling:** Clinical service that advises couples of the probable risk of having a child with a particular hereditary disorder.

17. _____: Photograph made through a microscope showing the chromosomes when they are separated and aligned for cell division; the chromosomes are displayed according to a standard array.

18. **amniocentesis:** Prenatal diagnostic procedure for examining the chromosomes of a fetus; sample cells are withdrawn from the _____ in which the fetus floats and are examined for signs of birth defects.

19. **chorionic villus sampling (CVS):** Prenatal diagnostic procedure for obtaining sample villi from the _____ surrounding the embryo and then examining the embryo's chromosomes for birth defects.

20. _____: Medical procedure using high-frequency _____ waves to detect the outlines of a fetus and determine whether the pregnancy is progressing normally.

21. **heritability:** Statistical estimate of contribution of heredity to individual differences in a specific _____.

22. _____: In genetics, a potential variability, depending on environmental conditions, in the expression of a hereditary trait.

23. **canalization:** Limitation on some _____ characteristics so that their expression can take, at most, only a few outcomes.

24. _____: Unfolding of a biologically based sequence of physical changes and behaviors.

25. _____: Person's unique way of behaving, feeling, and reacting.

26. _____: Person's style of approaching other people and situations.

LEARNING OBJECTIVES FOR SECTION III

After reading and reviewing this section of Chapter 2, you should be able to do the following.

1. Briefly explain the role of genes and chromosomes in inheritance of characteristics.

2. Explain how the sex of a child is determined.

3. Describe two new techniques for selecting the sex of a child and state circumstances under which they are likely to be used.

4. Identify two important physical differences between the sexes, other than genital or chromosomal structure, that show up during the prenatal period and persist up to or into adulthood.

5. Contrast dominant and recessive inheritance and explain how each occurs.

6. Explain how a person can be either homozygous or heterozygous for an expressed trait.

7. Explain the difference between a person's phenotype and that person's genotype.

8. List and describe four types of inheritance other than simple dominant and recessive inheritance.

9. List and describe three methods of transmission of defects, and give at least one example of each.

10. Name two ways in which chromosomal abnormalities occur.

11. Identify the causes and characteristics of Down syndrome and discuss the outlook for a child born with this disorder.

12. Explain how a genetic counselor assesses the probability that a child will be born with an inherited defect.

13. Discuss various options available to a couple weighing their risk of bearing a defective baby.

14. List and describe five techniques for prenatal diagnosis of defects or abnormalities.

15. Explain how researchers determine the heritability of a trait.

16. Explain the concepts of reaction range, canalization, and maturation and give at least one example of each.

17. Explain why siblings tend to be more different than alike and why each experiences a unique environment within the family.

18. List and describe three types of studies of the influences of hereditary and environmental factors in development.

19. Discuss the influence of heredity and environment on physical appearance, obesity, longevity, intelligence, personality traits, temperament, and various personality disorders.

20. Identify the characteristics and probable causes of schizophrenia.

CHAPTER 2 QUIZ

Matching—Numbers: Match each item at the left with the correct number in the right-hand column.

1.	Percentage of American women who have a first child after age 30 _____	6
2.	Number of days in the female ovulation cycle _____	16
3.	Number of chromosomes in body cells _____	21
4.	Number of chromosomes in sex cells (gametes) _____	23
5.	Number of males born for every 100 females in the United States _____	28
6.	Number of males per 100 females in the United States population _____	46
7.	Percent of offspring of hybrid pea plants showing the dominant trait in Mendel's	50
	cross-breeding experiments _____	75
8.	Percentage of babies born in the United States who have birth defects _____	95
9.	Number of the chromosome associated with Down syndrome _____	106
10.	Maximum percentage of heritability for most traits _____	

Multiple-Choice: Circle the choice that best completes or answers each item.

1. Women who choose the latest "ideal ages" for having a first child tend to be *all but which* of the following?
   a. recently married
   b. well educated
   c. financially struggling
   d. strongly feminist

2. Fertilization normally occurs in the
   a. uterus
   b. vagina
   c. cervix
   d. fallopian tube

3. A newborn girl has approximately how many immature ova in her ovaries?
   a. none
   b. 40
   c. 4000
   d. 400,000

4. A normal mature male's ejaculation contains approximately how many sperm?
   a. 50
   b. 500
   c. 500 million
   d. 500 billion

5. The incidence of fraternal twins has been increasing because of
   a. increased use of fertility drugs
   b. increased rate of sexual activity
   c. aftereffects of birth control pills
   d. none of the above; such births are accidental

6. The chemical called DNA
   a. tells the cells to manufacture proteins that control body functions
   b. tells the cells to produce testosterone
   c. causes a fetus to develop female body parts
   d. causes a fetus to develop a sex-linked disorder

7. Which of the following statements about genes is true?
    a. Each gene acts independently of other genes in determining a trait.
    b. Most inherited defects are transmitted by dominant genes.
    c. Each gene seems to have a fixed position on a particular chromosome.
    d. Genes are made of proteins.

8. A male zygote can result from which combination of sex chromosomes?
    a. YY
    b. XY
    c. XX
    d. any of the above

9. Which of the following hypotheses has been advanced to explain why male babies are more vulnerable to miscarriage and disorder than female babies?
    a. The Y chromosome contains genes which protect females against stress.
    b. The X chromosome contains harmful genes.
    c. The mechanisms for immunity in males are inferior.
    d. The male body develops earlier in the prenatal period than the female body.

10. Mendel's experiments proved that
    a. Traits are transmitted independently of each other.
    b. All inherited traits are expressed.
    c. Traits blend into each other over time.
    d. Most traits are inherited multifactorially.

11. The pattern of alleles underlying a person's observable traits is called his or her
    a. allelic type
    b. prototype
    c. phenotype
    d. genotype

12. The blood type AB is an example of
    a. incomplete dominance
    b. sex-linked inheritance
    c. polygenic inheritance
    d. multifactorial inheritance

13. Approximately what proportion of newborns in the United States each year have physical or mental disabilities?
    a. 1 percent
    b. 6 percent
    c. 10 percent
    d. 16 percent

14. A man and woman each carry the same harmful recessive allele. If they have four children, the probabilities are that how many of the children will have the disorder associated with the abnormal gene?
    a. 1
    b. 2
    c. 3
    d. 4

15. Chromosomal abnormalities are the result of
    a. inheritance
    b. prenatal accidents
    c. either a or b
    d. neither a nor b

16. African Americans are at higher-than-average risk of carrying genes for
    a. sickle-cell anemia
    b. Tay-Sachs disease
    c. cystic fibrosis
    d. beta thalassemia

17. A technique that allows a doctor to draw a blood sample from a fetus to diagnose the presence of certain disorders is
    a. chorionic villus sampling
    b. umbilical cord assessment
    c. alpha fetoprotein (AFP) test
    d. amniocentesis

18. The Human Genome Project is designed to
    a. map the location of genes, particularly those that cause disorders
    b. conduct genetic tests to identify people who carry harmful genes
    c. perform gene therapy to repair abnormal genes
    d. all of the above

19. The heritability of a trait generally does not exceed _____ percent.
    a. 10
    b. 25
    c. 50
    d. 75

20. A human characteristic that is highly canalized is
    a. body size
    b. sequence of motor development
    c. rate of language development
    d. shyness

21. Which of the following is a method of studying relative effects of heredity and environment?
    a. prenatal study
    b. adoption study
    c. case history
    d. breeding study

22. Which of the following behavioral and personality disorders appears to have only a modest genetic component?
    a. alcoholism
    b. autism
    c. depression
    d. schizophrenia

23. Which of the following statements about heredity and intelligence is true?
    a. Intelligence is controlled by a few specific genes.
    b. The influence of heredity on intelligence decreases with age.
    c. Heredity plays a more important role in differences in intelligence within ethnic groups than between them.
    d. Because of the strength of genetic influences on intelligence, little can be done to improve IQ scores.

True or False? In the blank following each item, write T (for *true*) or F (for *false*). In the space below each item, if the statement is false, rewrite it to make it true.

1. In preindustrial societies, large families were frowned upon. ___

2. The ovum is the largest cell in the adult human body. ___

3. Only one sperm can penetrate an ovum. ___

4. Monozygotic twins are always of the same sex. ___

5. Every cell in the human body has 46 chromosomes (23 pairs). ___

6. Mitosis is a process of cell division normally resulting in exact duplicates of the original cell. ___

7. DNA gives each cell the biochemical instructions to make the proteins it needs to perform its functions. ___

8. Twenty-two of the twenty-three pairs of chromosomes are known as autosomes. ___

9. The father's sperm normally determines a child's sex. ___

10. In preimplantation genetic diagnosis, a woman is artifically inseminated with either X or Y sperm. ___

11. Male babies are stronger than female babies and more likely to survive. ___

12. Most normal human traits can be explained by Mendel's law of dominant inheritance. ___

13. Because red hair is a recessive trait, a redheaded child must have two redheaded parents. ___

14. Red-green color blindness is a sex-linked trait. ___

15. Multifactorial transmission is the result of the interaction of several different genes.
_____

16. The most common inherited lethal defect among white people is Tay-Sachs disease.
_____

17. The son of a man with hemophilia has a 50 percent chance of inheriting the abnormal gene from his father and being a carrier of the disorder. _____

18. The risk of Down syndrome rises with the age of either parent. _____

19. If a couple's first child has a recessive defect, the second child is unlikely to have it. _____

20. Chorionic villus sampling can be performed earlier in a pregnancy than amniocentesis.
_____

21. The locations of several thousand human genes have been identified. _____

22. Maturation is programmed by the genes and cannot be affected by environmental factors.
_____

23. Differences in personalities of siblings who grow up in the same household are due to genetic differences. _____

24. Family (kinship) studies provide a good way to distinguish hereditary from environmental influences. _____

25. Temperament is the result of parental responsiveness during early infancy. ___

26. Schizophrenia appears to be transmitted multifactorially. ___

TOPICS FOR THOUGHT AND DISCUSSION

1. A 1989 survey found that almost half of the young couples in the sample rated other values equal to or above having children. Do you think these couples, if they have children, are likely to be good parents?

2. The more educated a woman is, the older she is likely to be when she has her first child. What developmental effects do you suppose the age and educational level of a mother might have on her children?

3. Why might Nepalese villagers believe that the woman determines the sex of the child? Why do you suppose that this belief has been prevalent in many societies?

4. In India, many abortions have resulted after amniocentesis was performed solely to determine whether a baby would be a boy or a girl. In the United States, too, many parents have definite preferences regarding the sex of an expected child. If it was established that amniocentesis which is motivated by such preferences has prompted an increase in abortions, would you favor a law (as was passed in India) banning amniocentesis except when a risk of birth defects can be shown? Would you favor a ban on disclosure of the sex of the fetus to the parents? Why or why not? How would you answer the Indian obstetrician, quoted in Box 2-1 of your text, who seemed to defend the frequent aborting of female fetuses in his country on the basis of cultural norms?

5. In view of the facts that females have a better chance of survival and are less vulnerable to disorders than males, why do you think women have been considered the "weaker sex" in most cultures throughout history?

6. A genetic counselor has informed you and your spouse that there is a 25 percent chance that a child conceived by the two of you would be born with sickle-cell anemia. What factors and alternatives might you consider, and what would your likely decision be?

7. According to your text, amniocentesis is generally recommended for pregnant women if they are at least 35 or if there is reason to suspect the likelihood of certain genetic or chromosomal disorders or complications. If you were in that position, and knowing that some research has found a slightly higher risk of miscarriage in women who had amniocentesis, would you have the procedure? Why or why not?

8. Critics of universal genetic testing claim that the risks outweigh the benefits. On the basis of the pros and cons outlined in your text, what is your opinion?

9. Imagine that you are a researcher trying to assess the relative influence of heredity and environment on a child's rate of language development. Would you be more likely to do a family (kinship) study, a twin study, or an adoption study? What would be the

advantages and disadvantages of each type of study? Remembering what you learned about research methods in Chapter 1, how would you design your study?

10. Although most human traits appear to be transmitted multifactorially with the influences of heredity and environment intertwined, the authors of your text argue that there is value in attempting to determine the relative influence of these two factors on specific traits because such knowledge can affect how people act toward children. Applying that principle to the findings on shyness in Box 2-4, what lessons might parents draw about the treatment of children who tend to be shy or bold?

11. According to your text, heredity seems to become more influential on intelligence as children grow older, partially overcoming the influence of the shared family environment. Yet the authors also state that each child in a family experiences a unique, nonshared environment. Can you reconcile these two points?

CHAPTER 2 READING

INTRODUCTION

Although genetic testing is new and controversial (as discussed in Box 2-3 of your text), its use is quickly becoming widespread. Among the issues still unresolved is the appropriateness of such testing for children and adolescents. This article is reprinted from the January-February 1995 issue of *Health* magazine.

GENETIC TESTING: KIDS' LATEST RITE OF PASSAGE

by Terence Monmaney

Not yet an adult, no longer a child, Melissa Drake[*] was 16, and sure she would get breast cancer. Her mother had died of the disease when Melissa was 12 years old. A grandmother and favorite aunt were also afflicted, not to mention numerous other women in her mother's family tree. "I'm going to get it," Melissa told her boyfriend, preparing him and testing his strength of heart. And she steeled herself for the day in her twenties when she would take the only step that offers a chance of preventing the disease: double mastectomy.

But because of their family history, Melissa and four generations of maternal relations were taking part in a study led by oncologist Barbara

---

[*] These names have been changed.

Weber, then at the University of Michigan in Ann Arbor. Weber and coworkers collected the women's blood and searched the DNA in the white cells for evidence of a gene that confers an 85 percent likelihood of developing breast cancer. Since the gene had not yet been identified, the researchers sought it indirectly, looking instead for so-called marker genes that in Melissa's family seemed to be inherited along with it.

One fall day in 1993, Melissa, her father, an aunt, and a cousin gathered at the medical center to hear the results of their tests. Actually, the researchers hadn't wanted to include Melissa. Little was known about how minors cope with such news, and since a girl who tested positive couldn't do anything about her breast cancer risk for years, why not wait and tell her when she turned 18? But Melissa's consent form said nothing about withholding results. And Melissa insisted she wanted to know.

The researchers gently gave the results: Melissa did not appear to have the gene. As whoops and tears sprang from her loved ones, Melissa just sat there. "Stunned," recalls genetic counselor Barbara Biesecker. "She was in shock. It took her a long, long time to really believe it."

Once she did, Melissa stopped thinking of her breasts as harboring disease and quit dreading her sexuality, another Michigan researcher says. "It was quite liberating for her."

Given recent developments, it looks [as if] such momentous exchanges will soon become commonplace. Last fall, an international research team based at the University of Utah managed to pinpoint the actual gene, named BRCA1, responsible for inherited breast cancer of the sort that appears in Melissa Drake's family. Barring unforeseen difficulties, a routine test for BRCA1 should be available in clinics in as little as two years. And though BRCA1 is responsible for only 5 percent of breast-cancer cases, it affects many lives: It's estimated that about half a million American women carry BRCA1, making it one of the world's most common disease-causing genes.

The gene's discovery grabbed headlines, but several hundred other disease genes have also been found in the past decade or so—from one that gives newborns a rare metabolic disorder to another that plunges senior citizens into a type of Alzheimers's. And since researchers are hotly pursuing many more disease genes, it's not farfetched to think DNA testing labs will someday be as common as fortune-telling parlors or at least the cholesterol-screening vans that visit malls.

At its best, genetic soothsaying offers a child or teen a shot at a whole new future. After researchers found the gene for retinoblastoma, an inherited childhood cancer of the eye, they developed new methods for treating the tumors and preventing the blindness that once was all but inevitable.

But unavoidable or untreatable diseases pose a dilemma. "We need an extra layer of caution when dealing with young people," says Katherine Schneider, a genetics counselor at the Dana-Farber Cancer Institute in Boston. "There are questions about their ability to give informed consent to these tests or to understand the tests' implications. Until we get more experienced in telling people about their genes, we'd rather work with adults."

Some researchers go further. In 1990, the International Huntington Association issued guidelines against subjecting minors to DNA tests for Huntington's disease, which strikes in middle age. Inherited and incurable, it eventually robs sufferers of mind and personality. "You endanger a young person's ability to dream about an unlimited future by telling them at an early age what's in store," says Kimberly Quaid, a psychologist at the Indiana University Medical School in Indianapolis, where she counsels families with the neurological disorder.

Quaid also worries that young people whose genes predispose them to serious diseases will be cast off as damaged goods. Recently, she says, a New York woman asked her local school board to subject special education students to the genetic test for fragile X syndrome, which causes mental retardation. The woman figured the school could save money by weeding out the kids with the syndrome.

Even parents don't necessarily have their children's best interests in mind, researchers have found. They tell of a man who asked that his two young children be tested for Huntington's because he assumed that one must have the gene—and he couldn't afford to send both to college. His request was denied. Other requests, while less disturbing, may nevertheless be prompted by the parents' needs, not the child's. "Parents feel guilty that they might have passed a disease gene on to a child," Biesecker says, "and many want a test to relieve them of that guilt."

"It may sound paternalistic," she says, "but sometimes we have to protect children from their parents." In the *Journal of the American Medical Association* last fall, geneticist Dorothy Wertz and her colleagues argued that a parent's request for testing could justifiably be turned down if the researcher or doctor believes that a child won't derive any medical benefit from the knowledge.

Inevitably, though, that hard line would deprive a lot of young people of vital information. Like Melissa Drake, many adolescents would rather have a clear picture of the future, even if it includes hardship, than to live in limbo. Parents also can benefit, emotionally and practically, as they budget, make decisions about insurance, and plan for the family.

Partly for that reason, Mary Pelias, a geneticist and lawyer at Louisiana State University, argues that unless parents are known to be negligent or abusive, they should have the final word.

"Who are geneticists to be guardians of the world?" Pelias says. "We need to make sure the family understands that this kind of information has an upside and a significant downside. That's all we can do. We shouldn't step between a parent and child."

Geneticist Gloria Petersen believes kids can handle heavy-duty genetic information. At Johns Hopkins University in Baltimore, she has worked with young children at high risk for a type of colon cancer, called familial adenomatous polyposis, or FAP. If a child inherits a gene for the disease, the first polyps typically appear on the colon around age 12.

Often, the colon is removed by age 20 to prevent tumors from taking hold.

"Usually, children are very well aware that the disease runs in the family and that they're at risk of getting it," she says. "They look to the test with tremendous hope. Resolving the uncertainty is the biggest boost they can have. Whether the result is positive or negative, it's an enormous relief."

Although Betty Farnsworth[*], age 41, has FAP, none of her children had shown any symptoms by the time she drove them to Baltimore from their home in North Carolina for testing. "If you don't want to know, tell me now," Farnsworth told the kids, aged 19, 12, and ten, a last time on the way up. Yes, they said, they wanted to know.

They all cried when they found that the two oldest, both girls, have the gene, while the youngest, a boy, does not. "I told them I was sorry," Farnsworth says. "But they're doing fine now, going on with their lives." Far from keeping the bad news a secret, the 19-year-old is doing a project on FAP for her high school class. "I think you live an easier life knowing than not knowing," says Farnsworth.

It's not in scientists' nature to argue that ignorance is bliss; the word *science*, after all, means "to know." But breast-cancer researchers at the University of Michigan and elsewhere now refuse to perform genetic analysis on minors, even though the test freed Melissa Drake from her prison of worry. It's an uneasy compromise; but for now scientists have decided to withhold the good news from some teens to spare others the bad.

QUESTIONS ABOUT THE READING

1. Does the article present a balanced treatment of the arguments for and against doing genetic tests on young people? Which side do you think has a stronger case?

2. If you were genetically at risk for breast cancer or some other life-threatening disease, at what age would you want to know, if at all?

3. A genetic counselor quoted in the article questions young people's ability to give informed consent to genetic testing. Thinking back to the discussion of informed consent in Chapter 1, do you see this as a good reason to deny children or teenagers knowledge about medical conditions that may affect them? Does it make a difference whether or not a disease is treatable?

ANSWER KEY FOR CHAPTER 2

Note: Numbers in parentheses refer to pages in the textbook where answers can be found.

CHAPTER 2 REVIEW

Important Terms for Introduction and Section I

1. heredity (page 65)
2. outside (65)
3. nature, nurture (65)

Learning Objectives for Section I

1. (page 66)
2. (66)

Important Terms for Section II

1. fertilization (page 67)
2. fertilization (67)
3. dizygotic (68)
4. monozygotic (68)

Learning Objectives for Section II

1. (page 67)
2. (67-68)

Important Terms for Section III

1. chromosome (page 68)
2. gene (69)
3. proteins (69)
4. allele (72)
5. identical (72)
6. different (72)

7. dominant inheritance (72)
8. homozygous (72)
9. alleles (73)
10. observable (73)
11. recessive (74)
12. expressed (74)
13. polygenic (75)
14. multifactorial (75)
15. extra (81)
16. genetic (82)
17. karyotype (83)
18. amniotic fluid (84)
19. membrane (84)
20. ultrasound, sound (86)
21. trait (87)
22. reaction range (87)
23. inherited (89)
24. maturation (89)
25. personality (94)
26. temperament (95)

Learning Objectives for Section III

1. (pages 68-69)
2. (69-70)
3. (70-71)
4. (71-72)
5. (72-73)
6. (72-73)
7. (73)
8. (74-75)
9. (75-80)
10. (80)
11. (81-82)
12. (83-84)
13. (84)
14. (84, 85-86)
15. (87)
16. (87-90)
17. (90-91)
18. (91-92)
19. (92-97)
20. (95-97)

CHAPTER 2 QUIZ

Matching—Numbers

1. 16 (page 66)
2. 28 (67)
3. 46 (68)
4. 3 (69)
5. 106 (71)
6. 95 (71)
7. 75 (72)
8. 6 (75, 84)
9. 21 (81)
10. 50 (87)

Multiple-Choice

1. c (page 66)
2. d (67)
3. d (67)
4. c (67)
5. a (68)
6. a (69)
7. c (69)
8. b (70)
9. c (72)
10. a (72)
11. d (73)
12. a (74-75)
13. b (75)
14. a (78-79)
15. c (80)
16. a (83)
17. b (86)
18. a (86)
19. c (87)
20. b (89)
21. b (91)
22. a (93)
23. c (94)

True or False?

1. F—In preindustrial societies, large families served economic and social needs. (page 53)
2. T (67)
3. F—More than one sperm may penetrate an ovum, but only one sperm can fertilize it. (67)

4. T (68)
5. F—Every cell in the human body except the sex cells has 46 chromosomes; the sex cells have 23 chromosomes. (68-69)
6. T (69)
7. T (69)
8. T (70)
9. T (70)
10. F—In preimplantation genetic diagnosis, DNA from three-day-old zygotes conceived by in vitro fertilization is analyzed to determine sex and possible genetic defects before implantation in the uterus. (70, 86)
11. F—Male babies are more vulnerable to death and disorders. (71)
12. F—Hardly any normal human traits are transmitted by simple dominant inheritance. (72)
13. F—A redheaded child may be born to dark-haired parents, both of whom gave the child a recessive allele for red hair. (72)
14. T (74)
15. F—Multifactorial transmission is the result of the interaction of genetic and environmental factors. (75)

16. F—The most common inherited lethal defect among white people is cystic fibrosis. (76)
17. F—The man cannot pass on the gene for hemophilia to his son, because it is carried on the X chromosome. (79-80)
18. T (81)
19. F—Since both parents are carriers, each child of the couple has a 1 in 4 chance of inheriting a recessive defect. (84)
20. T (85)
21. T (84-86)
22. F—Extreme environmental deprivation can interfere with maturation. (89)
23. F—Differences between siblings are due in part to nonshared environmental effects. (90)
24. F—Family studies alone do not clearly distinguish hereditary from environmental influences. (91)
25. F—Temperament appears to be largely inborn. (94-95)
26. T (95-97)

PRENATAL DEVELOPMENT

OVERVIEW

Chapter 3 explores the development of the child from conception to birth. In this chapter, the authors:

- Describe the experience of pregnancy and the psychological changes men and women go through as they approach parenthood

- Outline three stages of prenatal development

- Describe the developing capabilities of the fetus

- Discuss environmental factors that can affect the fetus and explain the importance of prenatal care

- Identify causes of infertility

- Discuss alternative ways for infertile couples to become parents

- Describe how the transition to parenthood affects family life

CHAPTER 3 REVIEW

Section I   The Experience of Pregnancy

LEARNING OBJECTIVES FOR SECTION I

After reading and reviewing this section of Chapter 3, you should be able to do the following:

1. Describe psychological changes prospective parents undergo.

Section II   Prenatal Development

FRAMEWORK FOR SECTION II

A.   The Three Stages of Prenatal Development
    1.   Germinal Stage (Fertilization to 2 Weeks): The Period of the Zygote
    2.   Embryonic Stage (2 to 8-12 Weeks)
        a.   Development during the Embryonic Stage
        b.   Spontaneous Abortion in the Embryonic Stage
    3.   Fetal Stage (from 8-12 Weeks to Birth)
B.   Prenatal Abilities and Activities
    1.   Fetal Therapy
    2.   Fetal Hearing
    3.   Fetal Learning

IMPORTANT TERMS FOR SECTION II

Completion: Fill in the blanks to complete the definitions of key terms for this section of Chapter 3.

1.   **gestation:** Period of time from conception to birth; normally _____ days.

2.   _____ **stage:** First 2 weeks of development of a conceptus, beginning at fertilization, characterized by rapid cell division and increasing complexity, and ending when the conceptus attaches to the wall of the uterus.

3.   _____: Conceptus between 2 weeks and 8 to 12 weeks after conception.

4.   **embryonic stage:** Second stage of pregnancy (2 to 8-12 weeks), characterized by differentiation of body parts and systems and ending when the _____ begin to appear.

5.   **critical period:** Specific time during development when an event has its greatest _____.

6.   **spontaneous abortion:** Natural expulsion from the uterus of a conceptus that cannot survive outside the womb; also called _____.

7.   **fetus:** Conceptus between _____ to _____ weeks and birth.

8.   _____ **stage:** Final stage of pregnancy (from ___ to ___ weeks to birth), characterized by increased detail of body parts and greatly enlarged body size.

LEARNING OBJECTIVES FOR SECTION II

After reading and reviewing this section of Chapter 3, you should be able to do the following.

1.   Identify the main activity that takes place during all three stages of prenatal development.

2. Summarize the development of the conceptus during the germinal stage.

3. Define the following terms: *mitosis, blastocyst, embryonic disk, ectoderm, endoderm, mesoderm, placenta, umbilical cord, amniotic sac, trophoblast, embryo, morphogens*.

4. Identify three functions of the placenta.

5. Explain why the embryonic stage is considered a critical period.

6. Summarize the development that occurs during the embryonic stage.

7. Explain why some pregnancies terminate in spontaneous abortion and what complications may occur.

8. Summarize the development that takes place during the fetal stage.

9. Discuss findings about fetal sensory, motor, and cognitive abilities.

10. List three techniques for correcting fetal disorders.

Section III The Prenatal Environment

FRAMEWORK FOR SECTION III

A. Maternal Factors
   1. Prenatal Nutrition
   2. Maternal Drug Intake
      a. Medical Drugs
      b. Nonmedical Drugs
         (1) Alcohol
         (2) Marijuana
         (3) Nicotine
         (4) Opiates
         (5) Cocaine
         (6) Caffeine
   3. Other Maternal Factors
      a. Illness
      b. Acquired Immune Deficiency Syndrome (AIDS)
      c. Incompatibility of Blood Type
      d. Medical X-Rays
      e. Maternal Age
      f. Environmental Hazards
      g. Physical Activity
B. Paternal Factors

C.   A Note on Prenatal Hazards
D.   Prenatal Care

IMPORTANT TERMS FOR SECTION III

Completion: Fill in the blanks to complete the definitions of key terms for this section of Chapter 3.

1.   **teratogenic:** Descriptive of an environmental factor that produces birth _____.

2.   _____ (**abbreviated** ___): Combination of mental, motor, and developmental abnormalities affecting the offspring of some women who drink heavily during pregnancy.

3.   **Acquired immune deficiency syndrome (AIDS):** Viral disease that undermines effective _____ of the immune system.

4.   **Rh factor:** Protein substance found in the blood of most people; when it is present in the blood of a(n) _____ but not in the blood of the _____ , death of the fetus can result.

LEARNING OBJECTIVES FOR SECTION III

After reading and reviewing this section of Chapter 3, you should be able to do the following.

1.   Describe effects of malnutrition on fetal development, and list the elements of good nutrition during pregnancy.

2.   Discuss factors to be weighed in considering the issue of "fetal abuse."

3.   Explain how drug intake during pregnancy can harm an embryo or fetus and list effects of medical drugs, alcohol, marijuana, nicotine, opiates, cocaine, and caffeine.

4.   Name at least three illnesses that can be passed from mother to fetus and describe their consequences.

5.   Discuss the risks of a fetus' contracting AIDS from the mother, and what screening and treatment are possible.

6.   Explain how incompatibility of blood type can arise between a mother and child and briefly discuss consequences, prevention, and treatment.

7.   Explain why medical X-rays during pregnancy should be avoided.

8.   Discuss the risks of complications for expectant mothers over the age of 30, as well as some benefits of delayed motherhood.

9. Identify the prenatal risks involved in exposure to industrial chemicals, lead contamination, and radiation.

10. Summarize the relationship between exercise during pregnancy and the health of the fetus.

11. Identify several ways in which a man can contribute to the risk of birth defects in his child.

12. List eleven ways of ensuring a healthy prenatal environment.

13. Compare access to, and prevalence of, prenatal care in the United States, Europe, and Israel.

Section IV When Conception Is an Issue

FRAMEWORK FOR SECTION IV

A. Infertility
   1. Causes of Infertility

B. Alternative Ways to Conceive
   1. Artificial Insemination
   2. In Vitro Fertilization
   3. Ovum Transfer
   4. Surrogate Motherhood
   5. Technology and Conception: Ethical Issues
C. Adoption

IMPORTANT TERMS FOR SECTION IV

Completion: Fill in the blanks to complete the definitions of the key terms for this section of Chapter 3.

1. _____: Inability to conceive after 12 to 18 months of trying to have a baby.

2. **artificial insemination:** Injection of sperm into a woman's _____.

3. _____ **fertilization:** Fertilization that takes place outside the mother's body.

4. **ovum transfer:** Implantation of a fertilized donor egg from another woman in the recipient mother's _____.

5. _____ **motherhood:** Pregnancy carried to term by a woman impregnated by the prospective father, usually by artificial insemination. She then gives the infant to the father and his wife; involves mutual agreement before conception.

LEARNING OBJECTIVES FOR SECTION IV

After reading and reviewing this section of Chapter 3, you should be able to do the following.

1. Discuss possible reasons for the increase in infertility during the past 30 years, its causes, treatment, and effects on a marriage.

2. List four alternative ways for infertile people to conceive, explain how each works, and point out some of the ethical questions involved.

3. Summarize trends in adoption in the United States since 1970 and briefly discuss its effects on children and attitudes toward it.

Section V The Transition to Parenthood

FRAMEWORK FOR SECTION V

A. The Marital Relationship
B. Relationship with the Baby

LEARNING OBJECTIVES FOR SECTION V

After reading and reviewing this section of Chapter 3, you should be able to do the following:

1. Describe two common patterns of change in marital relationships after the birth of a baby.

2. Discuss how a mother's attitudes during pregnancy may affect her baby's security of attachment.

3. Compare the adjustment of adoptive parents and biological parents.

CHAPTER 3 QUIZ

Matching—Month by Month: Match each month of gestation in the left-hand column with the appropriate description (a typical development during that month) in the right-hand column.

1. First month ___
2. Second month ___
3. Third month ___
4. Fourth month ___
5. Fifth month ___
6. Sixth month ___
7. Seventh month ___
8. Eighth month ___
9. Ninth month ___

a. Sex can first be easily determined.
b. First signs of individual personality appear.
c. Body begins to catch up to head, growing to same proportions as at birth.
d. Fetus stops growing.
e. Growth is more rapid than at any other time during prenatal or postnatal life.
f. Reflex patterns are fully developed.
g. Layer of fat begins developing over entire body.
h. Skin becomes sensitive enough to react to tactile stimulation.
i. Fetus is first able to hear.

Multiple-Choice: Circle the choice that best completes or answers each item.

1. Mitosis, or rapid cell division, begins within how many hours after fertilization?
   a. 2
   b. 12
   c. 24
   d. 36

2. The conceptus implants itself in the wall of the uterus during which stage of prenatal development?
   a. germinal
   b. embryonic
   c. fetal
   d. uterine

3. During the germinal stage, the fertilized ovum moves from the
   a. uterus to the fallopian tube
   b. fallopian tube to the uterus
   c. ovary to the fallopian tube
   d. fallopian tube to the ovary

4. Which of the following protects the unborn child?
   a. embryonic disk
   b. endoderm
   c. amniotic sac
   d. blastocyst

5. The placenta does *all but which* of the following?
   a. provides immunity
   b. produces hormones
   c. nourishes the fetus
   d. promotes cell division

6. Which of the following is (are) most likely to cause a spontaneous abortion?
   a. chromosomal abnormalities
   b. uterine abnormalities
   c. defective sperm
   d. infection

7. The fetal stage is characterized by
   a. high risk of miscarriage
   b. rapid growth and increased complexity
   c. occurrence of developmental birth defects
   d. all of the above

8. Doctors can give fetuses blood transfusions through the
   a. placenta
   b. amniotic fluid
   c. uterine walls
   d. umbilical cord

9. Which statement about fetal learning is true, according to research?
   a. Newborns prefer male voices to female voices.
   b. Newborns cannot yet distinguish between the mother's voice and that of another woman.
   c. Newborns recognize stories that were read to them before birth.
   d. Newborns show no preferences that suggest fetal learning has taken place.

10. Babies are less at risk when their mothers gain approximately how many pounds during pregnancy?
    a. 10 to 15
    b. 16 to 20
    c. 22 to 46
    d. none of the above; there is no known correlation between the mother's weight gain and the health of the baby

11. Pregnant women need how many extra calories daily?
    a. about 200
    b. 300 to 500
    c. 800 or more
    d. none—extra calories may make the baby obese

12. A test for the presence of drugs in a newborn's system analyzes the baby's
    a. blood
    b. breath
    c. lanugo
    d. meconium

13. Which of the following statements about fetal alcohol syndrome (FAS) is true?
    a. It affects about 1 infant in 2,000 in the United States.
    b. It is characterized by extreme passivity.
    c. In infancy, it can involve sleep disturbances and weak sucking.
    d. Although severe in early childhood, its effects rarely persist into adulthood.

14. Which of the following has *not* been found to be an effect of a mother's heavy smoking during pregnancy?
    a. low birth weight
    b. stillbirth
    c. facial abnormalities
    d. retarded growth and cognitive development

15. The use of which of the following drugs by a mother during pregnancy has been linked to neurological problems?
    a. cocaine
    b. marijuana
    c. both a and b
    d. neither a nor b

16. The effects of which of the following, when ingested during pregnancy, are still in question?
    a. caffeine
    b. birth control pills
    c. DES
    d. codeine

17. AIDS can be passed to an unborn child through the mother's
    a. amniotic fluid
    b. genes
    c. blood
    d. none of the above—AIDS can be passed only through sexual contact

18. Fetal exposure to which of the following can cause gene mutations?
    a. incompatible maternal blood type
    b. lead
    c. X-rays
    d. semiconductor chips

19. One study reported in your text found that women who delay parenthood until their thirties tend to
    a. have trouble adjusting to the change in lifestyle
    b. be lax in discipline
    c. be more affectionate with their babies than younger mothers
    d. spend less time on parenting due to job demands

20. If a father is in his late thirties or older when his baby is conceived, the child may have an increased risk of
    a. Down syndrome
    b. dwarfism
    c. bone malformations
    d. all of the above

21. Which of the following women is *least* likely to obtain prenatal care?
    a. Mexican American
    b. African American
    c. White American
    d. Cuban

22. The most common cause of male infertility is
    a. low sperm count
    b. inability to ejaculate
    c. blocked passage for sperm
    d. low mobility of sperm

23. In vitro fertilization is
    a. a form of artificial insemination
    b. conception outside the body
    c. most likely to be used when the cause of infertility is insufficient ovulation
    d. still in the experimental stage

24. One study reported in your text found that, in comparison with nonadopted children, adopted children tend to
    a. be less confident
    b. view the world more negatively
    c. view their parents as less nurturing
    d. none of the above

True or False? In the blank following each item, write T (for *true*) or F (for *false*). In the space below the item, if the statement is false, rewrite it to make it true.

1. A mother's emotional attachment to her unborn baby normally occurs immediately upon her discovery that she is pregnant. ___

2. It usually takes 1 week for the fertilized ovum to reach the uterus. ___

3. The embryonic disk differentiates into three layers from which the various parts of the body will develop. ___

4. Most developmental birth defects occur during the first trimester of pregnancy. ___

5. Differences in fetal activity seem to indicate temperamental patterns that may continue into adulthood. ___

6. Research has shown that fetuses can hear. ___

7. Gaining too much weight during pregnancy is riskier than gaining too little. ___

8. It is unsafe for a pregnant woman to take aspirin. ___

9. Any ill effects on a fetus of drugs taken during pregnancy will show up at or soon after birth. ___

10. An expectant mother who takes as little as one alcoholic drink per day may harm the fetus. ___

11. Cutting down on smoking during pregnancy can increase the baby's birth weight. ___

12. If a mother contracts German measles at any time during her pregnancy, her baby is almost certain to be born deaf or with heart defects. ___

13. If the Rh factor is present in a mother's blood but not in the fetus's blood, death of the fetus can result. ___

14. Women who delay childbearing until their thirties are more likely to have complications of pregnancy than younger mothers. ___

15. Jogging, swimming, bicycling, or playing tennis is likely to overstrain a pregnant woman and endanger the fetus. ___

16. An unborn child can be harmed by the mother's smoking but not by the father's smoking. ___

17. In the United States, nearly 1 in 4 pregnant women do not receive prenatal care in the first three months. ___

18. Infertility rates have tripled since 1960. ___

19. Ovum transfer is the female equivalent of artificial insemination by a donor. ___

20. Surrogate motherhood is another name for adoption. ___

TOPICS FOR THOUGHT AND DISCUSSION

1. Some expectant fathers experience physical symptoms of pregnancy. What are some possible reasons for this phenomenon?

2. In ancient times, people believed that a clap of thunder or a jolt could cause a woman to miscarry. How do you imagine this belief might have affected the treatment and behavior of women during pregnancy?

3. Why would correspondence between levels of fetal activity and levels of activity in infancy or adulthood support the hypothesis that temperament is inborn? Can you think of any other explanations for this finding?

4. The authors of your text state that ethical considerations prevent controlled experiments to study prenatal hazards. Why? Does the fact that findings regarding these hazards must be based largely on animal research and mothers' self-reports affect your confidence in these findings?

5. The first Rh-positive baby of an Rh-negative mother is usually not in danger, but the risk is greater for each succeeding child. What hypothesis can you suggest to explain this increasing risk? How might you test your hypothesis?

6. In one 1982 study cited in your text, interviews and observations of 105 new mothers aged 16 to 38 found that the older women were more satisfied, affectionate, and effective parents than those who became mothers at an earlier age. Do you think this research gives adequate grounds for the conclusion that "the trend toward late motherhood seems to be a blessing for babies"? If not, how would you design further research on this subject? What factors would you consider?

7. According to your text, ten western European countries and Israel offer free or very low cost prenatal and postnatal care (generally from a midwife, unless the birth is high-risk); and the state of New Jersey now provides full prenatal health services for all women in the state. Do you think all states should establish similar benefits?

8. Surrogacy contracts, such as the one ultimately invalidated by the New Jersey Supreme Court in the "Baby M" case, have raised much controversy over such issues as "child buying" and whether a surrogate has a right to change her mind and keep the baby. The discussions of prenatal hazards and "fetal abuse" in this chapter suggest another concern: to what extent can or should a surrogate mother be held responsible for avoiding these hazards and contributing positively to fetal development? (Note: The "Baby M" contract provided that the surrogate, Mary Beth Whitehead, would not smoke, drink, or take drugs while pregnant, would assume all medical risks, and would undergo amniocentesis or abortion upon demand of the father, William Stern.)

CHAPTER 3 READING

INTRODUCTION

As your text points out, researchers are turning attention to the father's responsibility for birth defects. This article by health and medical writer Trisha Thompson, which appeared in *Child* magazine in June/July, 1992, examines the father's role in prenatal health.

PARTNERS IN PREGNANCY

by Trisha Thompson

I am sitting on the paper-wrapped examining table in my nurse-midwife's office, engaged in preconception counseling. I've come here for my annual Pap smear, but also for advice about what I should and shouldn't do over the next six months to prepare for pregnancy. As we talk, I glance down at my dangling legs, and for some reason that's when it dawns on me: Why isn't my husband here? If I'm in the preconception stage, then he is, too. As if by ESP the midwife begins to ask about my husband's health and lifestyle: Is he on any medication? (No.) Where does he work? (At home, as a writer.) Does he smoke? (No.) How old is he, and is he in basically good health? (He's 35, and yes.)

To the relief of most women and the surprise of some men, the father's role in fetal health is finally gaining the attention it deserves—or perhaps regaining it. Specialists in this burgeoning field are fond of pointing out that the ancient Carthaginians had a wedding ritual that forbade both the bride and the groom from drinking wine on their wedding night for fear of conceiving a deformed child. Without the benefit of laboratory mice or epidemiology, the Carthaginians knew instinctively what doctors and couples are starting to realize fully today: If it takes two to make a baby, it probably takes two to make a *healthy* baby.

Sperm Power

In the past year alone, studies have suggested that men exposed to pesticides, industrial solvents, and radiation, as well as men who drink heavily, smoke, and are over 35, may be at increased risk of fathering sick babies—babies with birth defects, babies of low birthweight, babies who are stillborn, babies who grow up to have childhood cancer—regardless of how health-conscious their female partners are. "Historically, there's been some attention given to male reproductive hazards," says Gladys Friedler, Ph.D., associate professor of psychiatry and pharmacology at Boston University School of Medicine. "But the focus was on male fertility, not on reproductive outcome. The assumption was that if the sperm got to the egg, the sperm was okay—the rest was up to the female."

This rationale seemed to make sense—after all, a fetus is housed for nine months in its mother's body, not its father's. For a long time, then, the only real concern for men was to stay clear of toxins, such as the farm pesticide dibromochloropropane, or DBCP, that could render their sperm dead or immobile. In the late Seventies, this pesticide was banned after being found to cause high rates of infertility and sterility in the men who worked at the plants that manufactured it. Radiation to the testes and chemotherapy have long been known to make men sterile, and certain medications, such as anti-cancer drugs, can temporarily lower a man's sperm count or motility (swimming ability). Despite such well-known obstacles to male fertility, these are often the last factors considered when a couple has trouble conceiving. Generally, obstetricians still look to the woman first to identify possible problems.

Dana Richards, 32, of Syracuse, New York, faced this double standard last year when she and her husband Mark Eston, 30, were trying to conceive, and hadn't had any success after six months of trying. Richards's obstetrician asked no questions about Eston, and simply advised her to get a basal thermometer to better predict her ovulatory cycles. But after talking to her family practitioner about the problem, and mentioning that for the past year Eston had been on a muscle relaxant, Chlorzoxazone, for his arthritis, her doctor "said the medication could be the problem and that he should stop using it," says Richards. A month later, she was pregnant. "I'm surprised that the arthritis doctor didn't think to tell Mark the medication might have side effects like this," says Richards.

One double standard that has been broken down, however, is the age factor: Men must also be concerned about a possible link between older age and an increased risk of siring children with birth defects. A recent controversial study suggested that men who are over 35 are 1 1/2 to 2 times more likely to father children with rare genetic defects. After much public concern, however, the author of the study, David A. Savitz, Ph.D., associate professor of epidemiology at the School of Public Health at the University of North Carolina at Chapel Hill, amended his findings: "The greatest risk is with men over 40 or 50," he now emphasizes. But it is also important to remember that an increased risk of a birth defect that's extremely rare to begin with means the incidence is still very uncommon.

Men at Work

It's not surprising that certain toxic agents can make a man infertile. What *is* surprising is that sperm can seem perfectly normal and then turn out to be horribly damaged. At least a dozen recent studies, many funded by The March of Dimes, have shown connections between birth defects and men who work in occupations in which they are continuously exposed to pesticides, lead, gasoline, and radiation, among other hazards. These men have higher-than-average rates of siring children with spina bifida, cleft palates, heart defects, or childhood cancer (brain cancer, leukemia)—although they may have had no trouble conceiving.

"We're just starting to find out how agents can cause changes in a man's genes that allow his sperm to be mutated but fertile, and then affect the health of his baby," explains Dr. Savitz. Basically, there are three ways a man's exposure to a toxic agent can affect his unborn child: The substance alters a man's sperm to the extent that his DNA is mutated, and these mutated genes go into conceiving his baby; the man brings home the substance on his clothes, and his pregnant wife inhales it; or the substance gets into the man's bloodstream and eventually his seminal fluid, which is then deposited in his pregnant wife's vagina during sex, entering her bloodstream and ultimately the fetus.

Most Hazardous Occupations for Dad*

OCCUPATION	HAZARD
1. Nonorganic farmer, pesticide plant worker	1. Pesticides like phenoxy herbicides (exposure is 1,000 times greater than from eating an apple)
2. Anesthesiologist	2. Anesthetic gases
3. Battery plant worker	3. Lead
4. Nuclear reactor plant worker, X-ray technician	4. Ionizing radiation
5. Gas station attendant, petrochemical industry worker	5. Gaseous fumes like benzene
6. House painter, paint factory worker (even "weekend" painter)	6. Lead, mercury, and solvents
7. Carpenter, logger, sawmill worker	7. Glue, wood solvents
8. Janitor	8. Industrial cleaning fluids
9. Fire fighter	9. Chemicals from smoke
10. Cab or truck driver	10. Constant road vibration may lower sperm count

*according to research by Drs. Friedler, Savitz, and Legator. For more information on male and female reproductive hazards, write: "Father," March of Dimes Birth Defects Foundation, 1275 Mamaroneck Ave., White Plains, NY 10605.

Most experts believe, however, that the first two pathways—sperm mutation and inhalation—are the most plausible because they are a man's most direct routes to his unborn child. If the sperm's germ cell (the essential building block) is mutated, the mutation is permanent. If other sperm cells are damaged, the mutation lasts only until a new batch of sperm is grown and matured, every three to four months. However, if a child is conceived during this temporary period of mutation, the effects

may last more than one generation, according to research by Dr. Friedler. In a study of male mice injected with morphine before procreation, not only were the children of these father mice born with defects, but so were their grandchildren.

Fortunately, there is a lot that can be done to avoid the legacy of sperm mutation. At the University of Massachusetts Reproductive Hazards Center in Worcester, director Maureen Paul, M.D., recently treated a house painter who came in prior to conception complaining of stomach cramps. "The man worked for a small contractor and spent most of his time scraping lead-based paint off old houses," says Dr. Paul, who is a combined specialist in obstetrics/gynecology and occupational health. The man turned out to have had lead poisoning, which was successfully treated with chelation therapy—an ingested calcium compound leaches lead out of bones; the lead is excreted in urine. Within four months, this man could safely conceive a child.

However, it's important to remember that lead poisoning may also be an occupational hazard for soon-to-be parents who are preparing the nursery, possibly stripping an old house in which the paint chips contain lead, or using new paint that contains its own toxic solvents.

Pregnant women should have as little contact with questionable substances as possible, says Marvin S. Legator, Ph.D., director of the Division of Environmental Toxicology at the University of Texas Medical Branch in Galveston. And their partners should "use these chemicals for only short periods, say half an hour at a time, and air the house out," he says.

Bottom-line advice on reproductive health hazards in the workplace is even more clear-cut. For male and female workers in risky occupations, Dr. Paul suggests taking the following steps, preferably *before* you are pregnant. First, ask your employer for "Material Safety Data Sheets" on the chemicals in your workplace. Industries under regulation by the federal Occupational Safety and Health Administration (OSHA) are required to furnish

---

12 Steps to Growing a Healthier Baby

Here are the steps both [prospective parents] should take roughly 6 months before trying to conceive—and, of course, during pregnancy.

WOMEN

1. Don't smoke, and avoid other people's cigarette smoke.

2. Don't drink, especially not during the first 12 weeks of pregnancy, when the fetus's major organs begin to develop.

3. Avoid exposure to lead, pesticides, and noxious fumes.

4. Take iron, folic acid, and calcium supplements (consult your doctor for specific amounts). Pregnancy depletes a woman's stores of these three nutrients, and a deficiency of any one can cause her baby neurological and bone disorders.

5. If you work on a personal computer, maintain a distance of three feet (arm's length) from your VDT.

6. Avoid eating salmon, swordfish, tuna, shark, and lake whitefish, which may contain toxic levels of chemicals and mercury.

MEN

1. Don't smoke—at the very least, don't smoke when you're around your pregnant wife.

2. Drink only in moderation (no more than two drinks a day), since alcohol may even reach a fetus via seminal fluid.

3. Avoid exposure to lead, pesticides, and noxious fumes.

4. Take vitamin C supplements, about 500 mg. a day; a recent study found that a deficiency can cause genetic damage in sperm, which may be passed along to a baby at conception.

5. Go to as many obstetrician appointments with your wife as possible—you too are having a baby.

6. Be a calming influence on your family; the less stress your wife feels, the more hospitable her uterine environment.

---

these. If not, find out the generic (not just the brand) names of the substances in your workplace and have the levels of exposure measured by a professional (contact your building manager).

Give your doctor this information, and if he or she doesn't have access to a toxicology data base, researchers at the National Institute for Occupational Safety and Health (NIOSH), at

(800) 356-4674, may have some answers. You can also call OSHA in the largest city near you and ask them to inspect your job site.

Habit Hazards

Although occupational hazards are a serious matter, experts agree that the closer-to-home hazards of cigarette smoking and excessive drinking are a much greater concern. Several studies have shown that the children of fathers who smoked and drank (roughly more than two drinks a day) before conception had higher rates of birth defects and low birthweight, regardless of their mothers' abstinence.

"If you look at cigarette smoke as a toxic chemical soup, many ingredients in it are exactly those you find in industrial toxins—benzene, trichloral etholene," says Dr. Legator. As yet, no one is sure of the amount of smoking that causes damage, and whether the damage results from the mother's passive inhalation, the fact that toxic byproducts find their way into a man's semen, or both. In any case, most experts echo the stern advice of Dr. Legator: "If you're trying to have a kid or you're already pregnant, both you *and* your spouse should stop smoking." As for drinking, it is unlikely that we'll see warnings for fathers-to-be on beer bottles anytime soon, but these men should nonetheless avoid heavy drinking—limiting their intake to a drink or two a day—during the few months before they plan to conceive. It's also wise to refrain from heavy drinking throughout pregnancy to avoid the possibility that during intercourse alcohol-affected semen may enter the bloodstream of the mother and child.

The Stress Factor

While a couple's health habits and physical environment can be reformed, their emotional environment is tougher to control. Some of the newest research is exploring how stress can affect an unborn baby. One recent study shows that stressed-out pregnant women are most likely to fall into depression, causing biochemical changes in the womb that may influence a baby's developing nervous system. Many of these babies enter the world "jittery and apt to cry more," says study leader Barry Zuckerman, M.D., a professor of pediatrics at Boston University School of Medicine. The point, says Dr. Zuckerman, is for couples to recognize when this is happening and get help from family, friends, and community resource centers as early as possible.

More recently, a provocative study conducted by researchers at Boston City Hospital and Boston University School of Medicine found that Type A mothers—rated so because of their high level of job involvement—had babies who cried more and were more intense than babies born to more relaxed Type B mothers. Researcher Steven Parker,

M.D., speculated that while genetics may play a part in shaping the babies' temperaments, the high levels of stress a Type A woman typically feels may "alter the intrauterine environment in a way that affects her baby's behavior."

Until the verdict is in on stress during pregnancy, couples are wise to keep tensions in check by focusing their energies on what is truly most important in their lives at this time: growing a healthy baby. Perhaps the best thing about the new emphasis on a teamwork approach to conception and pregnancy is that it lays the groundwork for a teamwork approach to parenting—something that will come in handy over the next 18 years or so.

QUESTIONS ABOUT THE READING

1. What factors do you suppose may have led to the recent attention to men's responsibility for problems in conception, birth defects, and fetal health?

2. The article does not tell how *great* an increase in risk is associated with the conduct discussed, except in one instance in which a study concludes that the increased risk remains negligible. Is any risk, no matter how minimal, enough to call for a change in conduct? How would you imagine that the categories of conduct discussed—occupation, lifestyle habits, and stress—compare in degree of risk? In difficulty of alteration?

3. What would you do if you believed that your spouse might be endangering the health of your unborn child by occupation, habits, or other conduct?

4. Dr. Maureen Paul, director of the University of Massachusetts Reproductive Hazards Center, suggests how prospective parents can ascertain whether they are being exposed to reproductive health hazards in the workplace. Do you think most employers would cooperate with such an investigation? If not, what could be done to obtain their cooperation? What practical steps could an employee take if such an

investigation determined that he or she was being exposed to unsafe levels of toxic chemicals?

5.   Is Dr. Parker's speculation regarding the roles of genetics and environment in shaping the temperaments of babies of Type A mothers consistent with the treatment of influences on temperament in Chapter 2 of your text? (Note: The subject of temperament is treated in more depth in Chapter 7.)

6.   Your text, in Box 3-1, discusses issues involved in balancing fetal health against the personal freedom of the mother.

Considering the hazards discussed in this article, what should be a child's legal rights, if any, against parents who jeopardize fetal health? To what degree should parents' legal responsibility reflect their moral responsibility?

7.   The article touches on a "double standard" regarding which partner is responsible for infertility. If, as the article states, at least some obstacles to male fertility are well-known, why do you suppose doctors tend to look first to the woman to identify the source of the problem?

ANSWER KEY FOR CHAPTER 3

Note: Numbers in parentheses refer to pages in the textbook where answers can be found.

CHAPTER 3 REVIEW

Learning Objectives for Section I

1.   (pages 102-103)

Important Terms for Section I

1.   266 (page 104)
2.   germinal (104)
3.   embryo (107)
4.   bone cells (107)
5.   impact (107)
6.   miscarriage (107)
7.   8, 12 (108)
8.   fetal, 8, 12 (108)

Learning Objectives for Section II

1.   (pages 104)
2.   (104-107)
3.   (104-107)
4.   (106-107)
5.   (107)
6.   (105, 107)
7.   (107)
8.   (105-106, 108)

9.   (108-110)
10.   (109)

Important Terms for Section III

1.   defects (page 110)
2.   fetal alcohol syndrome (FAS) (page 114)
3.   functioning (119)
4.   fetus, mother (119)

Learning Objectives for Section III

1.   (pages 110-113)
2.   (112)
3.   (113-118)
4.   (118)
5.   (119)
6.   (119-120)
7.   (120)
8.   (120)
9.   (120-121)
10.   (121)
11.   (122)
12.   (123)
13.   (123-125)

Important Terms for Section IV

1.   infertility (page 125)
2.   cervix (126)
3.   in vitro (126)

4. uterus (127)
5. surrogate (127)

Learning Objectives for Section IV

1. (pages 125-126)
2. (126-128)
3. (128-129)

Learning Objectives for Section V

1. (pages 129-130)
2. (130-131)
3. (131)

CHAPTER 3 QUIZ

Matching—Month by Month
(All answers can be found on pages 105-106.)

1. e
2. h
3. a
4. c
5. b
6. i
7. f
8. g
9. d

Multiple-Choice

1. d (page 104)
2. a (104-107)
3. b (104)
4. c (106-107)
5. d (106-107)
6. a (107)
7. b (108)
8. d (109)
9. c (109-110)
10. c (110-111)
11. b (113)
12. d (113)
13. c (114)
14. c (116)
15. c (115-116, 117)
16. a (118)
17. c (119)
18. c (120)
19. c (120)
20. d (122)
21. a (124)
22. a (125)
23. b (126)
24. d (129)

True or False?

1. F—It takes time for emotional attachment to an unborn baby to develop. (page 103)
2. F—It normally takes 3 or 4 days for the fertilized ovum to reach the uterus. (104)
3. T (104-106)
4. T (107)
5. T (108)
6. T (109)
7. F—Gaining too little weight during pregnancy is riskier than gaining too much. (110-111)
8. T (113)
9. F—The effects of some drugs, such as the synthetic hormone DES, may not show up for many years. (113-114)
10. T (114)
11. T (116)
12. F—If a mother contracts German measles before the eleventh week of pregnancy, her baby is almost certain to be born deaf and to have heart defects. (118)
13. F—When the Rh factor is present in the fetus's blood but not in the mother's blood, death of the fetus can result. (119)
14. T (120)
15. F—Regular, moderate exercise can contribute to a more comfortable pregnancy and an easier, safer delivery and seems to have no ill effects on the fetuses of healthy women. (121, 123)
16. F—The father's smoking is associated with lower birthweight and a greater likelihood of his child's contracting cancer as an adult. (122)
17. T (124)
18. T (125)
19. T (127)
20. F—Surrogate motherhood is impregnation of a woman who for a fee carries a baby to term and gives it to the biological father and his wife. (127-128)

BIRTH AND
THE NEWBORN BABY

OVERVIEW

Chapter 4 begins with the drama of birth: the climax of fetal development and the curtain raiser on child development in the world outside the womb. In this chapter, the authors:

- Describe what happens during the four stages, or phases, of childbirth

- Discuss the pros and cons of various methods of, and alternative settings for, childbirth and of electronic fetal monitoring

- Identify factors affecting women's and men's reactions to childbirth

- Discuss potential complications of childbirth, including low birthweight, postmaturity, birth trauma, and stillbirth

- Describe the physical characteristics of a newborn baby and the changes in functioning of body systems that occur with the cutting of the umbilical cord

- Explain how the Apgar scale, the Brazelton scale, and other neonatal screening instruments are used to check the health and functioning of the newborn

- Describe the typical alternation of newborns' states of arousal

- Discuss whether there is a critical time for bonding between infants and their mothers

---
CHAPTER 4 REVIEW

Section I The Birth Process

FRAMEWORK FOR SECTION I

A. Birth and Biology: The Phases of Childbirth
   1. The First Stage of Childbirth
   2. The Second Stage of Childbirth
   3. The Third and Fourth Stages of Childbirth
B. Birth and Society: Helping the Mother and Baby
   1. Methods of Childbirth
      a. Medicated Delivery
      b. Natural and Prepared Childbirth
      c. Cesarean Delivery
   2. Medical Monitoring
   3. Alternative Settings for Giving Birth
C. Parents' Reactions to Childbirth
D. Complications of Childbirth
   1. Low Birthweight
      a. Who Is Likely to Have a Low-Birthweight Baby?
      b. Cross-Cultural Aspects of Low Birthweight
      c. Consequences of Low Birthweight
      d. Treatment of Low-Birthweight Babies
      e. The Impact of the Social Environment
   2. Postmaturity
   3. Birth Trauma
   4. Stillbirth

IMPORTANT TERMS FOR SECTION I

Completion: Fill in the blanks to complete the definitions of key terms for this section of Chapter 4.

1. _____ **delivery:** Surgical procedure to remove the baby from the uterus.

2. **electronic fetal monitoring:** Use of machines that track the baby's _____ during labor and delivery.

3. **low birthweight:** Substandard weight at birth—below _____ grams (_____ pounds).

4. **preterm infants:** Infants born early, that is, prematurely, before the _____ period is complete.

5. **small-for-date infants:** Infants weighing less than 90 percent of all babies born at the same _____ age.

6. **birth** _____: Injury sustained at the time of birth.

7. _____: Oxygen deprivation at birth.

LEARNING OBJECTIVES FOR SECTION I

After reading and reviewing this section of Chapter 4, you should be able to do the following.

1. Describe what occurs during each of the four stages, or phases, of labor.

2. Discuss considerations that should enter into a woman's decision whether or not to have a medicated delivery.

3. Explain the principles of natural and prepared childbirth and describe some elements of the Lamaze method.

4. Discuss some common reasons for and risks of cesarean delivery.

5. Discuss reasons for using electronic fetal monitoring during childbirth and drawbacks of its use.

6. Discuss considerations in choosing whether to give birth in a hospital, at home, or in a birth center or maternity center, and in choosing attendance by a physician or a midwife and a doula.

7. Cite factors that affect parents' reactions to childbirth.

8. Explain the difference between preterm (premature) and small-for-date infants.

9. Name four types of factors that put some women at risk of bearing low-birthweight babies, and give an example of each type.

10. Compare low-birthweight rates among various cultural groups and cite possible reasons for the high rates among African-Americans.

11. Discuss immediate and long-term consequences of low birthweight.

12. Describe methods of care and treatment of low-birthweight babies immediately after birth that can improve their chances of survival.

13. Discuss the impact of the home environment on the long-term outlook for low-birthweight babies.

14. Identify considerations involved, when a baby is postmature, in deciding whether to induce labor or deliver by the cesarean method.

15. Discuss environmental factors affecting the long-term outlook for children who have suffered birth trauma.

16. Describe the typical process of grieving for a stillborn baby.

Section II   The Newborn

FRAMEWORK FOR SECTION II

A. Who Is the Newborn?
B. How Does the Newborn Function?
    1. The Newborn's Body Systems
        a. Circulatory System
        b. Respiratory System
        c. Gastrointestinal System
        d. Temperature Regulation
    2. Medical and Behavioral Screening: Is the Baby Healthy?
        a. Immediate Medical Assessment: Apgar Scale
        b. Screening Newborns for Medical Conditions
        c. Assessing Responses: The Brazelton Scale
    3. Infants States of Arousal
C. The Mother-Infant Bond
    1. Imprinting
    2. Is There a Critical Period for Forming the Bond between Infants and Their Mothers?

IMPORTANT TERMS FOR SECTION II

Completion: Fill in the blanks to complete the definitions of key terms for this section of Chapter 4.

1. **neonate:** Newborn up to _____ month(s) of age.

2. **Apgar scale:** A method of assessing the baby's health immediately after _____.

3. **states of _____:** Conditions of alertness in a baby; the sleep-wake cycle.

4. **imprinting:** Rapid learning process early in life that establishes a behavior _____.

5. **mother-infant _____:** Feeling of close, caring connection between mother and newborn.

LEARNING OBJECTIVES FOR SECTION II

After reading and reviewing this section of Chapter 4, you should be able to do the following.

1. Describe the typical appearance of a neonate.

2. Contrast the circulatory, respiratory, gastrointestinal, and temperature-regulation systems in a fetus with those in a newborn.

3. Identify three tests given to newborns to assess their health or the normality of their responses or to identify babies with specific correctable defects.

4. Describe typical patterns of eating, sleeping, and waking and explain the developmental effects of individual variations in these early patterns.

5. Suggest several methods of comforting a crying baby and explain why providing such comfort assists the baby's healthy development.

6. Describe the current state of research on the question of a critical period for mother-infant bonding.

CHAPTER 4 QUIZ

Matching—Numbers: For each of the items in the column at the left, fill in the correct number from the column at the right.

1. Number of weeks in the neonatal period ___	1
2. Age below which a woman is at risk of bearing an underweight infant ___	4
3. Age above which a woman is at risk of bearing an underweight infant ___	7
4. Number of weeks of gestation at which a birth is considered postmature ___	16
5. Approximate length in inches of the average newborn ___	17
6. Number of minutes after delivery when Apgar scale is first administered ___	20
7. Minimum score attained by 90 percent of normal infants on Apgar scale ___	34
8. Average number of hours per day a newborn sleeps ___	42

Multiple-Choice: Circle the choice that best completes or answers each item.

1. Normal full-term gestation is ___ days.
   a. 66
   b. 166
   c. 266
   d. 366

2. During the first stage of labor
   a. the mother's cervix dilates to permit passage of the baby's head out of the uterus
   b. the mother experiences "false" labor pains
   c. the mother bears down to permit passage of the baby
   d. the baby's head begins to move through the cervix and vaginal canal

3. The movement of the baby through the cervix and vaginal canal generally takes approximately
   a. 10 minutes
   b. 30 minutes
   c. 1 1/2 hours
   d. 12 to 24 hours

4. The umbilical cord and placenta are expelled from the womb
   a. during the first stage of labor
   b. during the second stage of labor
   c. during the third stage of labor
   d. as soon as the cervix is fully dilated

5. Research has established that medicated delivery
   a. causes permanent deficits in motor and physiological response
   b. causes mothers to feel more positive toward their babies
   c. has no effect on babies
   d. none of the above; studies have yielded contradictory results

6. Natural childbirth involves educating and training women in order to eliminate
   a. the need for attending physicians
   b. severe contractions
   c. fear and pain
   d. the need for medical monitoring

7. Which of the following is *not* an element of the Lamaze method of childbirth?
   a. education about childbirth
   b. control of breathing
   c. coaching
   d. concentration on birth contractions

8. Which of the following tends to be a problem with elective cesarean deliveries as opposed to vaginal deliveries?
   a. Risk of infection is higher.
   b. Stress hormones are not released in the baby.
   c. The mother's recovery takes longer.
   d. each of the above

9. "False positive" readings on electronic fetal monitors during childbirth suggest that fetuses
   a. are in trouble when in fact they are not
   b. have normal heartbeats when in fact they do not
   c. are at risk of premature expulsion when in fact they are not
   d. are in position for delivery when in fact they are not

10. A doula is
    a. another term for midwife
    b. an experienced companion who provides emotional support during childbirth
    c. needed chiefly during forceps deliveries
    d. called upon to administer anesthesia

11. Men who are present at the birth of their babies
    a. often see the event as a peak emotional experience
    b. tend to be better fathers than men who are not present during childbirth
    c. are more emotionally committed to their children
    d. all of the above

12. Low-birthweight babies are defined as weighing less than
    a. 3 pounds
    b. 4 1/2 pounds
    c. 5 1/2 pounds
    d. 7 pounds

13. Other things being equal, which of the following women would be *least* likely to deliver a low-birthweight baby?
    a. 23-year-old bearing her second child 2 years after the birth of the first
    b. 23-year-old smoker
    c. 35-year-old bearing twins
    d. woman who was herself low-birthweight

14. According to current rates, which of the following women is *least* likely to deliver a low-birthweight baby?
    a. African American
    b. Asian American
    c. Hispanic American
    d. white American

15. Which of the following is *not* a common problem for low-birthweight babies?
    a. high body temperature
    b. irregular breathing
    c. infection
    d. immature reflexes

16. Studies of very low-birthweight Dutch and American children found that the most important factor in their cognitive development was
    a. the mother's educational level
    b. stimulation in the home environment
    c. health during the neonatal period
    d. family income

17. The number of stillborn infants is
    a. nearly 1 in 25
    b. fewer than 1 in 100
    c. about 1 in 1000
    d. none of the above; the number is unknown

18. The weight of an average newborn is about
    a. 5 pounds
    b. 6 1/2 pounds
    c. 7 1/2 pounds
    d. 9 pounds

19. The umbilical cord is essential to *all but which* of the following fetal body systems?
    a. circulatory
    b. respiratory
    c. gastrointestinal
    d. temperature regulation

20. Which of the following is *not* assessed by the Brazelton Neonatal Behavioral Assessment Scale?
    a. alertness
    b. respiration
    c. muscle tone
    d. startle reaction

21. Which of the following sleep patterns is typical of neonates?
    a. six to eight sleep periods of 2 to 3 hours each
    b. four or five sleep periods of approximately 4 hours each
    c. shorter sleep periods in the daytime and longer sleep periods at night
    d. none of the above; sleep patterns are so individual that no typical pattern can be described

22. Research on mother-infant bonding has established that babies who are separated from their mothers immediately after birth are more likely to
    a. die in infancy
    b. show cognitive deficits
    c. have difficulty bonding with the mother
    d. none of the above; most research found no long-term effects

True or False? In the blank following each item, write T (for *true*) or F (for *false*). In the space below each item, if the statement is false, rewrite it to make it true.

1. The first stage of labor typically lasts 12 hours or more for a first baby. ____

2. The first stage of labor is painful because of the stretching of the vagina as the baby's head pushes against it. ____

3. The mother has no control over the baby's progress through the vaginal canal. ____

4. In most childbirths, general anesthesia is routinely administered to the mother. ____

5. Research confirms that a maternal instinct causes mothers to respond positively to their babies' needs. ____

6. In the Lamaze method, an expectant mother is conditioned to alternately relax and tense her muscles in response to the voice of her husband or another labor "coach." ____

7. The rate of cesarean deliveries in the United States is lower than the rate in Greece or Czechoslovakia. ___

8. Uterine contractions apparently trigger release of hormones that help babies survive the stress of birth. ___

9. It is safer for a woman who has had a cesarean delivery to have vaginal delivery in subsequent births. ___

10. Electronic fetal monitoring has led to fewer cesarean births. ___

11. In the Netherlands, more than one-third of babies are born at home, with midwives rather than physicians attending. ___

12. More than 6 out of 10 infants who die during the first year had low birth weight. ___

13. A woman who gains less than 14 pounds during pregnancy risks bearing a low-birthweight baby. ___

14. When socioeconomic status and age of pregnancy are controlled, African American women are no more likely than white women to bear low-birthweight babies. ___

15. A baby weighing less than 2 pounds at birth is almost certain to die in infancy. ___

16. Stroking low-birthweight babies increases the amount of weight they are likely to gain. ___

17. Not much can be done to prevent cognitive deficits in children who were low-birthweight babies. ___

18. The longer the gestation period, the healthier an infant is likely to be. ___

19. Birth trauma is irreversible. ___

20. Newborns lose weight during the first few days of life. ___

21. A newborn who has thin skin, has hair covering its body, and has swollen breasts with secretions is probably unhealthy. ___

22. About half of all babies develop neonatal jaundice a few days after birth. ___

23. A low Brazelton score means that a newborn needs help to establish breathing. ___

24. Parents should not pick up and hold a crying infant, or the baby will become spoiled and cry for attention. ___

25. Research supports the idea of a critical period for mother-infant bonding. ___

TOPICS FOR THOUGHT AND DISCUSSION

1. Critics of conventional American childbirth practices charge that some of these practices meet the concerns of doctors and medical institutions more than the needs of mothers and babies. What practices described in this chapter seem to substantiate this charge? What defenses might medical professionals offer?

2. The authors state that a woman in labor is the "only person who can gauge her pain and is the most concerned about her child's well-being." In the light of mixed research findings about the effects on babies of anesthetics administered to the mother during childbirth, how should a woman weigh those two factors in deciding whether or not to have a medicated delivery? What voice, if any, should the father have in the decision? Considering recent attempts to prosecute mothers who used drugs such as cocaine while pregnant, does a pregnant woman owe it to her child to avoid intake of potentially harmful substances under *any* circumstances?

3. Why do you think the Lamaze method has become popular in the United States, where medicated deliveries are common?

4. Given the risks associated with cesarean deliveries, why are they performed so frequently in the United States? Your text suggests some reasons doctors may have for performing them; what factors might motivate women to have them?

5. If a father's emotional commitment to his child does not depend on the father's presence during delivery, what benefits, if any, may nonetheless be gained from the father's presence?

6. Your textbook mentions that a favorable environment may be able to overcome or ameliorate effects of low birthweight or birth trauma. That being so, would you favor a systematic program of interventions such as those tested in the Infant Health and Development Program (IHDP) studies? In a time of budgetary cutbacks, how much priority, if any, should be given to establishing such a program?

7. Can you suggest possible reasons for the finding that mother-child bonding immediately after birth may not be as critical for human babies as for ducks, sheep, and goats?

CHAPTER 4 READING

INTRODUCTION

Louise Erdrich is an award-winning author of fiction and poetry; among her novels are *Love Medicine* (1984) and *The Crown of Columbus* (1991), the latter written with her husband, Michael Dorris. After their marriage, Erdrich adopted Dorris's three children, and they have had three more children together. *The Blue Jay's Dance: A Birth Year*, published in 1995, is presented as a mother's diary. Erdrich relates her experiences during her third daughter's first year of life to the creative patterns of writing and the rhythms of nature outside the New Hampshire farmhouse where she and her husband live and work. In this excerpt, she describes her feelings during the baby's birth.

EXCERPTS FROM "THE BLUE JAY'S DANCE: A BIRTH YEAR"

by Louise Erdrich

Women's Work

Rocking, breathing, groaning, mouthing circles of distress, laughing, whistling, pounding, wavering, digging, pulling, pushing—labor is the most involuntary work we do. My body gallops to these rhythms. I'm along for the ride, at times in some control and at others dragged along as if foot-caught in a stirrup. I don't have much to do at first but breathe, accept ice chips, make jokes—in fear and pain my family makes jokes, that's how we deal with what we can't change, how we show our courage.

Even though I am a writer and have practiced my craft for years, and have experienced two natural childbirths and an epidural-assisted childbirth, I find women's labor extremely difficult to describe. In the first place, there are all sorts of labor and no "correct" way to do it. I bow to the power and grandeur of those who insist on natural childbirth, but I find the pieties that often attend the process irritating. I am all for pain relief or cesareans when women want and need these procedures. Enduring pain in itself doesn't make one a better person,

though if your mind is prepared, pain of this sort—a meaningful and determined pain based on ardor and potential joy—can be deeply instructive, can change your life.

Perhaps there is no adequate description for something that happens with such full-on physical force, but the problem inherent to birth narratives is also historical—women haven't had a voice or education, or have been overwhelmed, unconscious, stifled, just plain worn out or worse, ill to the death. Although every birth is a story, there are only so many outcomes possible. Birth is dictated to the consciousness by the conscious body. There are certain frustrations in approaching such an event, a drama in which the body stars and not the fiction-making mind. In a certain way, I'm jealous. I want to control the tale. I can't—therein lies the conflict that drives this plot in the first place. I have to trust this body—a thing inherently bound to betray me, an unreliable conveyance, a passion-driven cab that tries its best to let me off in bad neighborhoods, an adolescent that rebels against my better self, that eats erratically and sleeps too much, that grows another human with my grudging admiration, a sensation grabber, unpenitent, remorseless, amoral.

Birth is intensely spiritual and physical all at once. The contractions do not stop. There is no giving up this physical prayer. The person who experiences birth with the closest degree of awareness is the mother—but not only am I physically programmed to forget the experience to some degree (our brains "extinct" fear, we are all programmed to forget pain over time, and hormones seem to assist), I am overwhelmed by what is happening to me. I certainly can't take notes, jot down my sensations, or even have them with any perspective after a while. And then, once our baby is actually born, the experience of labor, even at its most intense, is eclipsed by the presence of an infant.

The problem of narrative involves, too, more than just embarrassment about a physical process. We're taught to suppress its importance over time, to devalue and belittle an experience in which we are bound up in the circular drama of human fate, in a state of heightened awareness and receptivity, at a crux where we intuit connections and, for a moment, unlock time's hold like a brace, even step from our bodies. Labor often becomes both paradigm and parable. The story of the body becomes a touchstone, a predictor. A mother or a father, in describing their labor, relates the personality of the child to some piece of the event, makes the story into a frame, an introduction, a prelude to the child's life, molds the labor into the story that is no longer a woman's story or a man's story, but the story of a child.

The first part of labor feels, to me anyway, like dance exercises—slow stretches that become only slightly painful as a muscle is pulled to its limit. After each contraction, the feeling subsides. The contractions move in longer waves, one after another, closer and closer together until a sea of physical sensation washes and then crashes over. In the beginning I breathe in concentration, watching Michael's eyes. I feel myself slip beneath the waves as they roar over, cresting just above my head. I duck every time the contraction peaks. As the hours pass and one wave builds on another there are times the undertow grabs me. I struggle, slammed to the bottom, unable to gather the force of nerve for the next. Thrown down, I rely on animal fierceness, swim back, surface, breathe, and try to stay open, willing. Staying *open and willing* is difficult. Very often in labor one must fight the instinct to resist pain and instead embrace it, move toward it, work with what hurts the most.

The waves come faster. Charlotte [the midwife] asks me to keep breathing *yes, yes*. To say yes instead of shuddering in refusal. Whether I am standing on the earth or not, whether I am moored to the dock, whether I remember who I am, whether I am mentally prepared, whether I am going to float beneath or ride above, the waves pound in. At shorter intervals, crazy now, electric, in storms, they wash. Sometimes I'm gone. I've poured myself into some deeper fissure below the sea only to be dragged forth, hair streaming. During transition, as the baby is ready to be pushed out into life, the waves are no longer made of water, but neons so brilliant I gasp in shock and flourish my arms, letting the colors explode from my fingertips in banners, in ribbons, in iridescent trails—of pain, it is true, unendurable sometimes, and yet we do endure.

Some push once, some don't push at all, some push in pleasure, some not and some, like me, for hours. We wreak havoc, make animal faces, ugly bare-toothed faces, go red, go darker, whiter, stranger, turn to bears. We choke spouses, beat nurses, beg them, beg doctors, weep and focus. It is our work, our body's work

that is involved in its own goodness. For, even though it wants at times to lie down and quit, the body is an honest hard-working marvel that gives everything to this one task.

Archery

During a time of grief in my father and mother's house, during a period when their adolescent children seemed lighted with a self-destructive fire beyond their control, I found the quote so often used about children written on a scrap of paper in my father's odd and lovely handwriting.

You are the bows from which your children as living arrows are sent forth . . . . Let your bending in the archer's hand be for gladness.

Because my parents for a time practiced archery, I know what it is to try to bend a bow that was too massive for my strength. In the last stages of labor, gathering into each push and bearing the strange power of transition, a woman bends the great ash bow with an unpossessed power. She struggles until her body finds the proper angle, the force, the calm. The fiberglass, the burnished woods, increase in tension and resilience. Each archer feels the despairing fear it cannot be done. But it will, somehow. Walking in the streets or the trails sometimes, now, looking at the women and their children as they pass, I think of them all as women who have labored, who have bent the bow too great for their strength.

QUESTIONS ABOUT THE READING

1. How does Erdrich's description of the physical sensations of the first two stages of childbirth compare with that in your text?

2. Erdrich mentions that she has experienced two natural childbirths and one epidural-assisted childbirth (what your text calls regional, or local, anesthesia). Which type of birth does she seem to be describing here?

3. Erdrich does not mention the setting in which the birth occurred, though she does mention the presence of a midwife. Can you guess or infer where the birth may have taken place?

4. In what ways do Erdrich's statements about natural versus medicated childbirth and cesarean delivery appear to be consistent or inconsistent with the information presented in your text? What do you think Erdrich means when she refers to the "pieties" that often attend natural childbirth? In what ways do you imagine that "pain of this sort . . . can be deeply instructive, can change your life"?

5. According to your text, exultation, relief, pride, and wonder—as well as pain and anxiety—are typical maternal reactions to childbirth. In what passages does Erdrich seem to express each of these emotions? If you have ever had a baby, how did your experience and your reactions compare to Erdrich's?

6. Erdrich writes of her frustration at being unable to control her "unreliable" body in the birth process; in another passage, she compares the experience of labor to bending a bow too great for one's strength. According to your text, are there any ways in which women can exercise some control over the outcome of childbirth?

ANSWER KEY FOR CHAPTER 4

Note: Numbers in parentheses refer to pages in the textbook where answers can be found.

CHAPTER 4 REVIEW

Important Terms for Section I

1. cesarean (page 142)
2. heartbeat (144)
3. 2500, 5 1/2 (147)
4. gestation (147)
5. gestational (147)
6. trauma (152)
7. anoxia (152)

Learning Objectives for Section I

1. (pages 137-139)
2. (139-140)
3. (140-142)
4. (142-144)
5. (144-145)
6. (145-146)
7. (146-147)
8. (147)
9. (147-148)
10. (148-149)
11. (149-150)
12. (150-151)
13. (151-152)
14. (152)
15. (152-153)
16. (153)

Important Terms for Section II

1. 1 (page 153)
2. birth (156)
3. arousal (158)
4. pattern (159)
5. bond (160)

Learning Objectives for Section II

1. (pages 153-154)
2. (155-156)
3. (156-158)
4. (158-159)
5. (160)
6. (160-161)

CHAPTER 4 QUIZ

Matching—Numbers

1. 4 (page 153)
2. 17 (148)
3. 34 (148)
4. 42 (152)
5. 20 (153)
6. 1 (156)
7. 7 (156)
8. 16 (158)

Multiple-Choice

1. c (page 136)
2. a (137)
3. c (138)
4. c (138)
5. d (139-140)
6. c (140-141)
7. d (141)
8. d (142, 144)
9. a (144)
10. b (145)
11. a (147)
12. c (147)
13. a (148)
14. b (149)
15. a (149)
16. b (151)
17. b (153)
18. c (153)
19. d (155-156)
20. b (157-158)
21. a (158)
22. d (160)

True or False?

1. T (page 137)
2. F—The first stage of labor is painful primarily because of the stretching, or dilation, of the cervix. (138)
3. F—The mother's bearing down with her abdominal muscles during each contraction helps the baby leave her body. (138)
4. F—General anesthesia is rarely used today. (139)
5. F—Many professionals believe there is no "maternal instinct"; a mother's response to her baby largely depends on the baby's behavior. (139)
6. T (141)
7. F—The rate of cesarean deliveries in the United States is among the highest in the world and is higher than in Greece or Czechoslovakia. (143)
8. T (144)
9. F—Two studies found a risk of rupturing the uterus when vaginal delivery follows an initial cesarean delivery. (143-144)
10. F—Electronic fetal monitoring often produces "false-positive" readings that lead doctors to deliver babies by cesarean section rather than vaginally. (144)
11. T (145)
12. T (147)
13. T (148)
14. F—While poverty and age are factors in the high rates of low birth weight among African American babies, even college-educated black women are more likely than white women to bear low-birthweight babies. (149)
15. F—In one study, 36 percent of babies weighing less than 1.76 pounds survived. (150)
16. T (151)
17. F—Studies show that socioeconomic circumstances, especially a stimulating home environment, can favorably influence cognitive development of low-birthweight babies. (151-152)
18. F—Postmature babies tend to have received insufficient blood and oxygen toward the end of gestation and are at higher risk of brain damage or death. (152)
19. F—The effects of birth injuries often can be counteracted by a favorable environment. (152-153)
20. T (154)
21. F—Thin skin, body hair, and swollen breasts with secretions are normal attributes of many newborns. (154)
22. T (156)
23. F—A low Apgar score means that a newborn needs help to establish breathing. (156-157)
24. F—Babies whose cries bring relief tend to become more self-confident and to communicate more without crying than babies whose cries are ignored or punished; it is particularly important to quiet low-birthweight babies, because quiet babies maintain their weight better. (159, 160)
25. F—Research has largely discredited the idea of a critical period for mother-infant bonding. (160-161)

PHYSICAL DEVELOPMENT AND HEALTH IN INFANCY AND TODDLERHOOD

OVERVIEW

Chapter 5 describes babies' physical growth and their rapidly developing sensory capabilities and motor skills, as well as threats to life and health. In this chapter, the authors:

- Identify the principles that govern physical development

- Describe the growth of body and brain and explain how this growth may be affected by environmental influences

- Explain the significance of inborn reflexes

- Discuss how babies should be nourished

- Trace highlights of infants' sensory and motor development

- Discuss factors that contribute to infant mortality and possible causes and prevention of Sudden Infant Death Syndrome (SIDS)

- Discuss trends in, and social policies regarding, immunization against childhood diseases

CHAPTER 5 REVIEW

Section I How Physical Development Takes Place

FRAMEWORK FOR SECTION I

A. Two Principles of Physical Development
B. Physical Development of the Two Sexes

IMPORTANT TERMS FOR SECTION I

Completion: Fill in the blanks to complete the definitions of key terms for this section of Chapter 5.

1. **maturation:** The unfolding of patterns of behavior in a biologically determined, age-related _____.

2. _____ **principle:** Principle that development proceeds in a "head-to-tail" direction: The upper body parts develop before the lower parts.

3. _____ **principle:** Principle that development proceeds in a near-to-far manner: The parts of the body near its center (spinal cord) develop before the extremities.

LEARNING OBJECTIVES FOR SECTION I

After reading and reviewing this section of Chapter 5, you should be able to do the following.

1. Explain the role and significance of maturation.

2. Give two examples of the cephalocaudal principle of physical development and two examples of the proximodistal principle.

3. Compare the physical development of boys and girls during infancy and toddlerhood.

Section II Growth

FRAMEWORK FOR SECTION II

A. Growth of the Body
    1. Height and Weight
    2. Influences on Growth
B. Growth of the Brain
    1. Development of the Nervous System
    2. How the Environment Influences Brain Development
    3. Reflex Behaviors
C. Nutrition in Infancy
    1. Breastfeeding
        a. Benefits of Breastfeeding
        b. The Cultural Context of Breastfeeding
        c. Encouraging Breastfeeding
    2. Bottle-Feeding
    3. Cow's Milk and Solid Foods

IMPORTANT TERM FOR SECTION II

Completion: Fill in the blank to complete the definition of the key term for this section of Chapter 5.

1. **reflex behavior:** _____ reaction to stimulation.

LEARNING OBJECTIVES FOR SECTION II

After reading and reviewing this section of Chapter 5, you should be able to do the following.

1. Describe typical changes in weight, height, body shape, and tooth development during the first 3 years.

2. Identify genetic and environmental influences on body growth.

3. Describe the growth and development of an infant's brain and nervous system.

4. Describe animal studies that support the idea of plasticity of the brain, and give one negative and one positive example of the effect of environment on brain development in humans.

5. Name at least four primitive reflexes; explain their purpose and the significance of their disappearance during infancy; and give examples of ethnic and cultural variations in reflex behavior.

6. Explain why breast milk has been described as the "ultimate health food" for babies.

7. List at least four signs of a well-nourished baby and at least four signs of a malnourished baby.

8. Discuss the incidence of breastfeeding among various demographic groups, the relative merits of breastfeeding and bottle-feeding, and ways to encourage breastfeeding.

9. Explain at what ages it is advisable to introduce cow's milk, fruit juices, and solid foods.

10. Summarize research on the long-term effects of obesity in infancy.

Section III   Early Sensory Capacities

FRAMEWORK FOR SECTION III

A. Sight
    1. Depth Perception
    2. Visual Preferences
B. Hearing
C. Smell
D. Taste
E. Touch
F. Pain Sensitivity

IMPORTANT TERMS FOR SECTION III

Completion: Fill in the blanks to complete the definitions of key terms for this section of Chapter 5.

1. **visual cliff:** Apparatus for testing _____.
2. **visual _____:** An infant's tendency to look longer at certain stimuli than at others, which depends on the ability to differentiate between sights.

LEARNING OBJECTIVES FOR SECTION III

After reading and reviewing this section of Chapter 5, you should be able to do the following.

1. Summarize research on the capacities of the five senses at birth and in the early weeks and months thereafter.

2. Discuss research findings about the origin of depth perception.

3. Explain the significance of very young babies' visual preferences.

4. List four milestones of response to sounds and the typical age for each.

5. Summarize findings on the development of auditory discrimination, smell, taste, and touch.

6. State practical implications of findings regarding newborns' ability to feel pain.

Section IV Motor Development of Infants and Toddlers

FRAMEWORK FOR SECTION IV

A. Milestones of Motor Development
1. Head Control
2. Hand Control
3. Locomotion

B. Environmental Influences on Motor Development
1. Cross-Cultural Differences
2. How Environment Can Slow Development
3. Can Motor Development Be Speeded Up?
a. Classic Research
b. More Recent Research
C. The Far-Reaching Effects of Motor Development
1. How Motor Development Influences Perception
a. Haptic Perception
b. Depth Perception
2. The Impact of Crawling

IMPORTANT TERM FOR SECTION IV

Completion: Fill in the blank to complete the definition of the key term for this section of Chapter 5.

1. _____ **Screening Test:** Screening test given to children (1 month to 6 years old) to identify abnormal development; it assesses gross motor skills, fine motor skills, language development, and personal and social development.

LEARNING OBJECTIVES FOR SECTION IV

After reading and reviewing this section of Chapter 5, you should be able to do the following.

1. List at least five milestones of motor development in infancy and toddlerhood and the average age at which each is attained.

2. Give examples of differing rates of development of motor skills in different societies or cultures and suggest reasons for these differences.

3. Discuss research findings on the extent to which environmental factors can or cannot retard or speed up motor development.

4. Explain how motor development influences haptic perception and depth perception.

5. Explain how crawling is significant for physical, intellectual, and emotional development.

6. Describe cultural differences in sleeping arrangements for infants.

Section V   Death in Infancy

FRAMEWORK FOR SECTION V

A. Infant Mortality
B. Sudden Infant Death Syndrome (SIDS)
    1. Causes of SIDS
        a.   Risk Factors for SIDS
        b.   Current Theories
    2. Effects on the Family
    3. Preventing SIDS

IMPORTANT TERMS FOR SECTION V

Completion: Fill in the blanks to complete the definitions of key terms for this section of Chapter 5.

1. **infant mortality rate:** Proportion of babies who die within the first _____ of life.

2. **sudden infant death syndrome (SIDS):** Sudden and unexpected death of any infant under 1 year of age, in which the cause of death remains unexplained after a thorough investigation that includes an autopsy; also known as _____ death.

LEARNING OBJECTIVES FOR SECTION V

After reading and reviewing this section of Chapter 5, you should be able to do the following.

1. Compare the infant mortality rate in the United States with rates in other populous nations.

Section VI   Immunizations for Better Health

FRAMEWORK FOR SECTION VI

A. Lower Immunization Rates: Implications for Social Policy
B. Immunization Worldwide

LEARNING OBJECTIVES FOR SECTION VI

After reading and reviewing this section of Chapter 5, you should be able to do the following.

1. Explain the relationship between disease rates and immunization rates for preventable childhood illnesses; state reasons for the decline in immunizations and discuss social policy implications.

2. List at least four of the leading causes of infant mortality in the United States, give reasons for its decline, and analyze differences among various population groups.

3. Cite possible explanations and risk factors for sudden infant death syndrome (SIDS), effects on the family, and recommendations for prevention.

2. Explain why immunization rates are higher in several European countries than in the United States.

CHAPTER 5 QUIZ

Matching—Numbers: Match each description in the left-hand column with the correct number in the right-hand column.

1.	Percent by which the weight of a 1-year-old baby's brain compares with its full adult weight ___	2
		3
2.	Age in months at which the average baby's birthweight doubles ___	4
3.	Number of teeth the average child has by age 2 1/2 years ___	5
4.	Height in inches of the typical 1-year-old ___	6
5.	Age in months by which an infant's vision typically reaches 20-20 ___	12
6.	Age in months at which the average baby can build a tower of two cubes ___	17
7.	Age in months at which the average baby can walk well ___	20
8.	Age in days at which infants can distinguish new speech sounds from familiar ones ___	30
9.	Age in months at which the average baby can walk up steps ___	70
10.	Earliest age in months at which babies should begin eating solid foods ___	

Multiple-Choice: Circle the choice that best completes or answers each item.

1. According to the cephalocaudal and proximodistal principles, it would take longest for a baby to develop the ability to
   a. focus the eyes
   b. wiggle the toes
   c. hold a rattle
   d. kick the legs

2. Body growth is fastest in which of these periods?
   a. birth to 1 year
   b. 1 year to 2 years
   c. 2 years to 3 years
   d. 13 years to 15 years

3. At birth, the cells in the brain
   a. number fewer than half the quantity present in adulthood
   b. are fully connected but not yet functioning
   c. are more developed in the subcortex than in the cerebral cortex
   d. are developed only in the cerebral cortex

4. The brain grows from about what percent of its adult weight at birth to about what percent of its adult weight at 1 year?
   a. 1 to 10
   b. 10 to 50
   c. 25 to 70
   d. 50 to 100

5. *All but which* of the following are reflex behaviors?
   a. coughing
   b. crawling
   c. shivering
   d. yawning

6. The group of reflexes which are present at birth but disappear during the first year are called
   a. subcortical
   b. Darwinian
   c. infantile
   d. primitive

7. *All but which* of the following are considered benefits of breastfeeding over bottle-feeding for newborns?
   a. promotes better tooth and jaw development
   b. contains less fat
   c. protects against respiratory infections
   d. is more digestible

8. One study shows that the ability of newborns to differentiate between patterns is predictive of their
    a. intelligence
    b. artistic talent
    c. visual acuity
    d. independence

9. According to research, *all but which* of the following statements about infants' hearing are true?
    a. Newborns show signs of having heard sounds in the womb.
    b. Hearing improves immediately after birth.
    c. A 3-day-old baby can distinguish the mother's voice from a stranger's.
    d. Auditory discrimination at 4 months predicts IQ at 5 years.

10. Which of the following tastes would most newborns prefer?
    a. pure water
    b. sugar solution
    c. lemon juice
    d. none of the above; newborns cannot discriminate among these tastes

11. It appears that the first sense to develop is
    a. sight
    b. hearing
    c. touch
    d. taste

12. *All but which* of the following are present in newborns?
    a. precision grip
    b. directional smell
    c. visual preference
    d. auditory discrimination

13. A child's failure to pass an item on the Denver Developmental Screening Test is considered a sign of developmental delay if what percent of children the same age ordinarily pass it?
    a. 50
    b. 75
    c. 80
    d. 90

14. The average baby begins to roll over at about
    a. 3 weeks
    b. 2 months
    c. 3 months
    d. 5 months

15. Which of the following is likely to walk earlier?
    a. African baby
    b. Asian baby
    c. American baby
    d. Mexican baby

16. According to research, which of the following statements about the environment and motor development is true?
    a. Because many aspects of motor development are genetically programmed, the environment cannot retard it.
    b. Control of elimination is unlikely to occur before a child is ready.
    c. Early training based on a "stepping" reflex has no effect on the age at which walking begins.
    d. Infant "walkers" have helped many children to walk early.

17. Crawling helps to promote "social referencing," meaning that a crawling baby is more likely than one who does not yet crawl to
    a. interact with other babies
    b. perceive how near or far away a person or object is
    c. compare his or her size with that of adults
    d. look at the mother to check whether a situation is safe

18. The infant mortality rate in the United States is lower
    a. than ever before
    b. among black babies than among white babies
    c. than in any other industrialized nation
    d. than the rate in Singapore

19. Almost two-thirds of infant deaths occur within how long after birth?
    a. 10 hours
    b. 4 weeks
    c. 3 months
    d. 1 year

20. Research suggests that one possible explanation for sudden infant death syndrome may be
    a. choking
    b. vomiting
    c. contagious infection
    d. parental smoking

21. Immunization rates in the United States
    a. are higher than in most European countries
    b. have increased steadily since 1980
    c. follow a disease cycle of "alarm-action" and "relaxation-inaction"
    d. are falling among minority groups only

True or False? In the blank following each item, write T (for *true*) or F (for *false*). In the space below each item, if the statement is false, rewrite it to make it true.

1. Normal physical development seems to follow a predetermined sequence. ____

2. Research has established that baby boys are more active than baby girls. ____

3. By the second birthday, the average child weighs 4 times as much as at birth. ____

4. Most babies get the first tooth at about 4 months. ____

5. The subcortex controls thinking and problem solving. ____

6. About 250,000 brain cells per minute form in the developing fetus. ____

7. Undernourishment before or just after birth can result in brain damage. ____

8. If a baby does not outgrow the rooting reflex by approximately 9 months, the cerebral cortex may not be developing properly. ___

9. Breastfeeding is more popular than bottle-feeding among poor and minority women. ___

10. AIDS can be transmitted to a breastfeeding baby through the mother's milk. ___

11. Long-term studies have found no significant differences in physical or mental health of breastfed and bottle-fed babies. ___

12. Pediatric nutritionists recommend starting solid foods by 2 months to foster healthy growth and help babies sleep through the night. ___

13. Babies should not be given skim milk or low-calorie diets. ___

14. A fat baby or toddler is more likely than a thin one to become a fat adult. ___

15. Babies cannot perceive colors in the first few months. ___

16. Babies at 2 to 3 months can perceive heights but do not fear them. ____

17. Newborns prefer complex patterns to simple ones. ____

18. A typical 6-month-old baby may voluntarily ignore a loud sound. ____

19. Within the first week of life, infants learn to recognize the smell of their mothers. ____

20. Circumcision is not painful for an 8-day-old baby, because nerve endings are not yet developed. ____

21. A baby who never saw anyone walk would be unlikely to learn how to walk. ____

22. Babies in all cultures develop basic motor skills at about the same rates. ____

23. Perceptual abilities are limited by a child's level of motor development. ____

24. Black babies are about twice as likely as white babies to die within the first year. ___

25. Sudden infant death syndrome is a leading cause of postneonatal death. ___

26. Fewer than 6 out of 10 schoolchildren have had all their required immunizations. ___

TOPICS FOR THOUGHT AND DISCUSSION

1. Research shows that baby boys and girls typically are very similar in physical development. However, as you will see in Chapter 7, some parents encourage baby boys to be more active than baby girls. Given the findings discussed in Chapter 5 on the influence of environmental factors, what effect, if any, do you think such parental treatment might have?

2. Research on animals has shown that brain growth and functioning can be enhanced by environmental stimulation. A stimulating environment also can promote the physical and mental development of retarded children, aging people, and victims of brain damage. If these findings are generalizable to normal children, what are the practical implications for parents? Can you suggest some simple, inexpensive ways to enrich a baby's environment? (Note: Keep these findings, and these questions, in mind as you read about environmental influences on cognitive development in Chapter 6.)

3. Since some primitive reflexes seem to serve no purpose, why do you think babies are born with them?

4. Remembering the ethical limitations on research with humans, which type of experiment described in Chapter 1 would be most feasible in investigating the long-term effects of breastfeeding and bottle-feeding—a natural experiment, a field experiment, or a laboratory experiment? What would be the difficulties and drawbacks of such an experiment?

5. Given the advantages of breastfeeding, why do you think this feeding method declined in popularity between 1984 and 1989, and what might explain its resurgence? Why do you suppose that breastfeeding remains less popular than bottle-feeding among young, poor, and minority women?

6. Were you surprised to read about the sensory capabilities of very young infants? How might you design an infant's environment with these capabilities in mind?

7. The authors of your text refer to the need to "child-proof" a home when infants learn to crawl. Yet the text also points out the importance of an enriched environment. How can parents reconcile these needs?

8. What social policy changes might effectively reduce infant mortality, especially among minority groups?

9. Since nearly all babies in the United States receive their first immunizations on schedule, and nearly all 5-year-olds are fully inoculated, what measures (other than those mentioned in your text) can you suggest to increase immunization rates for younger children?

CHAPTER 5 READING

INTRODUCTION

What goes on inside a baby's head? Is the baby contented? Hungry? Irritated? Excited? Angry? Since babies can't tell us, parents and other caregivers try to guess by observing their behavior. In recent years, researchers using sophisticated techniques such as those described in your text have begun to ask—and answer—more precisely questions about how infants perceive and interpret sensory information. What causes an infant to pay attention to one stimulus rather than another? What do babies know about their surroundings, and how soon do they know it? In this selection from *Diary of a Baby* (Basic Books, 1990), Daniel N. Stern, M.D., an infant psychiatrist and a father of five, takes us on a fanciful journey—based on his own and others' research—into the sensory world of a six-week-old infant named Joey. Stern also is the author of *The First Relationship* and *The Interpersonal World of the Infant*.

JOEY AT SIX WEEKS: AN EXCERPT FROM "DIARY OF A BABY"

by Daniel N. Stern, M.D.

Step into Joey's earliest world and recall what you have never really forgotten. Imagine that none of the things you see or touch or hear have names or functions, and few any memories attached to them. Joey experiences objects and events mainly in terms of the feelings they evoke in him. He does not experience them as objects in and of themselves, or for what they do or are called. When his parents call him "honey," he doesn't know that honey is a word and refers to him. He doesn't even particularly notice it as a sound distinct from a touch or a light. But he attends carefully to how the sound flows over him. He feels its glide, smooth and easy, soothing him; or its friction, turbulent and stirring him up, making him more alert. Every experience is like that, having its own special feeling tone—for infants as for adults. But we pay less attention to it. Our sense of being is not focused on it as Joey's is.

Now, pretend that weather is the only medium. Pretend that chairs, walls, light, and people all make up a weatherscape, a special moment of a day or night, its unique mood and force deriving from its own combination of wind, light, and temperature. And pretend that there are no objects for the weather to affect, no trees to be blown, no field or harbor for the rain to pelt. And, finally, that there is no you to stand outside the weather and watch it happen. You are part of the weatherscape. The prevailing mood and force can come from inside you and shape or color everything you see outside. Or, they can start outside and resonate inside you. In fact, the distinction between inside and outside is still vague: both may seem to be part of a single continuous space. As adults, we have many moments when the inside and the outside worlds seem to influence one another directly, almost flow freely one into the other. For instance, the inside moves to the outside when someone close to you does something hateful and looks for that moment intensely ugly. Or, the outside moves inside when you walk out into an unexpectedly sunny and clear morning, and your spirits lift and your body lightens. In adults, these partial breaches in the inside-outside barrier are short-lived. In infants, they are almost constant.

A human weatherscape is a unique moment of feelings-in-motion. It is not static like a photograph. It has duration, like a chord or several notes or even a musical phrase. It can last from a split second to many seconds. And during the time that fills a moment, Joey's feelings and perceptions change together. Each moment has its own sequence of feelings-in-motion: a sudden increase in interest; a rising, then a falling wave of hunger pain; an ebbing of pleasure. It is as a sequence of these moments strung together that Joey experiences life.

Like shots in a movie, one moment may be continuous with the next, or fade into it, or cut abruptly against it, or be separated from it by a blank pause. It is not clear to Joey how he gets from one moment to the next or what, if anything, happens between them. (Is it so clear for us?) But all his senses are focused on each one, and he lives each intensely. Many are the prototypes of moments that will recur over and over throughout his life.

A Patch of Sunshine: 7:05 A.M.

Joey has just awakened. He stares at a patch of sunshine on the wall beside his crib.

. . .

A space glows over there,
A gentle magnet pulls to capture.
The space is growing warmer and coming to life.
Inside it, forces start to turn around one another
in a slow dance.
The dance comes closer and closer.
Everything rises to meet it.
It keeps coming. But it never arrives.
The thrill ebbs away.

. . .

For Joey, most encounters with the world are dramatic and emotional—a drama whose elements and nature are not obvious to us as adults. Of all the things in the room, it is the patch of sunshine that attracts and holds Joey's attention. Its brightness and intensity are captivating. At six weeks of age, he can see quite well, though not yet perfectly. He is already aware of different colors, shapes, and intensities. And he has been born with strong preferences about what he wants to look at, about what pleases him. Among these preferences, intensity tops the list. It is the most important element in this scene. A baby's nervous system is prepared to evaluate immediately the intensity of a light, a sound, a touch—of anything accessible to one of his senses. How intensely he feels about something is probably the first clue he has available to tell him whether to approach it or to stay away. Intensity can lead him to try to protect himself. It can guide his attention and curiosity and determine his internal level of arousal. If something is only mildly intense (like a lamp lit in daylight), his attraction to it is weak. If too intense (like direct sunlight), he avoids it. But if it is moderately intense, like the patch of sunshine, he is spellbound. That just-tolerable intensity arouses him. He immediately alters in response to it. It increases his animation, activates his whole being. His attention is sharper. The patch of sunshine is a "gentle magnet," whose force he feels.

At this age, Joey is also drawn to areas enclosed in a clearly marked frame. The edges of the square sunpatch catch his eye at the line where lighter and darker wall meet. In a sense, the sunlight pulls, and the edges capture.

How does Joey know that the glowing space is "over there"? How does he know that it is not, for example, "over here," close at hand? Even at this young age, Joey is able to calculate distances and quadrants of space. Soon he will divide all space into two distinct areas: a near world within the reach of his extended arm, and a far world beyond it. Not for another few months will Joey be able to reach for, and grasp, what he wants with precision. Nonetheless, he is preparing at six weeks to distinguish between reachable and nonreachable space in this way. (This ability will help him learn the crucial act of reaching by defining for him which things are actually within reach. It would not be useful if he tried to reach for the moon—or even for things far across the room.) His space is not continuous and seamless like an adult's. It is as though a bubble were to form around him at the radius of his arm's length. Even blind babies, when starting to reach, reach for a sound-making object only when it comes within that radius. They carve up distance the same way as the sighted babies do, but with their ears, not their eyes. Thus the sunpatch, being beyond Joey's future reach, is "over there."

Why does the sunpatch "come to life" for Joey and reveal to him forces that turn around one another in a slow dance? These effects depend on how Joey explores the sunpatch with his eyes and his attention. At this age, babies often stare at things as if their gaze has indeed been captured and they are obliged to stare at one spot. A baby in this state appears, as Joey does, to be active mentally—not lost in a vague reverie, as an adult would be.

Parents can feel challenged, even upset by such moments in a baby's life. Imagine holding your six-week-old baby girl in your arms. You're face to face. You want to play, but she is transfixed by a spot where your forehead and your hairline meet. You, wanting her to look into your eyes, smile at her to divert her gaze. But your smile is not successful. You may—as most parents do—go on trying to divert her. You may make silly faces or even shake your baby from side to side, hoping the physical movement will unhook her gaze. But she may well continue to gaze at your hairline. Many parents interpret this gaze aversion as real rejection and may even give up trying for the moment to make eye contact. This is not any kind of rejection, however, but a normal phenomenon. It has been called obligatory attention.

Now, sometimes you succeed in changing and capturing your baby's gaze; sometimes you don't. But even when you don't—even when she never lets go visually of your hairline, of the "edge" where it meets your forehead—you often get the impression she is taking in your antics in some way. And so she is. She is paying attention to your face, but peripherally. She is transfixed by the frame, not by the picture. And that's the point.

Joey is staring at the edge made by the square of light against the wall. But just because he is staring at one point on the edge of the sunpatch doesn't mean that he is paying attention only to that one spot. Although we are usually not aware of it, we can easily separate our focus of vision (exactly what our eyes are looking at) from our focus of attention (exactly what our mind is paying attention to). Think of driving a car. Your eyes are fixed on the road ahead, but your attention can wander from side to side (to objects in peripheral vision) or far away or into the past. Or, better, choose one spot on a blank white page and stare at it. When after a while the spot becomes boring, your focus of attention, but not your eyes, will start to wander outside the fixed spot to other areas just around it. As your attention hovers over these new areas, they appear to change, even to disappear. The colors may start to drift. What initially appeared all white has now a hint of green or red in it. And these two colors may flip-flop. Or, the brightness and shading of the areas may shift like a slow play of light falling on a hillside through drifting clouds. Or, the flat page can appear to change its shape around the spot: it can buckle or melt or curve away. Such illusions occur when our focal attention and our visual fixation separate and play off each other.

Joey, too, will soon get bored looking at the exact same spot at the edge of the sunpatch. Probably his focal vision gets stuck on one spot, while his focus of attention starts to wander away from it. He begins to explore, with his attention, the interior of the sunpatch which appears in his peripheral vision. And as soon as he does that, he experiences illusions like an adult's. The patch of sunshine starts to "come alive" for him. It begins to move, to change color and shape. He does not know that these are just tricks played on the mind by the tension between vision and attention. For Joey, the patch of sunshine, in coming to life, reveals a play of forces. He sees dancing. He enters into a dynamic relationship with the patch of sunshine, each acting upon the other. All Joey's perceptions are like this. There are no "dead," inanimate objects out there. There are only different forces at play. As Joey engages with them, the sunpatch becomes dynamic and starts a slow turning dance.

The sunpatch appears to grow warmer and to keep coming closer as a result of the play of colors. Infants by this age have color vision. The patch of sunshine is, of course, yellowish against the white wall; the latter, by comparison, looks slightly bluish where the sun does not strike it. "Warm" intense colors, like yellow, appear to come forward; and "cooler" colors like blue, to recede and move back. So, to Joey, the sunshine patch appears to advance toward him, while the space immediately surrounding the patch appears to move away. The space has both a center that constantly approaches, like a note slowly rising higher, but never disappearing out of range; and a surrounding area that slowly recedes. This center, alive with the spectacle of dancing forces, appears to keep approaching him but never reaches him. Also, the advancing sunpatch against the retreating wall appears to be continually turning inside out.

In this interaction with a sunpatch, Joey feels everything rising "to meet it," a sort of promise ("It keeps coming"), and finally an "ebbing" of the "thrill" of suspense. The play of illusions and feelings fascinates Joey. It is a light show that captures not only his eyes but his entire nervous system. Infants love experiences where stimulation and excitation mount—if not too fast or too high. (When you want to grab and hold your baby's attention, you intuitively jazz up your voice and facial expressions.) And they tend to get bored and move away from situations where the stimulation is low, or stops changing. So, after a while, Joey gets bored by the play of appearances he sees in the sunpatch. Its infinite approach stops being new and suspenseful. His attention suddenly dies away, and he looks elsewhere for a different experience. At this point, he turns his head away from the sunlit wall.

QUESTIONS ABOUT THE READING

1. Imagine yourself awakening and observing a patch of sunshine on the wall. How would your experience differ from Stern's description of Joey's? In what ways, if any, would it be similar? Why?

2. Since it is impossible for an adult to actually observe the world the way a six-week-old baby does, the author presents conjectures based on research. Thinking back to Chapter 1, as well as to studies described in Chapter 5, what types of methods seem best suited to investigating the sensory world of babies?

3. Does the description in this selection seem consistent with the information in your text about babies' early sensory capacities, regarding (for example) peripheral vision, color perception, depth perception, and visual preferences? (Keep in mind the description of how Joey's attention shifts away from the sunpatch, at the end of the selection, when you read about habituation in Chapter 6.)

4. What does the discussion of "reachable" and "unreachable" space suggest about a relationship between visual and motor development? The author refers to blind babies' ability to differentiate between reachable and unreachable space. If Joey were blind, how might he experience the patch of sunlight? If he were deaf?

5. In the introductory material, the author describes how Joey reacts to his parents' calling him "honey." From the description, does his response to auditory experience seem to have anything in common with his response to visual experience?

6. Think back to the discussion in Chapter 4, about babies' states. In what state does Joey seem to be while looking at the sunpatch?

7. How do you think Joey's experience of viewing the patch of sunshine might differ if he were being held by an adult rather than lying in his crib? Does your answer suggest any relative benefits of a baby's having time alone as well as with others, or any desirable approach for an adult interacting with a baby?

ANSWER KEY FOR CHAPTER 5

Note: Numbers in parentheses refer to pages in the textbook where answers can be found.

CHAPTER 5 REVIEW

Important Terms for Section I
1. sequence (page 167)
2. cephalocaudal (168)
3. proximodistal (168)

Learning Objectives for Section I
1. (page 167)
2. (167-168)
3. (168-169)

Important Term for Section II
1. involuntary (page 174)

Learning Objectives for Section II
1. (pages 169-170)
2. (170)

3. (171-173)
4. (173-174)
5. (174, 175)
6. (176-177)
7. (176)
8. (177-179)
9. (179)
10. (180)

Important Terms for Section III

1. depth perception (page 181)
2. preference (182)

Learning Objectives for Section III

1. (pages 180-184)
2. (181-182)
3. (182)
4. (183)
5. (183-184)
6. (185)

Important Term for Section IV

1. Denver Developmental (page 186)

Learning Objectives for Section IV

1. (pages 186-189)
2. (189-190)
3. (191-193)
4. (193-194)
5. (194-195)
6. (196)

Important Terms for Section V

1. year (page 196)
2. crib (198)

Learning Objectives for Section V

1. (pages 196-197)
2. (196-198)
3. (198-199)

Learning Objectives for Section VI

1. (pages 200-201)
2. (202-203)

CHAPTER 5 QUIZ

Matching—Numbers

1. 70 (page 168)
2. 5 (169)
3. 20 (170)
4. 30 (169)
5. 6 (180)
6. 14 (187)
7. 12 (186)
8. 3 (183)
9. 17 (186)
10. 4 (179)

Multiple-Choice

1. b (page 168)
2. a (169)
3. c (171)
4. c (173)
5. b (174)
6. d (174)
7. b (176-177)
8. a (182)
9. b (182-184)
10. b (184)
11. c (184)
12. a (182-186)
13. d (186)
14. c (186, 188)
15. a (189)
16. b (191-192)
17. d (195)
18. a (196)
19. b (197)
20. d (199)
21. c (201)

True or False?

1. T (page 167)
2. F—Although some research found baby boys to be more active, other studies suggest that baby boys and girls are equally active. (168)
3. T (169)
4. F—Most babies get the first tooth between 5 and 9 months. (170)
5. F—The subcortex controls basic biological functions such as breathing and digestion; the cerebral cortex controls thinking and problem solving. (171)

6. T (172)
7. T (173)
8. T (174)
9. F—Poor and minority women are more likely to bottle-feed. (177)
10. T (178)
11. T (178)
12. F—Pediatric nutritionists recommend withholding solid foods before ages 4 to 6 months. (179)
13. T (179, 180)
14. F—Research has found that any correlation between obesity in infancy and adulthood is related to obesity in the family. (180)
15. F—Infants can distinguish between primary colors within the first 4 months. (181)
16. T (181-182)
17. T (182)
18. F—Most babies do not develop voluntary control over response to sounds until about 12 months. (183)

19. T (184)
20. F—Even on the first day of life, babies can feel pain, and babies show signs of pain when circumcision is performed without anesthesia. (185)
21. F—Basic motor skills such as walking depend primarily on maturation of the central nervous system, muscles, and bones, though environmental factors may influence the pace of development. (186, 189)
22. F—Babies in various cultures have been found to develop basic motor skills at different rates. (189-190)
23. T (193-194)
24. T (196)
25. T (197)
26. F—Fewer than 60 percent of 2-year-olds have had all recommended immunizations, but 90 percent are fully inoculated by age 5. (200-201)

COGNITIVE DEVELOPMENT IN INFANCY AND TODDLERHOOD

OVERVIEW

Chapter 6 examines the rapid cognitive development that takes place during the first 3 years of life. In this chapter, the authors:

- Compare the Piagetian, psychometric, and information-processing approaches to understanding cognitive development and discuss how each approach addresses and assesses infants' and toddlers' intelligence

- Discuss the relationship between maturation and learning, describe ways in which babies learn, and discuss the role of memory in infants' learning

- Outline stages in language development during the first 3 years; compare theories about language development; and discuss genetic and environmental factors in language development and readiness for reading.

- Present findings on the growth of competence and how parents can foster it

- Highlight the developmental importance of parent-child play

---

CHAPTER 6 REVIEW

Section I Three Approaches to Studying Cognitive Development

FRAMEWORK FOR SECTION I

A. Piagetian Approach: Cognitive Stages
   1. Sensorimotor Stage (Birth to About 2 Years)
      a. Cognitive Concepts of the Sensorimotor Stage
      b. Substages of the Sensorimotor Stage
         (1) Substage 1: Use of Reflexes (Birth to 1 Month)
         (2) Substage 2: Primary Circular Reactions and Acquired Adaptations (1 to 4 Months)
         (3) Substage 3: Secondary Circular Reactions (4 to 8 Months)
         (4) Substage 4: Coordination of Secondary Schemes (8 to 12 Months)
         (5) Substage 5: Tertiary Circular Reactions (12 to 18 Months)
         (6) Substage 6: Beginning of Thought—Mental Combinations (18 to 24 Months)
   2. Evaluation of Piaget's Concept of a Sensorimotor Stage
      a. Support for Piaget's Theory
      b. Limitations of the Concept
B. Psychometric Approach: Intelligence Tests
   1. What Do Intelligence Tests Measure?
   2. Difficulties in Measuring Infants' and Toddlers' Intelligence
   3. Developmental Testing of Infants and Toddlers
   4. Can Infants' and Toddlers' Intelligence Test Scores Be Increased?
C. Information-Processing Approach: Perceptions and Symbols

   1. Information Processing during Infancy as a Predictor of Intelligence
      a. Habituation
         (1) How Habituation Is Measured
         (2) The Significance of Habituation
      b. Studying Infants' Information Processing
      c. Exploratory Behavior
   2. Influences on Information Processing and Cognitive Development

IMPORTANT TERMS FOR SECTION II

Completion: Fill in the blanks to complete the definitions of key terms for this section of Chapter 6.

1. _____ behavior: Behavior that is goal-oriented—conscious and deliberate rather than accidental—and adaptive: used to identify and solve problems.

2. _____ approach: Study of cognitive development based on describing qualitative changes in thinking that are typical of children at particular stages; named after its founder, _____.

3. _____ approach: Study of cognitive development based on attempts to measure the quantity of intelligence.

4. _____-processing approach: Study of cognitive development based on the mental capacities and processes that support thought.

5. _____ development: Changes in mental powers and qualities that permit understanding.

6. _____ stage: In Piaget's theory, the first stage in human cognitive development (birth to about age 2), during which infants acquire knowledge through _____ experience and _____ activity.

7. _____: In Piaget's theory, awareness that a person or thing continues to exist when out of sight.

8. **circular reaction:** In Piaget's theory, a simple behavior that is _____ often.

9. _____: Organized pattern of behavior.

10. _____ **Scales of Infant Development:** Standardized test of infants' mental and motor development.

11. **habituation:** Simple type of learning in which _____ with a stimulus reduces, slows, or even stops a response.

12. **dishabituation:** Increase in _____ after the presentation of a new stimulus; see habituation.

13. **visual-recognition memory:** Recognition of a visual _____.

14. **visual _____ preference:** Preference for new rather than familiar pictures.

15. **cross-modal _____:** Ability to identify by sight items earlier felt but not seen.

16. **exploratory behavior:** Activity prompted by _____ about the environment.

LEARNING OBJECTIVES FOR SECTION I

After reading and reviewing this section of Chapter 6, you should be able to do the following.

1. Compare the concerns and methods of the Piagetian, psychometric, and information-processing approaches to understanding and assessing intelligence.

2. Describe the major change that occurs during the sensorimotor stage, according to Piaget, and list two important concepts that have developed or have begun to develop by the end of that stage and one ability that is still relatively limited.

3. List the substages of Piaget's sensorimotor stage, describe the development that occurs during each substage, and give an example of typical behavior at each substage.

4. Trace the development of object permanence through the six substages of Piaget's sensorimotor stage, and explain why current researchers believe that Piaget may have underestimated the age at which infants achieve this capacity.

5. List at least four other abilities that may be achieved earlier than Piaget thought, according to recent research.

6. Give at least two reasons why it is difficult to measure infants' and toddlers' intelligence reliably.

7. State a purpose for administering developmental tests to infants and describe one such test.

8. Identify two factors that seem to increase infants' and toddlers' intelligence test scores.

9. Explain how efficiency of habituation, visual-recognition memory, visual novelty preference, cross-modal transference, and exploratory behavior are related to prediction of childhood intelligence.

10. Explain how responsiveness of parents or other caregivers can enhance babies' ability to process information.

Section II Infants' Learning

FRAMEWORK FOR SECTION II

A. Maturation and Learning
B. Types of Learning
    1. Classical Conditioning
    2. Operant Conditioning
C. Infants' Memory and Learning

IMPORTANT TERMS FOR SECTION II

Completion: Fill in the blanks to complete the definitions of key terms for this section of Chapter 6.

1. _____: Relatively permanent change in behavior that results from experience.

2. _____: Unfolding of patterns of behavior in a biologically determined, age-related sequence.

3. **classical conditioning:** Learning in which a previously neutral stimulus (_____ stimulus) acquires the power to elicit a response (_____ response) by association with a(n) _____ stimulus that ordinarily elicits a particular response (_____ response).

4. _____ **conditioning:** Learning in which a response continues to be made because it has been reinforced.

LEARNING OBJECTIVES FOR SECTION II

After reading and reviewing this section of Chapter 6, you should be able to do the following.

1. Distinguish between learning and maturation and give an example of how they interact.

2. Name two types of conditioning and describe how each occurs.

3. Summarize research findings about infants' memory capabilities.

Section III   Development of Language

FRAMEWORK FOR SECTION III

A. Stages in Development of Language
  1. Prespeech
    a. Crying
    b. Cooing
    c. Babbling
    d. Imitating Language Sounds
    e. Recognizing Language Sounds
    f. Gestures
  2. First Words
    a. How Vocabulary Grows
  3. Creating Sentences
    a. First Sentences
    b. Learning Grammar
  4. Characteristics of Early Speech
B. Theories of Language Acquisition
  1. Learning Theory
  2. Nativism
C. Individual Differences in Language Development
  1. Genetic and Temperamental Factors
  2. Environmental Factors
    a. Child-Directed Speech ("Motherese")
     (1) The Value of Child-Directed Speech
     (2) Cross-Cultural Patterns in Child-Directed Speech
    b. Other Environmental Factors
  3. The Development of Early Literacy

IMPORTANT TERMS FOR SECTION III

Completion: Fill in the blanks to complete the definitions of key terms for this section of Chapter 6.

1. **language:** _____ system that uses words and grammar.

2. **prelinguistic speech:** Communicative use of _____ by infants without using words or grammar.

3. **linguistic speech:** Spoken use of language; besides words and grammar, it relies on pronunciation, _____, and _____ to convey meaning.

4. **holophrase:** _____ that conveys a complete thought; the typical speech form of children aged 12 to 18 months.

5. _____ **a concept:** Using a word correctly but in too restricted a way.

6. _____ **a concept:** Using a word incorrectly because of a failure to restrict its meaning appropriately.

7. **learning theory:** Theory that most behavior is learned from _____.

8. _____: Theory that views human beings as having an inborn capacity for language _____.

9. **language _____ device (abbreviated ___)**: In _____ linguistics, the inborn "mechanism" that enables the human to learn a language.

10. **child-directed speech (CDS), or "_____"**: A simplified kind of speech used in talking to babies and toddlers; it includes a high-pitched tone, short words and sentences, slow tempo, repetition, and many questions.

LEARNING OBJECTIVES FOR SECTION III

After reading and reviewing this section of Chapter 6, you should be able to do the following.

1. Identify six forms or components of prelinguistic speech.

2. List in sequence at least six milestones in language development during the first 3 years.

3. Explain the role of symbolic gesturing in cognitive development, identify four types of symbolic gestures, and give an example of each.

4. Outline three stages of linguistic speech, and give an example of a typical utterance at each stage.

5. Name four types of words commonly spoken by 1- and 2-year-olds.

6. Describe the growth of language ability from the time children use their first sentences to approximately age 3.

7. List and give examples of five characteristics of early speech.

8. Contrast the views of learning theorists and nativists, identify the single most important factor in language acquisition according to each theory, and discuss research that supports and challenges each.

9. Cite two genetic influences that help account for individual differences in language development.

10. Discuss the influence of child-directed speech ("motherese") on language development and summarize pros and cons of its use.

11. Cite several ways in which parents' or caregivers' verbal interactions with toddlers can affect their language development.

12. Give at least four suggestions for stimulating babies' and toddlers' language development.

13. Describe a technique for advancing toddlers' preliteracy skills.

Section IV Competence

FRAMEWORK FOR SECTION IV

A. What Is Competence?
B. What Influences Competence?
C. HOME: Home Observation for Measurement of the Environment

LEARNING OBJECTIVES FOR SECTION IV

After reading and reviewing this section of Chapter 6, you should be able to do the following.

1. List at least two social skills and two cognitive skills of competent preschoolers.

2. Identify three major aspects of child rearing that can affect the development of competence.

3. List at least five guidelines for enhancing young children's competence.

4. Describe a measuring instrument used to assess the impact of the home environment on cognitive growth.

Section V   Play Between Parents and Their Infants and Toddlers

LEARNING OBJECTIVE FOR SECTION V

After reading and reviewing this section of Chapter 6, you should be able to do the following.

1. Explain how observations of parent-child play can be used to assess the development of infants and toddlers.

CHAPTER 6 QUIZ

Matching—Who's Who: Match each name in the left-hand column with the appropriate description at the right. (Note: Here, a description may be used to identify more than one name.)

1. Andrew Meltzoff ___
2. Noam Chomsky ___
3. Theodore Simon ___
4. Nancy Bayley ___
5. Jean Piaget ___
6. Karen Wynn ___
7. Rosalie Rayner ___
8. B.F. Skinner ___
9. Alfred Binet ___
10. Burton L. White ___
11. John B. Watson ___

a. studied mothers' influence on prechoolers' competence
b. devised an early psychometric intelligence test
c. used Mickey Mouse dolls to test infants' ability to count
d. developed a psychometric test of infants' and toddlers' developmental status
e. foremost proponent of learning theory of language acquisition
f. proposed the existence of an inborn language acquisition device
g. formulated a stage theory of cognitive development based on observation of children
h. conducted experiments on deferred imitation in babies
i. conducted a famous conditioning study, teaching a baby to fear a white rat

Multiple-Choice: Circle the choice that best completes or answers each item.

1. Which of the following is *not* something babies learn to do during the sensorimotor stage, according to Piaget?
    a. organize their behavior toward goals
    b. solve simple problems
    c. coordinate sensory information
    d. understand the concept of number

2. According to Piaget, a 10-month-old baby who plays peekaboo is developing the concept of
    a. object permanence
    b. causality
    c. invisible imitation
    d. circular reactions

3. In Piaget's terminology, thumb-sucking by a 2-month-old baby is a
   a. primary circular reaction
   b. secondary circular reaction
   c. tertiary circular reaction
   d. form of deferred imitation

4. According to Piaget, a 9-month-old baby who sees a toy on the floor, crawls to it, and picks it up is showing
   a. an acquired adaptation
   b. a tertiary circular reaction
   c. coordination of secondary schemes
   d. object permanence

5. According to Piaget, the approximate age at which babies typically begin to think is
   a. 8 months
   b. 12 months
   c. 15 months
   d. 18 months

6. Research discussed in your text has challenged Piaget's estimate of the age at which children develop *all but which* of the following abilities?
   a. object permanence
   b. invisible imitation
   c. deferred imitation
   d. trial-and-error problem solving

7. Which theoretical approach to cognitive development attempts to measure intelligence quantitatively?
   a. psychometric
   b. Piagetian
   c. information-processing
   d. nativist

8. Which of the following can reliably predict an infant's later intelligence?
   a. Stanford-Binet Intelligence Scale
   b. Bayley Scales of Infant Development
   c. both a and b
   d. neither a nor b

9. An infant's later intelligence can be predicted from his or her
   a. speed of habituation
   b. age of attaining object permanence
   c. visual novelty preference
   d. all of the above

10. An infant's fear of falling is an example of
    a. learning
    b. maturation
    c. instinct
    d. temperament

11. As a baby sucks on a dry nipple, an experimenter plays a tape of a woman singing a lullaby. When the baby stops sucking, the singing stops; when the baby resumes sucking, the singing resumes. This is an example of
    a. habituation
    b. classical conditioning
    c. operant conditioning
    d. complex learning

12. A baby's earliest means of communication is
    a. cooing
    b. babbling
    c. crying
    d. smiling

13. A 12-month-old baby who reaches for a ball and says "da" is using
    a. a holophrase
    b. prelinguistic speech
    c. telegraphic speech
    d. manual babbling

14. Telegraphic speech
    a. is universal among 1- and 2-year-olds
    b. is a form of prelinguistic speech
    c. conforms to some degree to the grammar a child hears
    d. consists of holophrases

15. The sentence "Mama goed bye-bye" is an example of a young child's tendency to
    a. overregularize rules
    b. speak ungrammatically
    c. underextend a concept
    d. overextend a concept

16. According to the nativist view of language acquisition, children learn to speak their native language by
    a. imitating their parents and caregivers
    b. analyzing the language they hear and figuring out its rules
    c. repeating sounds that receive positive reinforcement
    d. all of the above

17. Child-directed speech, or "motherese,"
    a. focuses on telling children what to do
    b. is most frequently used by working-class mothers
    c. is more common in the United States than in other cultures
    d. has shown positive correlation to language growth

18. Two-year-olds are most likely to develop preliteracy skills if their parents or caregivers do *all but which* of the following when reading to the children?
    a. ask yes-or-no questions
    b. ask open-ended questions
    c. correct wrong answers
    d. expand on the children's answers

19. Research shows that babies tend to become more competent when given
    a. strict rules regarding orderliness
    b. as much parental attention as possible
    c. freedom to explore
    d. all of the above

20. Parents can best influence a child's competence beginning when the child is how old?
    a. 3 to 5 months
    b. 6 to 8 months
    c. 10 to 12 months
    d. 2 years

21. HOME (the Home Observation for Measurement of the Environment) has found a combination of *all but which* of the following fairly reliable in predicting children's IQ?
    a. parents' responsiveness
    b. parents' educational level
    c. socioeconomic status
    d. parents' involvement in children's play

True or False? In the blank following each item, write T (for *true*) or F (for *false*). In the space below each item, if the statement is false, rewrite it to make it true.

1. According to Piaget, the sensorimotor stage typically lasts from birth to about 3 years of age. ____

2. Between about 1 to 4 months, according to Piaget, babies begin to take intentional actions. ____

3. Research has confirmed Piaget's belief that children younger than about 18 months are not yet capable of symbolic thought. ____

4. Research suggests that babies are born with the ability to imitate. ____

5. Research suggests that babies as young as 5 months have a rudimentary understanding of number. ___

6. Intelligence tests were originally developed to identify bright students. ___

7. IQ tests reliably predict 2-year-olds' intelligence test scores later in childhood. ___

8. Children's "self-righting tendency" is particularly strong for verbal abilities. ___

9. The Bayley Scales of Infant Development can help diagnose a neurological deficit. ___

10. According to information-processing research, a child's mental development is fairly continuous from birth. ___

11. Habituation occurs when a baby responds to a new stimulus. ___

12. Infants less than 1 week old can distinguish between certain sights and sounds. ___

13. Mothers' responsiveness to their babies' crying is related to individual differences in later cognitive development. ___

14. The first thing infants learn is to suck. ___

15. Maturation is essential to the development of speech. ___

16. Newborns can learn by classical conditioning. ___

17. Infants younger than 2 months cannot remember past events. ___

18. Accidental and deliberate imitation are forms of prelinguistic speech. ___

19. A baby's first word is typically said between the ages of 10 and 14 months. ___

20. A 16-month-old baby who spreads her arms to indicate an airplane, instead of using the word, shows slowed cognitive development. ___

21. The development of linguistic speech is closely tied to age. ___

22. Toddlers' speech is a simplified version of adult speech. ___

23. Parents can best foster young children's vocabulary development by giving them frequent requests and commands. ___

24. Repeating babies' babbled sounds slows their speech development by reinforcing meaningless utterances. ___

25. Parents' socioeconomic level is a major factor in the development of children's competence. ___

26. Parents who want to enhance their children's competence should direct their interests into constructive channels. ___

27. Children with developmental disabilities tend to play differently than normal children do. ___

TOPICS FOR THOUGHT AND DISCUSSION

1. In your view, does Piaget's apparent underestimation of the age of development of several abilities seriously undermine the concept of the sensorimotor stage and the value of his theory of cognitive development? Why or why not?

2. Meltzoff and Moore found that newborn babies can imitate adults' facial expressions, such as sticking out the tongue. Other research, however, contradicts their findings. Nevertheless, Meltzoff and Moore suggest that a primitive ability to imitate is present at birth and is reinforced by mutual imitation games with parents. Can you devise a method to more conclusively confirm or disprove these findings and interpretations?

3. Longitudinal research reported in your text found that infants' information-processing skills at 5 months predicted their exploratory competence at 13 months. Can you suggest other factors (genetic and/or environmental) that might affect exploratory competence, or underlying factors that might explain both information-processing skill and exploratory competence? What research design might be used to test your hypothesis[es]?

4. Aldous Huxley, in his novel *Brave New World*, envisions a society of the future in which conditioning is used to totally control human behavior. Babies destined to work in factories are conditioned to reject "time-wasting" books and flowers by associating those objects with frightening noises and painful electric shocks. Is this an example of classical conditioning or operant conditioning, or does it have elements of both? Do you think Huxley might have been caricaturing Watson and Rayner's conditioning of "Little Albert"? In what ways are the two situations similar? In what ways are they different? Does the purpose of conditioning affect the ethics involved? Can you think of a situation in which associating a stimulus with pain or discomfort for an infant might be warranted?

5. Which theory of language development—learning theory or nativism—appears from the discussion in your text to make the stronger case? Can you devise research that would help to confirm or disprove either theory? The authors of your text say that most developmentalists today draw on both theories. Is this consistent with the way most developmentalists today view the nature-versus-nurture argument discussed in Chapter 2?

6. Considering the points made by advocates and opponents of child-directed speech, or "motherese," as reported in your textbook, which side do you think has made the stronger case? Why? Do the authors seem to favor one point of view or the other? Which view is more consistent with your own observations?

7. Which of the research findings reported in this chapter would you consider most helpful in stimulating an infant's or toddler's cognitive development?

CHAPTER 6 READING

INTRODUCTION

How early should parents begin reading to a child? When should they stop? Jim Trelease, author of *The Read-Aloud Handbook* and *The New Read-Aloud Handbook* (Penguin) gives answers that may surprise you. Trelease, an educational consultant in Springfield, Massachusetts, was an award-winning cartoonist and writer for *The Springfield Daily News* and has frequently visited classrooms throughout the Connecticut River Valley, sharing his love of children's books. The article reprinted below is from the February 1991 issue of *Parents Magazine*.

READ ME A STORY

by Jim Trelease

Are we ever to become a nation of readers? The facts are sad and clear: There are five times as many video stores as there are public libraries in this country. Most American adults don't read even one book a year. And according to the latest statistics available from the A. C. Nielsen Company, our six- to eleven-year-olds watch an average of 23 hours and 39 minutes of television each week, while our two- to five-year-olds manage to clock a staggering 27 hours and 49 minutes.

Is there anything parents can do about this sorry state of affairs? The answer is a resounding yes! According to a landmark study by Dolores Durkin at Teachers College, Columbia University, in New York City, those children who entered school knowing how to read and those who learned without difficulty in the classroom had one thing in common: They had all been read to.

According to a report issued by the Center for the Study of Reading, at the University of Illinois, Urbana-Champaign, reading aloud to children is the single most important activity contributing to their eventual success in reading.

Reasons for Reading

We read to children for the same reasons we talk to them: to inspire, inform, stimulate, affirm, amuse, and guide. It's also important to realize that listening comprehension must come before reading comprehension. If a child has never heard the word "enormous," he or she will never say the word "enormous." And obviously, if you've never heard or said the word, reading and writing it will be extremely difficult.

Less obviously, the skill of reading involves more than just decoding words and mastering their meaning. According to Joan Brooks McLane and Gillian Dowley McNamee, authors of Early Literacy (Harvard University Press), learning to read incorporates an important and complex set of skills, emotions, attitudes, and expectations.

For this reason, children who come from homes where personal conversation is not encouraged–where "Go watch TV" becomes a regular response, and the blare of televisions and stereos drowns out the intimacy of private exchanges–are the ones who arrive at school already lacking several of the basic learning tools necessary for academic achievement: vocabulary, curiosity, the ability to question, and concentration.

The Center for the Study of Reading, which focuses not only on infants and preschoolers but also on older children, recommends that reading aloud "continue throughout the grades." The battle for literacy is far from over by the time a child reaches the fourth grade, when most basic skills have already been taught. Although most children eventually do learn these skills, they learn them in such a way–through workbooks and skill sheets–that by the middle grades, the excitement they initially experienced in learning to read in first grade has given way to boredom or frustration.

This, in turn, has an enormous negative impact on an accrued skill such as reading; if you don't read much, you simply won't improve. Once you have assimilated the basic skills, the only way to get from a fourth-grade reading level to a ninth- or twelfth-grade level is by reading. And since children, like adults, are members of a pleasure-seeking species, they will not read if they have come to hate it.

And there's where being read to makes one of its most important contributions to children's lives. It serves as a living commercial for the pleasures of reading. It advertises how much fun reading stories and books can be. Hearing Charlotte's Web read aloud inspires the child to want to work that magic the way Mom and Dad do, to want to savor those words and visit those places and meet those people all over again.

Getting Started

How soon can parents begin to explore the pleasures of reading aloud? Answer that for yourself: When did you start talking to your child? "Day one," you respond. "But I'd certainly feel pretty silly reading to a newborn." Why? If it's not silly to talk to the child, if you can justify using words and sentences with a child who doesn't understand one word of English, why not read to him too? If the child is old enough to be spoken to, he's old enough to be read to–it's all part of language learning.

Start with poetry, the first sounds children fall in love with. Even infants respond to the rhythms and cadences of Mother Goose nursery rhymes. Don't look for plots here. Mother Goose is simply there to take the endings and blendings and mix them with the rhythm and rhyme of language, all to be fed into a child's growing language bank.

The earlier you start, the easier it is for both parent and child. It's like bathing–if you wait until a child is four years old before you give her a bath, you'll probably have a hard time getting her into the tub. Children who are read to from infancy slip into the process of reading by themselves without experiencing stress. Their interest and attention span have been nurtured on books from the very beginning, so reading is as natural a part of their day as breakfast, lunch, and supper.

Infants are a captive audience. They're perfectly content to lie there and listen to you read. In fact, babies love the sounds, attention, and closeness–and so the conditioning process begins. Even at this early stage, beware of sending negative messages; namely, that the book is the center of your attention. Avoid pitting your child against the story. Hold the book with one hand, and use your free hand to hug or gently caress your baby.

Get into the habit of commenting to the child on what you're reading. "You fell down today just like Jack and Jill, didn't you, Sarah?" And even though she may be too young to reply, pause a second for an answer. Such comments establish a pattern of conversation that she will subconsciously absorb.

Don't be frustrated by the comparatively short attention span of your one-year-old. Studies such as "Mothers Reading to Infants: A New Observational Tool," which appeared in the journal The Reading Teacher in 1987, indicate that a very young child's attention span for stories is usually only a few minutes long. Rather than imprison the child and force the issue (and thereby create a negative relationship between your child and books), bide your time and read again later for another three minutes. Using this method, you can accumulate reading time, and it's stress-free for both parent and child. Focusing the child's attention by pointing to something on the page, and learning to vary your reading voice between whispers and excitement, are also helpful. Attention spans are not built overnight–they are built minute by minute, page by page, day by day.

Reading to Toddlers

Parents of children under two should also be forewarned that having a limited number of familiar books in the home is better than reading a different book every day. Young children love and need the repetition of familiar words, characters, and stories.

Reading aloud is a comforting ritual in many households. Children love not only the words and pictures of their favorite books but also the security that comes with a daily time for stories. Sitting on a parent's lap after a bath, listening to a familiar voice, winding down after a hectic toddler day, is an indelible and significant experience for most young children.

Nonetheless, many parents find the endless repetition extremely irritating. Perhaps they wouldn't be as bothered if they realized that children learn language in pieces. Books are like jigsaw puzzles, and some of the pieces are often missing until the child-listener's vocabulary and life experience provide those missing pieces. For example, the three-year-old listening to "A Visit From St. Nicholas" could possibly misinterpret the lines

"Away to the window, I flew like a flash,
Tore open the shutters and threw up the sash."

For the young listener who has never heard the term "sash" but who has heard the words "threw up," the poem evokes an image entirely different from the one a parent conjures! Repeated readings and discussions will clarify the meaning.

Many parents are often tempted to turn a relaxing read-aloud experience into a structured teaching session, quizzing their child for prescribed answers. This can turn the experience into something the child fails instead of enjoys.

That is not to say you cannot teach while reading aloud. Announcing the title and author each time you read aloud is covert instruction. "And James Stevenson drew these funny pictures" also instructs. Occasionally running your finger along the words as you read and pointing to objects as they are named are effective ways of teaching without being heavy-handed.

Another recommended method is to look at the cover of the picture book and say, "I wonder what this book is going to be about" or "This book was written and illustrated by Robert McCloskey. Have we read any other books by him?" You can also engage the child by stopping at a critical point in the story and asking, "What do you think is going to happen next?" Such nonthreatening questions also nurture children's important recall and predictive skills.

At the library, you might ask the librarian to help you and your child choose an author, such as Dr. Seuss, Ezra Jack Keats, or Tomie DePaola, each of whom has written many children's books. For one week, read only that author's books; declare it "Bill Peet Week" at your house. (If you haven't ready any of this award-winning author-illustrator's more than 30 books, you and your family are in for a special treat!) Look up information about the chosen author and tell your child something new about the person's life each day during "author week." You can supplement with tried-and-true favorites.

By the time children reach age three, their story appetites expand to more than a few favorites, especially if parents have been reading aloud more than one book each day. Illustrations are increasingly important, both as clues and as visual pleasures. And many parents of threes are astonished to discover that their prodigies have memorized favorite books verbatim. Young and preliterate children try to "read" books by picking up clues from the visual images on the page before, during, and after the parent reads the text aloud. Remember that visual literacy precedes print literacy.

The Social Aspects of Reading

Because reading and writing–done by, for, or with others–are about communicating, it's important to make reading as social an experience as possible. Let children know that books are not written by machines, that they don't "come" from libraries or stores any more than milk comes from supermarkets.

Parents sometimes overlook the obvious– that reading doesn't mean reading just books. Again tapping the social nature of print, share your shopping list with your child–"Is there anything you want me to get at the store? Here's what I'm getting so far"–and read it. Let the child see you write his request. Read aloud the print you encounter in the environment: bumper stickers, billboards, junk mail, the headlines, weather, and even the comics in the newspaper. Post notes by your phone, and stick postcards on the refrigerator.

Most children in the late primary grades are not read to regularly by their parents. In one middle-class Connecticut community, a recent random school sample disclosed that only 8 percent of the children in grades four to six had been read to the previous evening. The next-biggest mistake, after not reading at all, is made by the parent who stops reading aloud too soon.

Why read aloud to fourth-graders who can already read? Isn't that a waste of time? Not at all when you realize that, until eighth grade, children's reading levels are distinctly different from their listening levels. First-grade children can easily digest the vocabulary and plot of The Cosby Show when they hear it, but they would be lost if they had to read the script. Most first-graders are listening at a fourth- or fifth-grade reading level, and fourth-graders are listening at a sixth- or seventh-grade level. This means that all of them can comprehend books they're not yet able to read.

Listening to books exposes a child to new ideas and words, whets his appetite for more, reminds him that books get better as you get older, and offers him a target to strive toward.

Because picture books are so rich visually and contain some of the most treasured stories of our culture, by no means am I suggesting that you abandon them. But we do our children a grave disservice by waiting so long to read novels to them. You should certainly continue to read picture books aloud, but do add a chapter from a novel to the day's reading. Kindergarten children are entirely capable of enjoying novels such as E. B. White's Charlotte's Web and James and the Giant Peach, by Roald Dahl.

Books that don't end in just one sitting– chapter books–may require some adapting to by your child. You can help here by initially reading either short chapter books or picture books that are broken down into chapters. Hearing you read a series of picture books dealing with one family can also help your child make the transition to novels.

Through all this, you are building your child's vocabulary and attention span. But just as important, you are building bridges–cultural and emotional–between yourself and your child. Long before I knew what it would do for my children intellectually, I read to them daily. Why? Because my father had read to me, because I remember the special feeling I had when I sat in his lap and heard him read The Newark Evening News and The Saturday Evening Post to me. Once I was naive enough to think my feelings were unique, but I've since met many people who echo them.

As a California teacher wrote to me, "My dearest and clearest memories of my father are when he read to me from The Book House every evening. I remember each detail–the chair, the lamp, how I felt next to him, the way his eyes peered through his bifocals, and most of all, his voice. Fifty years later I can still hear exactly how he sounded....For those few minutes he was all mine, that voice was all for me."

QUESTIONS ABOUT THE READING

1. Trelease says, "We read to children for the same reasons we talk to them." What is special about reading to a child, as compared with other verbal activities like talking, singing, and making up stories?

2. Trelease suggests that parents begin reading to infants at birth. Do you consider this approach sensible? Are there differences between talking and reading to newborns?

3. According to Trelease, children who watch television constantly tend to enter school lacking basic learning tools: vocabulary, curiosity, the ability to question, and concentration. Does Trelease adequately explain this phenomenon? How would you explain it?

4. Why does Trelease suggest that parents continue to read to children after they have learned to read? Do you agree? Do you see any dangers in this approach?

5. Do you like Trelease's idea of discussing with young children the authors of books, including facts about the authors' lives? What value is served by doing so?

6. Trelease refers to the development of visual literacy, which comes before print literacy. Are his suggestions for how to read to toddlers consistent with the dialogic techniques for development of preliteracy skills reported in your text?

ANSWER KEY FOR CHAPTER 6

Note: Numbers in parentheses refer to pages in the textbook where answers can be found.

CHAPTER 6 REVIEW

Important Terms for Section I
1. intelligent (page 209)
2. Piagetian, Jean Piaget (209)
3. psychometric (209)
4. information (209)
5. cognitive (210)
6. sensorimotor, sensory, motor (210)
7. object permanence (210)
8. repeated (212)
9. scheme (212)
10. Bayley (222)
11. familiarity (224)
12. responsiveness (224)
13. stimulus (225)
14. novelty (225)
15. transference (225)
16. curiosity (226)

Learning Objectives for Section I
1. (page 209)
2. (210)
3. (212-216)
4. (212-217)
5. (217-219)

6.   (220-221)
7.   (221-222)
8.   (222-223)
9.   (223-226)
10. (226-227)

Important Terms for Section II

1.   learning (page 227)
2.   maturation (228)
3.   conditioned, conditioned, unconditioned, unconditioned (228)
4.   operant (229)

Learning Objectives for Section II

1.   (pages 227-228)
2.   (228-229)
3.   (229-231)

Important Terms for Section III

1.   communication (page 231)
2.   sound (231)
3.   intonation, rhythm (236)
4.   single word (236)
5.   underextending (238)
6.   overextending (238)
7.   experience (238)
8.   nativism, acquisition (238)
9.   acquisition, LAD, nativist (239)
10. motherese (241)

Learning Objectives for Section III

1.   (pages 231-235)
2.   (232)
3.   (234-235)
4.   (236-238)
5.   (236)
6.   (237-238)
7.   (238)
8.   (238-240)
9.   (240)
10. (240-243)
11. (243-244)
12. (244)
13. (244-245)

Learning Objectives for Section IV

1.   (page 245)
2.   (246)

3.   (247)
4.   (247-248)

Learning Objective for Section V

1.   (pages 248-249)

CHAPTER 6 QUIZ

Matching—Who's Who

1.   h (page 218)
2.   f (238, 239)
3.   b (220)
4.   d (221, 222)
5.   g (210)
6.   c (219)
7.   i (228)
8.   e (238)
9.   b (220)
10. a (245-246)
11. i (228)

Multiple-Choice

1.   d (pages 210, 218)
2.   a (210, 211)
3.   a (213)
4.   c (213)
5.   d (213, 215)
6.   d (216-218)
7.   a (209, 220)
8.   d (220, 222)
9.   d (216, 225)
10. a (228)
11. c (229)
12. c (232)
13. a (236)
14. c (237)
15. a (238)
16. b (239)
17. d (241)
18. a (244-245)
19. c (247)
20. b (246-247)
21. c (247-248)

True or False?

1.   F—The sensorimotor stage lasts from birth to about 2 years. (page 210)
2.   T (213-214)

3. F—Research suggests that infants can think symbolically much earlier than Piaget believed. (216)
4. T (218)
5. T (218-219)
6. F—Intelligence tests were originally developed to identify children who could not handle academic work. (220)
7. F—IQ tests are unreliable for children under age 2, and even then the relationship with later scores may be weak. (220)
8. F—The "self-righting tendency" begins to diminish between 18 and 24 months of age, when differences in sophisticated verbal abilities begin to develop. (221)
9. T (222)
10. T (223)
11. F—Habituation occurs when response to a familiar stimulus declines; dishabituation occurs when the baby responds to a new stimulus. (224)
12. T (224)
13. F—Mothers' responsiveness when babies are *not* in distress is related to later cognitive development. (226-227)
14. F—Infants are born with a sucking reflex; they learn to *use* sucking to relieve hunger. (227)
15. T (228)
16. T (229)

17. F—Research shows that infants younger than 2 months can remember past events, especially pleasurable ones. (230)
18. T (233)
19. T (232, 236)
20. F—Sixteen-month-old babies frequently use symbolic gestures for objects they cannot yet name. (234)
21. F—The development of prelinguistic speech is fairly closely tied to age; linguistic speech is not. (237)
22. F—Toddlers' speech is not just a simplified version of adult speech; it has its own special characteristics. (238)
23. F—Children learn new words faster when parents ask questions about objects than when parents tell them what to do. (243)
24. F—Repeating babies' babbled sounds helps them experience the social aspect of speech. (244)
25. F—In research on children's competence, mothers of various socioeconomic levels had children of comparable levels of competence. (246)
26. F—Parents who want to enhance children's competence should talk to them about whatever they are interested in at the moment. (247)
27. T (248)

PERSONALITY AND SOCIAL DEVELOPMENT IN INFANCY AND TODDLERHOOD

OVERVIEW

Chapter 7 begins the exploration of personality and social development with themes that continue, with variations, at each stage of childhood. In this chapter, the authors:

- Present Erikson's theoretical perspective on the development of trust and autonomy and discuss how children learn self-regulation

- Summarize what is known about infants' emotions, how they show these emotions, and the importance of emotional communication with adults

- Discuss the influences of temperament, gender, and the family on personality development, including attachment to the parents

- Portray disturbances in development that appear to have either a biological or environmental basis

- Describe sibling relationships in infancy and toddlerhood and trace the development of sociability in infants and toddlers

- Discuss the impact of early day care on cognitive, social, and emotional development and identify characteristics of good day care

CHAPTER 7 REVIEW

Section I Early Personality Development

FRAMEWORK FOR SECTION I

A. The Development of Trust
B. Self-Regulation
   1. The Development of Autonomy
   2. How Children Learn Self-Regulation

IMPORTANT TERMS FOR SECTION I

Completion: Fill in the blanks to complete the definitions of key terms for this section of Chapter 7.

1. **personality:** A person's unique and relatively consistent way of feeling, thinking, and _____ .

2. _____ **versus** _____ : In Erikson's theory, the first critical alternative of psychosocial development, in which infants (birth to 18 months) develop a sense of how reliable people in their world are.

3. **self-regulation:** Control of one's own behavior to conform to social _____ .

4. _____ **versus** _____ : In Erikson's theory, the second critical alternative of psychosocial development (18 months to 3 years), in which the child achieves a balance between self-determination and control by others.

5. **socialize:** To _____ children the behaviors their culture considers appropriate.

LEARNING OBJECTIVES FOR SECTION I

After reading and reviewing this section of Chapter 7, you should be able to do the following.

1. Describe the first two crises proposed by Erik Erikson.

2. Trace the development of self-regulation, factors that promote it, and its relationship to each domain of development.

3. List at least four suggestions for dealing with toddlers' negativism and developing self-regulation.

Section II Factors in Personality Development

FRAMEWORK FOR SECTION II

A. Emotions: The Basis of Personality and Social Development
   1. Studying Babies' Emotions
   2. How Emotions Develop: The Emerging Sense of Self
   3. How Infants Show Their Emotions
      a. Crying
         (1) Responding to Crying
         (2) Crying as a Diagnostic Tool
      b. Smiling
      c. Laughing

B. Emotional Communication Between Babies and Adults
   1. The Mutual Regulation Model
      a. "Reading" the Messages of Another Person
      b. How a Mother's Depression Affects Mutual Regulation
   2. Social Referencing
C. Individual Differences in Personality
   1. Temperamental Differences
      a. Components of Temperament
      b. Three Patterns of Temperament
      c. Influences on Temperament
      d. Effects of Temperament on Adjustment: "Goodness of Fit"
   2. Gender Differences
D. The Family and Personality Development
   1. Studying the Child in the Family
   2. Attachment: A Reciprocal Connection
      a. Studying Attachment
      b. Patterns of Attachment
         (1) Secure Attachment
         (2) Avoidant Attachment
         (3) Ambivalent, or Resistant, Attachment
         (4) Disorganized-Disoriented Attachment
      c. How Attachment Is Established
         (1) What the Mother Is Like
         (2) What the Baby Is Like
      d. Changes in Attachment
      e. Long-Term Effects of Attachment
      f. Critique of Attachment Research
   3. The Mother's Role
      a. What Do Babies Need from Their Mothers?
   4. The Father's Role
      a. Bonds and Attachments between Fathers and Infants
      b. How Do Fathers Act with Their Infants?
      c. What Is the Significance of the Father-Infant Relationship?
   5. Stranger Anxiety and Separation Anxiety
E. Disturbances in Development
   1. Autism
   2. Environmental Deprivation

IMPORTANT TERMS FOR SECTION II

Completion: Fill in the blanks to complete the definitions of key terms for this section of Chapter 7.

1. **emotion:** _____ feelings such as sadness, joy, and fear, which arise in response to situations and experiences and can be expressed through some kind of altered behavior.

2. **self-_____:** Ability to recognize one's own actions, intentions, states, and abilities.

3. **self-recognition:** Ability to recognize one's own _____.

4. _____ **model:** Process by which child and caregiver communicate emotional states to each other and respond appropriately.

5. **depression:** An emotional state characterized by _____ and such other symptoms as difficulties in eating, sleeping, and concentrating.

6. **social _____:** Understanding an ambiguous situation by seeking out another person's perception of it.

7. _____: A person's style of approaching other people and situations.

8. _____ **child:** Child with a generally happy temperament, regular biological rhythms, and a readiness to accept new experiences.

9. _____ **child:** Child who has an irritable temperament, irregular biological rhythms, and intense responses to situations.

10. _____ **child:** Child whose temperament is generally mild and who is hesitant about accepting new experiences.

11. _____: Active, affectionate, reciprocal relationship between two people; their interaction reinforces and strengthens the bond; the term often refers to an infant's relationship with his or her parents.

12. **Strange Situation:** A laboratory technique used to study _____.

13. _____ **attachment:** Attachment pattern in which an infant separates readily from the

primary caregiver and actively seeks out the caregiver when she or he returns.

14. _____ **attachment:** Attachment pattern in which an infant rarely cries when the primary caregiver leaves and avoids contact on his or her return.

15. _____ **(resistant) attachment:** Attachment pattern in which an infant becomes anxious before the primary caregiver leaves but both seeks and resists contact on the caregiver's return.

16. _____ **attachment:** Attachment pattern in which an infant shows contradictory behaviors and seems confused and afraid.

17. _____ **anxiety:** Wariness of unfamiliar people and places often shown by infants in the second half of the first year.

18. _____ **anxiety:** Distress shown by an infant when a familiar caregiver leaves.

LEARNING OBJECTIVES FOR SECTION II

After reading and reviewing this section of Chapter 7, you should be able to do the following.

1. Tell how researchers study babies' emotions; name at least five emotions babies seem to show during the first year; and explain the relationship between self-awareness and the development of emotions.

2. Identify four patterns of crying, describe the impact of mothers' responses to their babies' cries, and explain the value of crying as a diagnostic tool.

3. Trace changes, or stages, in what makes babies smile and laugh.

4. Explain the mutual regulation model and its relevance to babies' emotional development.

5. Explain how a mother's depression can affect her baby.

6. Describe how babies exhibit social referencing.

7. List nine aspects of temperament that show up soon after birth.

8. Describe three temperamental patterns and discuss hereditary and environmental influences that affect them.

9. Explain the significance of "goodness of fit" and its implications for parenting.

10. Summarize what is known about differences in baby boys' and girls' personalities.

11. Discuss the effects of cultural patterns and societal changes in family life on children's socialization, and identify two current trends in research on the family's influence on personality development.

12. Describe and evaluate the methodology of research on attachment.

13. Describe four patterns of attachment between infants and mothers; discuss influences on the development of these patterns and their long-term effects.

14. Compare infants' interactions with their mothers and with their fathers, and discuss the significance of the father-infant relationship.

15. Discuss factors influencing the development of stranger anxiety and separation anxiety.

16. Briefly discuss the cause(s), symptoms, and treatment of autism.

17. Report findings on effects of environmental deprivation in infancy.

Section III   Relationships With Other Children

FRAMEWORK FOR SECTION III

A.   Siblings
   1.   The Arrival of a New Baby
   2.   How Siblings Interact
B.   Changes in Sociability
   1.   Interest and Imitations
   2.   Sociability and Conflict

LEARNING OBJECTIVES FOR SECTION III

After reading and reviewing this section of Chapter 7, you should be able to do the following.

1.   Describe typical reactions to the arrival of a new baby and suggest ways to help siblings adjust.

2.   Describe the complex interactions between siblings in infancy and toddlerhood.

3.   Trace changes in typical interactions among babies during the first 2 years of life, and cite influences on individual differences in sociability.

Section IV   The Impact of Early Day Care

FRAMEWORK FOR SECTION IV

A.   What Is Good Day Care?
B.   Day Care and Cognitive Development
C.   Day Care and Social Development
D.   Day Care and Emotional Development

LEARNING OBJECTIVES FOR SECTION IV

After reading and reviewing this section of Chapter 7, you should be able to do the following.

1.   Identify characteristics of good day care and list suggestions for choosing a day care center.

2.   Report findings on the impact of early day care on cognitive, social, and emotional development and the significance of the timing of a mother's return to work.

3.   Describe Sweden's child care system.

CHAPTER 7 QUIZ

Matching—Who's Who: Match each name in the left-hand column with the appropriate description at the right. (Note: Here, a description may be used for more than one name or may not be used at all.)

1. Mary Ainsworth____
2. Stella Chess____
3. René Spitz____
4. Michael Lewis____
5. John Bowlby____
6. Harry Harlow and Margaret Harlow____
7. Carroll Izard____
8. E.Z. Tronick____
9. Erik H. Erikson____
10. Alexander Thomas____
11. Alison Clarke-Stewart____

a. studied infants' emotions by observing their facial expressions
b. proponent of mutual regulation model
c. studied emergence of self-recognition and self-awareness
d. believed that a child's good or bad conduct depends entirely upon the mother
e. using the ethological approach, studied mother-infant bonding in animals
f. pioneered in attachment research employing the Strange Situation
g. studied effects of institutionalization on babies
h. traced temperamental traits from infancy to young adulthood
i. described achievement of basic trust in infancy and of autonomy in toddlerhood
j. studied mothering needs of infant rhesus monkeys
k. studied impact of infant day care on social development

Multiple-Choice: Circle the choice that best completes or answers each item.

1. Personality is
   a. inherited
   b. developed through early experience
   c. both a and b
   d. neither a nor b; research has been unable to determine the origins of personality

2. Erikson maintained that the resolution of the crisis of trust versus mistrust occurs primarily in
   a. the first few hours after birth
   b. the period from 18 months to three years of age
   c. the feeding situation
   d. toilet training

3. According to Erikson, the proper balance of autonomy versus shame and doubt gives a child the virtue of
   a. will
   b. hope
   c. self-determination
   d. trust

4. Language is a key factor in personality development during Erikson's crisis of
   a. trust versus mistrust
   b. autonomy versus shame and doubt
   c. mutual regulation versus self-regulation
   d. independence versus negativism

5. Young children are most likely to comply with rules regarding
   a. safety
   b. fighting
   c. toileting
   d. eating

6. Which of the following emotions does *not* seem to appear during the first year?
    a. anger
    b. guilt
    c. fear
    d. surprise

7. An infant suddenly begins to cry loudly and then holds her breath. This is which pattern of crying?
    a. hunger cry
    b. pain cry
    c. frustration cry
    d. angry cry

8. The earliest smile of newborns is produced by
    a. gas
    b. pleasure
    c. recognition of parents
    d. spontaneous nervous system activity

9. Which of the following involves a baby's "reading" a caregiver's behavior or expression and adjusting his or her own behavior accordingly?
    a. mutual regulation model
    b. social referencing
    c. both a and b
    d. neither a nor b

10. Babies of depressed mothers tend to
    a. rock and squirm
    b. act upset when separated from the mother
    c. have trouble sleeping
    d. all of the above

11. As 12-month-old Emily plays in the sandbox, her mother sits nearby on a park bench. When another woman sits down on the bench, Emily looks at her mother uncertainly. Only after Emily sees her mother give the woman a friendly greeting does Emily smile and resume playing. This is an example of
    a. stranger anxiety
    b. separation anxiety
    c. insecure attachment
    d. social referencing

12. *All but which* of the following are probably attributable to temperament?
    a. insomnia
    b. frequent constipation
    c. creativity
    d. cheerfulness

13. The New York Longitudinal Study suggests that temperamental differences are largely influenced by
    a. heredity
    b. parental attitudes
    c. birth order
    d. gender

14. Which of the following 3-year-olds is likely to be best adjusted?
    a. Abbie, an "easy" child whose parents are in the midst of a contested divorce
    b. Ben, a "slow-to-warm-up" child whose family has had to move four times because of job changes
    c. Carol, a "difficult" child whose parents feed her on a flexible schedule
    d. none of the above; temperament is not a major factor in adjustment

15. Differences between infant boys' and girls' personalities
    a. are evident almost from birth
    b. reflect physiological differences between the sexes
    c. may reflect different treatment by adults
    d. show up consistently in a number of studies

16. Research suggests that the least securely attached babies may be those whose attachment pattern is characterized as
    a. disorganized-disoriented
    b. ambivalent
    c. avoidant
    d. resistant

17. Which of the following has been identified as a probable factor in secure attachment?
    a. absence of siblings close in age
    b. normal hearing in the baby
    c. mother's employment
    d. mother's relationship to her own mother

18. Experiments with rhesus monkeys, raised in cages with plain and cloth-covered wire-mesh surrogate "mothers," produced *all but which* of the following conclusions?
    a. Baby monkeys cling more to a surrogate "mother" that provides soft bodily contact than to one that feeds them.
    b. Baby monkeys will not take food from an inanimate "mother."
    c. Baby monkeys raised with inanimate "mothers" do not grow up normally.
    d. Baby monkeys remember a cloth surrogate "mother" better than a plain wire one.

19. Which of the following statements about fathers' relationships with their babies is true?
    a. The father-infant attachment develops later than the mother-infant attachment.
    b. Fathers tend to be about as responsive to babies as mothers are.
    c. Fathers' tendency to be less responsive than mothers is biologically based.
    d. In all cultures, fathers' style of playing with their babies is vigorous and highly physical.

20. Stranger anxiety seems to be related to *all but which* of the following?
    a. insecure attachment
    b. temperament
    c. quality and stability of substitute care
    d. caregiver's reaction to the stranger

21. Which of the following statements about infantile autism is true?
    a. It often develops as early as the fourth month of life.
    b. It affects more girls than boys.
    c. Its main cause is lack of parental responsiveness
    d. There is no effective treatment.

22. *All but which* of the following statements about sibling relationships in infancy and toddlerhood are true?
    a. Most behavioral problems of older siblings disappear by the time a new baby is 8 months old.
    b. Babies interact significantly with older siblings after the first 6 months.
    c. In many cultures, 4-year-olds have considerable responsibility for care of a baby brother or sister.
    d. Sibling relationships are characterized primarily by rivalry.

23. Which of the following is *not* necessarily a criterion for good day care?
    a. small groups of children
    b. college-educated caregivers
    c. child-related training of caregivers
    d. high staff-child ratio

24. When tested for intelligence and on other cognitive measures, 2-to-4-year-olds in good day care centers
    a. Score slightly lower than home-raised children.
    b. Score significantly lower than home-raised children.
    c. Score as high or higher than home-raised children, but this gain is often temporary.
    d. Appear to attain a permanent advantage over home-raised children.

25. At which of the following ages does the quality of substitute care appear to be most critical in affecting a baby's attachment to a working mother?
    a. 8 months
    b. 14 months
    c. 18 months
    d. 24 months

True or False? In the blank following each statement, write T (for *true*) or F (for *false*). In the space below each statement, if the statement is false, rewrite it to make it true.

1. According to Erikson, it is important for mothers to avoid creating mistrust on the part of their babies. ___

2. Self-regulation generally develops by the age of 2. ___

3. Negativism generally peaks at about age 3½ to 4. ___

4. Infants in different cultures show similar patterns of emotional development. ___

5. By 18 months, babies typically can recognize their own image. ___

6. Babies whose parents regularly respond soothingly to their cries tend to become spoiled and cry more to get what they want. ___

7. An 8-month-old baby may laugh at something unexpected. ___

8. Babies of depressed mothers tend to show signs of emotional withdrawal because of inability to elicit responses from the mother. ___

9. Recent research suggests that in the neonatal period, temperament is substantially influenced by the prenatal and birth experiences. ___

10. An "easy" child is one who is easy to raise. ___

11. According to Ainsworth, an essential part of human personality development is an infant's attachment to the mother. ___

12. Ainsworth found that attachment to the mother generally develops by 6 or 7 months. ___

13. The more secure an infant's attachment to the mother, the easier it is to leave her and explore the surroundings. ___

14. Studies have shown that mothers' employment has a negative effect on babies' security of attachment. ___

15. The relationship between attachment in infancy and personality development later in childhood is well established. ___

16. American fathers tend to play with their infants more than care for them. ___

17. Stranger anxiety is universal across cultures. ___

18. Longitudinal studies in Czechoslovakia found that children with adverse early environments fail to develop normally. ___

19. Babies become more sociable around the age of 1 year, when they start to walk. ___

20. More than 50 percent of American infants whose mothers work receive care outside the home. ___

21. Children who spent much of their first year in day care tend to be less competent than home-raised children. ___

22. In Sweden, most infants are in day care. ___

TOPICS FOR THOUGHT AND DISCUSSION

1. According to Erikson's theory, how can parents or caregivers tell when they are striking the "right" balance of trust versus mistrust, or autonomy versus shame and doubt? Can you suggest some guidelines based on your experience?

2. In your experience with children, how effective are the suggestions given in this chapter for reducing negativity and encouraging self-regulation? For choosing a good day care center? Do you have additional or better suggestions for dealing with these situations?

3. Izard and his colleagues have identified babies' emotions on the basis of their facial expressions. However, as your text points out, this evidence is inconclusive: agreement by a large number of observers that a baby *looks* angry does not establish that the baby *is* angry. Can you suggest any other basis for identifying babies' emotions?

4. According to the mutual regulation model, it is important for caregivers and babies to "read" each other's behavioral signals accurately and to respond appropriately. Your text discusses how babies learn to do this. How can parents and other caregivers improve their responsiveness and gauge the accuracy of their interpretations?

5. Research suggests that temperament is largely inborn and remains fairly stable, though it can be affected by environmental factors. In thinking about people you have known since childhood, do you consider this finding surprising or not?

6. Although research shows that differences in boys' and girls' behavior cannot be seen clearly before the age of 2, the authors of your text report other findings suggesting that differences in the ways parents treat baby boys and girls, particularly around the age of 18 months, may contribute to the shaping of personality differences. Might a proponent of the mutual regulation model have an alternative interpretation?

7. The authors of your text caution that almost all the research on attachment is based on the Strange Situation, which they say is artificial and focuses on a narrow range of behaviors. They add that it may be a particularly poor way to study attachment in children in some other cultures, in those who are accustomed to routine separations from the mother, and in those with disabilities such as Down syndrome. Can you suggest a better way to study attachment behavior, perhaps in a child's natural environment?

8. Thinking back to Chapter 1, why do you suppose the Harlows did their classic experiments on mothering with monkeys rather than with human babies? If their conclusions are applicable to humans, do they seem consistent with Erikson's theory?

9. The authors of your text suggest that when fathers assume the role of primary caregiver, the nature of father-infant attachment may change. The authors also suggest that differences in the way fathers and mothers behave with their babies may be influenced by societal expectations. What additional evidence would you look for in considering these points? Do you think the trend toward fathers serving as primary caregivers is likely to grow substantially? Do you see a value in fathers and mothers playing different roles in their infants' lives?

10. A Czechoslovakian study of children with emotionally deprived family backgrounds recommends that such families' social functioning be monitored and evaluated, and that assistance be provided where necessary. Would you favor such a program in this country? Do you see any possible dangers in it?

11. Why do you think there is little research on how to help children adjust to a new sibling? Can you suggest any way to test the popular advice reported in your text? On the basis of the other information given about sibling relationships, what additional suggestions would you give to parents?

12. Although the authors of your text say that day care is a complex issue, their main conclusion is that high-quality care can have positive effects on development, though gender and age of entering day care may make a difference. Do you agree that the evidence given in the text supports that conclusion? What other evidence, if any, would you like to see? Why do you think that in Sweden, where child care is "seen as every family's right," most parents of babies below 18 months take advantage of family leave to care for their own children? Given limited resources, would you prefer to see our society place more emphasis on providing high-quality day care or paid parental leave?

CHAPTER 7 READING

INTRODUCTION

Are the "terrible twos" as terrible as they are generally believed to be? Two researchers at Pennsylvania State University—Jay Belsky, professor of human development, and Keith Crnic, professor of psychology—have a surprising answer based on early findings from a longitudinal study of firstborn sons. This report of their research-in-progress is reprinted from the 1995 issue of *Health & Human Development Research/Penn State*. (Belsky also was one of the authors of a controversial study, cited near the end of Chapter 7 of your text, on how substitute care affects baby boys' attachment to their mothers.)

ARE THE TWOS SO TERRIBLE?

by Rita Rooney

As time-honored prophecies have it, a child learns the use of power sometime before his or her second birthday. That's when language first springs to command and the full impact of the word "no" is felt by parents immersed in one of childhood's most predictable episodes—the terrible twos. Early reports from a longitudinal study, however, suggest the toddler years may be getting a bad rap.

After four years of researching the terrible twos, Jay Belsky, professor of human development, and Keith Crnic, professor of psychology [both at Pennsylvania State University], conclude toddlerhood isn't necessarily more disruptive than other developmental stages. And when generational conflict does emerge, it is driven more by a parent's behavior than by the child's.

"Like adolescence, the years between two and four have a reputation for being traumatic for parents," Belsky says. "But the literature suggests that most adolescents get along fine with their parents, and the same is true of toddlers.

"At both times, we see kids trying to get their own way and parents exercising control. The question is, For whom are these years troublesome and why?"

Now in its fifth year, the study has focused on 130 intact White American families rearing firstborn sons. The researchers collected data during home visits to observe families when the children were 15 months of age, and continued their observations at regularly scheduled intervals until the child's third birthday. They now are following up with assessments of the child's social, emotional, and intellectual skills as the early enrollees in the study reach age 5.

Belsky says they chose a homogeneous sample so that extraneous factors would not affect the comparisons.

"We decided to work with sons because boys at that age are more likely to have problems managing their emotions," he adds. "Also, they probably respond more negatively to problems within the marriage—and we wanted to look at how marital relationships influence child behavior."

Families experiencing the most trouble during this developmental stage, the researchers found, were those in which parents practiced a type of simple control. For instance, a toddler amuses himself by opening and closing a refrigerator door and his mother scolds, "Stop that."

Belsky says this kind of control is generally ineffective because it doesn't show respect for the child. Parents in the study who exercised control plus guidance scored higher in gaining a positive response.

An admonition, "Stop that or you will get your fingers caught in the door," sends a message that the child is an individual who has rights and privileges and who deserves an explanation for the command.

Control without guidance is more likely to produce an escalation—beginning with non-compliance from the youngster, then more angry control by the parent, then even more negative behavior on the part of the child.

"It isn't that the untroubled families in our study never use simple control," Belsky says. "It's that they use it less often, and control coupled with guidance more often."

Keith Crnic, whose work has focused on stress processes in families, points out that even though there is considerable family stress during infancy, it doesn't affect the way parents think of or react to the baby.

"That changes during the toddler years," Crnic says. "Stress leads parents to become more irritated with the child, so that interaction is impaired."

The researchers identified three groups of families, ranging from less troubled to more troubled. The families having trouble in the second year all attempted to control their children 33 or more times during two hours of observation. They exercised the most simple or negative control of the three groups as well as the least control plus guidance. In return, they got the least compliance and the most defiance from their toddlers.

The study analyzed characteristics of the child, the marriage, parents, work, and social support to see how they might collectively explain what was going on within the families. While no single one of these factors is considered a stronger predictor of trouble, families showing more risk factors were more likely to be troubled.

Perhaps most surprising was that characteristics of the father (his personality and his experiences at work, for example) had the most impact, followed by those of the mother, while the child's own personality seemed less influential.

The role of fathers provides intriguing food for thought, Belsky contends. Since the study focused only on boys, he suggests it may be that fathers are more invested in and reactive to boys, or that their reaction is tied to an assertion of being the dominant male.

The marital relationship plays a role, too: How husbands and wives cooperate as parents seems to be significant, although the general quality of their marriage seemed less so. It was the couples who experienced problems co-parenting, not necessarily those with difficult marriages, who seemed to be creating a troubled environment.

But is the toddler himself really blameless in the family equation?

"We know without doubt that some kids, on their own, are more difficult than others," Belsky says.   "But that alone doesn't appear to determine how family members interact with each other. On the other hand, the character of the parents does play a major role—whether or not the child is problematic."

How the toddlers are affected by the family conflict is another question. "Youngsters at that age cannot express the clues that would lead us to an assessment of stress," Crnic says. "We can make some presumptions by looking at their behavior, but the real answers lie in the future."

The researchers hope that identifying troubled families during these early years will help predict long-term implications for behavioral and emotional development. They also are interested in why some parents behave in ways that don't seem effective in managing the toddler.

"The primary reason is that, in troubled families, fathers, and mothers to a lesser degree, are negatively emotional," Belsky says. "They tend to feel less supported by each other and by others, and they don't cooperate as parents.

"Although it doesn't look as if the children were more difficult initially, they become so in the process that ultimately creates a troubled family."

Belsky and Crnic point to the well-known fact that some children—especially boys—between ages 5 and 7 have problems managing emotions and controlling aggression. In 9- to 12-year-olds, there's the same pattern of anti-social behavior, along with the negative escalation: attempted control by parents, met by protest from kids. The question remains, Does such behavior have its origins in the toddler years?

"My guess is that it does," Belsky says. "It doesn't mean that every child in one of those families we have characterized as troubled will have problems later in life. But it does increase the likelihood."

As for the terrible twos, Belsky contends that when society attaches labels to a period of development, it exaggerates the challenge of parenting. He points out that fewer than one in four of the families studied were characterized as consistently troubled—hardly a disaster call for most parents.

QUESTIONS ABOUT THE READING

1. According to your text, the "terrible twos" are a normal manifestation of a toddler's drive toward autonomy, and what looks like negative behavior actually is healthy. On the basis of this article, would Belsky and Crnic agree or disagree? Do their comments seem consistent with the suggestions for reducing negativism in Box 7-1?

2. Do Belsky's and Crnic's tentative conclusions seem consistent or inconsistent with the discussion in your text of how children develop self-regulation? How do you suppose a proponent of Erikson's theory might interpret these findings?

3. Belsky and Crnic chose a homogeneous sample so as to prevent the intrusion of extraneous factors. Do you think that was a wise decision? Does the nature of the sample affect your evaluation of the findings?

4. Belsky says he and Crnic decided to study male toddlers because boys at that age are more likely to have problems than girls in managing their emotions. If that is true, how does it square with the discussion of gender differences in your text? If there are differences in boys' and girls' emotional control, might they be related to parents' gender-typing behavior? Can you suggest a way to test that hypothesis?

5. Were you surprised at the finding that the parents' characteristics (particularly the father's) have more impact than the child's personality on the degree of trouble within the family? How would you evaluate this finding in the light of the discussion in your text on "goodness of fit"?

6. According to Belsky, fewer than one in four families with toddlers are "consistently troubled." He also predicts that children in such families may be more likely to have problems as they grow older. In your view, do these statements suggest more cause for concern than the author of the article expresses?

7. Is Belsky's comparison of parent-toddler and parent-adolescent relationships consistent with your experience? Does conflict with teenagers often seem to spring from parental attempts to exercise "simple control"? (Keep this question, and your answer, in mind when you read Chapter 16 of your textbook.)

ANSWER KEY FOR CHAPTER 7

Note: Numbers in parentheses refer to pages in the textbook where answers can be found.

CHAPTER 7 REVIEW

Important Terms for Section I
1. behaving (page 255)
2. basic trust, basic mistrust (255)
3. expectations (256)
4. autonomy, shame and doubt (257)
5. teach (259)

Learning Objectives for Section I
1. (pages 255-256, 257)
2. (256, 257-259)
3. (258)

Important Terms for Section II
1. subjective (page 259)
2. awareness (261)
3. image (261)
4. mutual regulation (263)
5. sadness (264)
6. referencing (265)
7. temperament (266)
8. easy (267)
9. difficult (267)
10. slow-to-warm-up (267)
11. attachment (272)
12. attachment (273)
13. secure (274)
14. avoidant (274)
15. ambivalent (274)
16. disorganized-disoriented (274)
17. stranger (283)
18. separation (283)

Learning Objectives for Section II
1. (pages 260-261)
2. (262)
3. (262-263)

4. (263-264)
5. (264-265)
6. (265)
7. (266-267)
8. (267-268)
9. (268-269)
10. (269-271)
11. (271-272)
12. (272-273, 278-279)
13. (273-278)
14. (279-283)
15. (283-284)
16. (285-286)
17. (286)

Learning Objectives for Section III
1. (page 287)
2. (287-288)
3. (289-290)

Learning Objectives for Section IV
1. (pages 290-291, 292)
2. (291-296)
3. (295)

CHAPTER 7 QUIZ

Matching—Who's Who
1. f (page 273)
2. h (266)
3. g (284)
4. c (261)
5. e (272-273)
6. j (279-280)
7. a (260)
8. b (263-264)
9. i (255-256, 257)
10. h (266)
11. k (294)

Multiple-Choice

1. c (page 255)
2. c (256)
3. a (257)
4. b (257)
5. a (259)
6. b (261)
7. b (262)
8. d (263)
9. c (263-264, 265)
10. a (264)
11. d (265)
12. c (266-267)
13. a (267)
14. c (268-269)
15. c (269-271)
16. a (274)
17. d (274)
18. b (279-280)
19. b (281)
20. a (283-284)
21. a (285)
22. d (287-288)
23. b (291, 292)
24. c (291-292)
25. a (294-295)

True or False?

1. F—According to Erikson, although trust predominates in a healthy personality, some degree of mistrust is necessary for children to learn to protect themselves. (page 256)
2. F—A significant level of self-regulation typically does not develop until about the age of 3. (257)
3. T (258)
4. T (260)
5. T (261)
6. F—Research suggests that babies whose cries bring relief gain confidence in their ability to communicate and eventually cry less than other babies. (262)
7. T (263)
8. T (264-265)
9. T (267-268)
10. F—No temperamental type is immune to behavioral problems; a key factor is "goodness of fit" between the child's temperament and the demands made on the child. (268-269)
11. F—According to Ainsworth, an essential part of human personality development appears to be an infant's attachment to a mother figure, who may be any primary caregiver. (272)
12. T (272)
13. T (274, 277)
14. F—Studies of the relationship between mothers' employment and babies' security of attachment suggest that the mother's feelings about working, not the fact of employment itself, may affect attachment. (275)
15. F—Some researchers claim that the association between attachment in infancy and personality development later in childhood is weak and inconclusive and that later development may reflect the child's personality characteristics or parent-child interaction after infancy. (278-279)
16. T (281)
17. F—There are cross-cultural differences in stranger anxiety. (284)
18. F—Longitudinal studies in Czechoslovakia found that most environmentally deprived children developed normally, attesting to their resilience. (286)
19. F—Babies become less sociable around the age of 1 year, when they start to walk; their interest at that age becomes more focused on mastering physical coordination. (289)
20. T (290)
21. F—Children who spent much of their first year in day care tend to be at least as sociable, self-confident, persistent, achieving, and better at problem solving than home-raised children. (293)
22. F—In Sweden, a parent is entitled to paid leave for the first 18 months, and most babies below that age are cared for at home by a parent. (295)

PHYSICAL DEVELOPMENT AND HEALTH IN EARLY CHILDHOOD

OVERVIEW

Chapter 8 covers physical development and health in the three years following infancy and toddlerhood. In this chapter, the authors:

- Describe children's physical growth and change between ages 3 and 6 and summarize nutritional needs of this age group

- Trace the development of motor and artistic skills and discuss the significance of handedness

- Point out health issues that may arise during these predominantly healthy years, and environmental factors that may contribute to health problems

- Identify normal sleep patterns and common sleep problems

- Discuss causes and effects of child abuse and neglect and methods of prevention and treatment

CHAPTER 8 REVIEW

Section I Physical Growth and Change

FRAMEWORK FOR SECTION I

A. Appearance, Height, and Weight
B. Structural and Systemic Changes
C. Nutrition

LEARNING OBJECTIVES FOR SECTION I

After reading and reviewing this section of Chapter 8, you should be able to do the following.

1. Summarize how boys and girls change in appearance, height, and weight between ages 3 and 6.

2. Describe structural and systemic changes during this period.

3. Discuss nutritional needs in early childhood.

Section II Motor Development

FRAMEWORK FOR SECTION II

A. Motor Skills
    1. Gross Motor Skills
    2. Fine Motor Skills
B. Handedness
    1. Advantages of Left or Right Dominance
C. Artistic Development
    1. Stages of Children's Art Production
    2. Art Therapy

IMPORTANT TERMS FOR SECTION II

Completion: Fill in the blanks to complete the definitions of key terms for this section of Chapter 8.

1. _____ **skills:** Physical skills involving the large muscles (like jumping or running).

2. _____ **skills:** Abilities involving the small muscles (like buttoning or copying figures).

3. **handedness:** _____ for using a particular hand.

LEARNING OBJECTIVES FOR SECTION II

After reading and reviewing this section of Chapter 8, you should be able to do the following.

1. Outline the development of preschool boys' and girls' increasingly complex large-muscle skills, explain what causes that development, and suggest appropriate ways to foster it.

2. Summarize gender differences in young children's strength, musculature, and motor skills.

3. Give examples of 3-, 4-, and 5-year-olds' growing eye-hand and small-muscle coordination.

4. Explain what seems to cause handedness; discuss cultural attitudes toward it and advantages and disadvantages of being left- or right-handed.

5. Outline four stages in young children's drawing, and suggest how adults can best encourage children's artistic development.

6. Explain how art therapy can help children deal with emotional trauma.

Section III   Health

FRAMEWORK FOR SECTION III

A. Health Problems in Early Childhood
    1. Minor Illnesses
    2. Major Illnesses
        a. HIV and AIDS in Children
    3. Accidental Injuries
B. Dental Health
    1. Thumb-Sucking
C. Health in Context: Environmental Influences
    1. Exposure to Illness
    2. Stress
    3. Poverty
        a. Health Implications of Poverty
        b. Social Policy and Poverty
    4. Lead Poisoning

LEARNING OBJECTIVES FOR SECTION III

After reading and reviewing this section of Chapter 8, you should be able to do the following.

1. Explain the physical, cognitive, and emotional benefits of frequent minor respiratory illnesses in young children.

2. Summarize current trends in death rates from major childhood illnesses.

3. Describe effects of HIV infection in young children.

4. Identify the two most common sites of accidents fatal to young children; discuss the effectiveness of laws aimed at preventing such accidents; and list recommended precautions for reducing the risk of accidents.

5. Summarize dental development in early childhood and appropriate treatment for thumb-sucking.

6. Discuss five major environmental factors that may affect young children's health.

Section IV Sleep Patterns and Problems

FRAMEWORK FOR SECTION IV

A. Normal Sleep Behavior
B. Problems with Sleep
   1. Bedtime Struggles
   2. Night Terrors and Nightmares
   3. Nighttime Fears
   4. Bed-Wetting (Enuresis)

IMPORTANT TERMS FOR SECTION IV

Completion: Fill in the blanks to complete the definitions of the key terms for this section of Chapter 8.

1. _____ **objects:** Objects used repeatedly by a child as a bedtime companion.
2. **enuresis:** Bed-_____.

LEARNING OBJECTIVES FOR SECTION IV

After reading and reviewing this section of Chapter 8, you should be able to do the following.

1. Describe normal sleep behavior of preschoolers and state how it differs from that of infants and toddlers.

2. Name at least three conditions associated with bedtime struggles and list at least five suggestions for helping children sleep well.

3. Distinguish between night terrors and nightmares.

4. Describe an effective treatment for nighttime fears.

5. Identify factors that may be involved in bed-wetting and name four effective ways of treating it.

Section V Maltreatment of Children: Abuse and Neglect

FRAMEWORK FOR SECTION V

A. Causes of Abuse and Neglect
   1. The Microsystem: The Abuser or Neglecter and the Child
      a. The Abuser or Neglecter
      b. The Child
   2. The Exosystem: Jobs, Neighborhood, and Social Support
   3. The Macrosystem: Cultural Values and Patterns

B. Long-Term Effects of Abuse and Neglect
   1. Why Some Children Do Not Show Scars of Abuse
C. Helping Families in Trouble or at Risk
   1. Preventing Maltreatment
   2. Providing Help for the Abused and Their Families
      a. The Microsystem: The Family
      b. The Exosystem: The Community
      c. The Macrosystem: Cultural Values

IMPORTANT TERMS FOR SECTION V

Completion: Fill in the blanks to complete the definitions of key terms for this section of Chapter 8.

1. **child _____:** Maltreatment of children involving physical or psychological injury.

2. **_____ syndrome:** Condition showing symptoms of physical abuse.

3. **_____:** Sexual contact between a child and an older person.

4. **child _____:** Withholding of such necessary care as food, clothing and supervision.

5. **_____ failure to thrive:** Failure to grow and gain weight despite adequate nutrition, possibly due to emotional neglect.

6. **emotional abuse:** Action or _____ to act that damages children's behavioral, cognitive, emotional, or physical functioning.

LEARNING OBJECTIVES FOR SECTION V

After reading and reviewing this section of Chapter 8, you should be able to do the following.

1. Distinguish among physical abuse, sexual abuse, emotional abuse, and physical and emotional neglect.

2. Compare typical characteristics of abusive and neglectful parents.

3. Identify typical characteristics of children who are victims of abuse.

4. State ways in which community and culture may contribute to maltreatment of children.

5. Discuss factors affecting the long-term outlook for maltreated children.

6. Describe effective ways of preventing maltreatment and of helping abused children and their families.

CHAPTER 8 QUIZ

Matching—Numbers: Match each item at the left with the correct number in the right-hand column.

1.	Approximate percentage of 5-year-old boys who are bed-wetters ___	3
2.	Age at which all primary teeth are normally present ___	4
3.	Age at which permanent teeth generally begin to appear___	5
4.	Approximate percentage of American white children living in poverty ___	6
5.	Approximate percentage of African American children living in poverty ___	7
6.	Number of scribble patterns a 2-year-old typically can draw ___	13
7.	Average height in inches of a 6-year-old boy or girl ___	17
8.	Number of states that permit corporal punishment in school ___	30
9.	Age at which a child typically can hop four to six steps on one foot ___	40
10.	Age at which a child typically can walk downstairs unaided, alternating feet ___	46

Multiple-Choice: Circle the choice that best completes or answers each item.

1. Which of the following would *not* be a normal change after age 3?
    a.   faster growth rate
    b.   more slender appearance
    c.   increased stamina
    d.   decreased appetite

2. Which of the following is *not* among suggestions that, according to your text, may help in dealing with young children who are finicky eaters?
    a.   serving finger foods
    b.   introducing new foods one at a time
    c.   serving casseroles to "hide" rejected foods
    d.   giving the child a choice of foods

3. Children between the ages of 3 and 6 can perform increasingly complex motor behaviors in part because their
    a.   brain stem is better developed
    b.   muscles, bones, and lungs are stronger
    c.   reflexes are quicker
    d.   all of the above

4. Left-handed people tend to be
    a.   subject to brain damage
    b.   poor in spatial tasks
    c.   dyslexic
    d.   ambidextrous

5. According to Kellogg, a child's purpose in drawing shapes and designs is to
    a.   portray real objects
    b.   develop eye-hand coordination
    c.   explore form and design
    d.   please parents and teachers

6. The leading cause of death among infants and children worldwide is
    a.   cancer
    b.   respiratory illnesses
    c.   accidents
    d.   AIDS

7. According to an American Academy of Pediatrics task force, a child who carries the HIV virus but does not show symptoms
    a.   is likely to show developmental delays
    b.   is likely to have behavior problems
    c.   should be isolated to protect other children
    d.   should have no special treatment

8. Who of the following children is likely to be sick the least often?
    a.   child in small-group care (2 to 6 children)
    b.   child in day care (7 or more children)
    c.   child in large family, raised at home
    d.   child in small family, raised at home

9. Stressful family events appear to increase children's susceptibility to
    a.   illness
    b.   injury
    c.   both a and b
    d.   neither a nor b

10. Who of the following is more likely to repeat a grade in school?
    a.   middle-class child
    b.   poor child living at home
    c.   child whose family is homeless
    d.   none of the above; no relationship between socioeconomic status or homelessness and school failure has been found

11. Children in poor families are at high risk of
    a.   hearing loss
    b.   insomnia
    c.   lead poisoning
    d.   all of the above

12. Which of the following is (are) normal for preschoolers?
    a.   prolonged bedtime struggles
    b.   transitional objects
    c.   frequent nightmares
    d.   bed-wetting

13. Night terrors differ from nightmares in that night terrors
    a. usually occur within 1 hour after falling asleep
    b. are often remembered vividly
    c. are experienced more by girls than boys
    d. all of the above

14. According to the text, how can bed-wetting best be treated?
    a. Teach the child to control the sphincter muscles.
    b. Wake a child who begins to urinate.
    c. Reward the child for staying dry.
    d. all of the above

15. More than 90 percent of child abuse occurs
    a. in day care centers
    b. at home
    c. in parks or other secluded places
    d. in strangers' cars

16. Approximately what proportion of abusive parents were abused themselves as children?
    a. 10 percent
    b. one-third
    c. half
    d. more than 90 percent

17. Which of the following is (are) *not* characteristic of abusive parents?
    a. marital problems and physical fighting
    b. disorganized household
    c. large number of children closely spaced
    d. emotional withdrawal from spouse and children

18. Victims of child abuse are likely to be
    a. passive and compliant
    b. cold and unaffectionate
    c. needy and demanding
    d. none of the above; the parent's personality, not the child's, determines the likelihood of abuse

19. Preschoolers who have been sexually abused are likely to
    a. have nightmares
    b. be hyperactive
    c. run away from home
    d. all of the above

20. According to your text, which of the following is *not* generally recommended as a way to stop or prevent child abuse?
    a. separating children from abusive parents
    b. treating abusers as criminal offenders
    c. relieving parents who feel overburdened
    d. teaching parents how to manage their children's behavior

True or False? In the blank following each item, write T (for *true*) or F (for *false*). In the space below each item, if the statement is false, rewrite it to make it true.

1. Boys at age 3 tend to be a little taller and heavier than girls. ___

2. Preschoolers typically eat less in proportion to their size than infants do. ___

3. Five-year-old boys tend to be better than 5-year-old girls at catching a ball. ___

4. Handedness usually develops by age 3. ___

5. According to Rhoda Kellogg, adults should encourage children when they begin to draw more recognizable pictures. ___

6. By early childhood, the lungs are fully developed. ___

7. Major illnesses are more likely to be fatal in childhood than in adulthood. ___

8. Children with AIDS tend to show delayed development. ___

9. Children are more likely to be injured in day care centers than at home. ___

10. Care of "baby teeth" does not affect dental health because they are not permanent. ___

11. Thumb-sucking that continues past age 6 seems to result from emotional disturbance and should be treated with psychological counseling. ___

12. Children in high quality day care programs tend to be healthier than those not in day care. ___

13. Homelessness is closely related to low birth weight. ____

14. There is no treatment for lead poisoning. ____

15. Enuresis runs in families. ____

16. A baby who fails to grow and gain weight despite adequate nutrition may suffer from emotional neglect. ____

17. Most child abusers have psychotic or malicious personalities. ____

18. A neglectful mother is likely to have had complications during pregnancy. ____

19. Low-income urban neighborhoods have almost uniformly high rates of child abuse. ____

20. Cultural approval of spanking as punishment may be related to the incidence of child abuse. ____

21. Children who are sexually abused are likely to be raped or sexually assaulted as adults. ____

22. Most victims of child abuse grow up to become abusers themselves. ___

23. Apart from physical evidence of sexual abuse, it has few recognizable signs. ___

TOPICS FOR THOUGHT AND DISCUSSION

1. How would you expect differences in preschool boys' and girls' motor development to affect the extent to which, and the ways in which, they play with each other? (Keep this question, and your answer, in mind as you read Chapter 10.)

2. There seems to be room for more research on the causes of handedness and its connection to physical and intellectual abilities. How would you design such research? To what questions would you seek answers? What methods and types of experiments would you utilize?

3. In view of the lack of evidence to back up the prejudice against left-handedness, why do you think such prejudice has been so widespread?

4. The authors present one clinician's view that minor childhood illnesses are beneficial in that they promote competence, empathy, and understanding of language. Did you find this view surprising? Convincing?

5. Since low income is the chief factor associated with ill health, what steps should be taken to improve the health of poor children and to ensure that they receive proper medical care and immunizations against contagious illnesses? In view of the lower childhood death rates in European countries that have free health care, would you favor such a system for this country? If not, what other measures, if any, would you support?

6. According to your text, it is better to reward a bed-wetter for staying dry at night than to punish the child for bed-wetting. Does that recommendation reflect learning theory as described in Chapter 1 of your text? Would an advocate of the psychoanalytic perspective consider either of these methods effective? Why or why not?

7. According to your text, little is known about the effectiveness of various kinds of interventions in cases of suspected child abuse. Why do you think this might be so? Can you suggest ways to make such an evaluation?

CHAPTER 8 READING

INTRODUCTION

On the night of October 25, 1994, a distraught 23-year-old mother named Susan Smith, of Union, South Carolina, reported that her two young sons—Michael, age 3, and Alexander, age 14 months—had been abducted by a gunman who forced her out of her car and drove off with the children. Smith and her estranged husband, David, went on national television pleading for the boys' return. But after intensive police questioning and polygraph tests, Susan Smith confessed that she actually had drowned her children by driving her car to a nearby lake and allowing it to slide down a ramp into the water with the boys strapped in their car seats.

Killing a child may be the ultimate form of child abuse. Yet, to all appearances, Smith had not been an abusive mother. Reportedly, she was despondent over a failed romance; she had been abused by her stepfather; and she had previously attempted suicide. She claimed that she had intended to take her own life with her sons' but couldn't go through with it and jumped out of the car at the last minute. She was convicted of murder and sentenced to life imprisonment.

This article, slightly condensed from the November 14, 1994, issue of *Newsweek*, uses the Smith case as a springboard to examine psychological patterns that may help explain the unthinkable: why some parents kill their children.

WHY PARENTS KILL

by John McCormick, with Susan Miller and Debra Woodruff

The [Susan] Smith case captured the nation's attention, at first because it played on every parent's fear of a stranger abducting a beloved baby. That proved unfounded; the incidence of such stranger-kidnappings is, in fact, quite rare. The real explanation was even more terrifying because it was closer to home and harder to

fathom. What could prompt a mother to murder her own children?

Researchers know a lot more about why spouses kill each other than they do about why mothers and fathers kill. But they are collecting data, and the early discoveries are striking. Roughly 1,300 children are killed by their parents or close relatives each year—including about two thirds of homicide victims younger than 10. In the vast majority of cases, it is not a deliberate, premeditated act, but the final episode in a long pattern of violence. The youngest children seem to be the most vulnerable; half of last year's casualties were under the age of 1. Men kill slightly more often than women, though the National Center for Missing Exploited Children has found that when the child is under 2, the mother is more likely to be the murderer.

Homicide and child-abuse experts are beginning to recognize patterns in the circumstances that drive parents to kill. Most cases, they say, involve acts of discipline gone wrong. "Often, the kids are screaming bloody murder and the parents can't make them stop," says Dr. Katherine Kaufer Christoffel of the Violent Injury Prevention Center at Children's Memorial Hospital in Chicago. Most of these fatalities are infants; with slightly older children, toilet-training problems are frequently involved. "What these two have in common is that the child is not cooperating in a way that the parent finds tolerable," Christoffel says. "The parent loses it—sometimes because his own parents lost it and that's what he learned."

"Losing it," of course, can be shorthand for mental illness, which comes in a variety of forms. Postpartum depression is one. Experts are increasingly realizing that it can drive some mothers to kill their offspring months or even years after they are born. Drug abuse or financial problems can also distort a parent's ability to think and act normally. "Any big-time stress—a job loss, a death in the family, eviction—can set people off," says Christoffel.

Some severely depressed parents kill their children in a bungled attempt to kill themselves. Susan Smith told authorities that's what she had in mind when she drove to the lake: distraught over money and failed romances, unable to take her own life, she found herself rolling the car with her sons into the lake instead. Northeastern University criminologist James

Fox calls such acts "[suicide] by proxy." And as Richard Gelles, director of the University of Rhode Island's Family Violence Research Program, explains, they can involve a form of "boundary confusion" in which the mother "is overly enmeshed in the lives of her children. She doesn't know where her life ends and theirs begins." The phenomenon isn't limited to women. There are many cases of men who slaughter their families before turning the gun on themselves. "Frequently, the parent thinks this life is miserable," says Fox, "and rationalizes that the family will be happily reunited in the hereafter."

THE REASONS

A recent federal study examined 84 cases where children 11 and under were killed by parents. The most common explanations:

Child abuse, unspecified 21%
Angry with child's behavior 17%
Mental instability or handicap 11%
Unwanted infant...10%
Unintended result of another crime......................7%
Neglect...6%
Unable to handle the responsibility 4%

Source: Bureau of Justice Statistics

Other times, parents kill their kids in an attempt to strike at an estranged spouse—what Fox calls "murder by proxy." The murderous parent is often the loser in a bitter custody battle, and the rationale is a version of the jealous wife-beater's classic threat: "If I can't have you, then no one will." Researchers think men are more prone to such twisted logic than women, if only because women still win the majority of custody battles.

Murdering the kids and framing the mate is another variation. Late last month, 34-year-old Dora Buenrostro stormed into the police station in placid San Jacinto, Calif[ornia], pleading for help, she said, because her estranged husband had turned up and she feared for her kids. Police found 9-year-old Susana and 8-year-old Vicente stabbed to death in her apartment; they later discovered 4-year-old Diedra's body strapped in a car seat in an abandoned building. Buenrostro alleged that her husband must have killed them, but when his alibi checked out, police arrested her instead.

One of the most disturbing psychological explanations is associated with Munchausen's syndrome. Adults who suffer from the affliction typically invent or induce their own illnesses to win attention. In "Munchausen's syndrome by proxy," parents use their children instead, dragging them through countless tests and doctor visits to diagnose imaginary illnesses or murdering them outright in a twisted bid for sympathy. Experts first described the condition in 1977—and by 1992, some 200 cases had been uncovered, including a number of deaths previously attributed to natural causes.

One telltale sign is when more than one child in a family dies for unexplained reasons. A classic case is that of Marybeth Tinning of Schenectady, N[ew] Y[ork]. All nine of her children died mysteriously between 1972 and 1985. Tinning was convicted of murdering the last one in 1986. Waneta Hoyt, also of upstate New York, is now awaiting trial for the suspected murders of her five children between 1965 and 1971. A local prosecutor read about the case in a medical journal theorizing that sudden infant death syndrome might run in families; he suspected homicide instead. Last spring, 23 years after the death of her last baby, Hoyt was interrogated by police for the first time and, after two hours, she began to confess details of how she suffocated her kids, one by one, with pillows, a towel or her shoulder. Hoyt has since recanted the confession. [1]

"Shaggy Stranger"

Still another unsettling finding is the frequency with which stepfathers or boyfriends kill the kids they inherit in romantic relationships. Gelles estimates that one-quarter to one-third of child murders are committed by the new men in the mothers' lives. Scientists note that this mimics the behavior of some chimps, apes and monkeys: a male joining a group picks a mate and frequently kills her offspring. Anthropologist Susan Hrdy at the University of California, Davis, says that both the male primate and the male human may be annoyed that their females are spending time and energy on another male's progeny. Anne Cohn Donnelly, of the Chicago-based National Committee to Prevent Child Abuse, puts it more bluntly: "The new man is trying to romance a woman who's spending half her time changing diapers."

Though Susan Smith's precise motives are still emerging, she may fit into the sad subset of

---

[1] Hoyt was subsequently convicted.

mothers who kill their kids in a vain attempt to win approval from their new men. Gelles says this type of killer typically feels powerless, and was often abused herself as a child: "Her identity comes from pleasing the men in her life. The boyfriend says 'Jump!' and she says, 'How high?'"

That may explain the motive of Elizabeth Diane Downs of Eugene, Ore[gon]. In a 1983 case eerily similar to Susan Smith's, Downs told police that a "shaggy-haired stranger" had demanded her car on a dark, isolated road, then shot her three sleeping children when she refused. Cheryl, 7, died at the hospital; Christy, 8, suffered a stroke and Danny, 4, was permanently paralyzed. Police were skeptical of Downs's account—particularly when she mentioned a boyfriend in Arizona who did not want to raise children. She was convicted largely on the basis of Christy's wrenching testimony, and sentenced to life imprisonment. Downs escaped briefly in 1987, explaining she was still searching for the shaggy-haired stranger to prove her innocence. Farrah Fawcett played her part in the made-for-TV movie version, "Small Sacrifices."

Hedda Nussbaum may be the textbook example of still another pattern—victims of "battered-woman syndrome" who kill their children or stand by, helplessly, while their mates inflict fatal blows. Last month Nussbaum went back to court seeking $12.6 million in damages from her ex-lover Joel Steinberg for what she said was physical and emotional pain during a decade of assaults that culminated in 6-year-old Lisa's beating death in 1987. Last week, Nussbaum's psychiatrist, Dr. Samuel Klagsbrun, warned against drawing parallels between his patient and Susan Smith: "By the time Lisa was killed by Steinberg, Hedda had been reduced to a robotlike state of existence where she wasn't able to go to the fridge without first asking permission from Joel." That's quite different, Klagsbrun said, from the kind of woman "whose own identity hasn't developed sufficiently [and she] fills that void by clumping onto a man."

Abuse Victims

There were ample signs that Lisa Steinberg was being beaten before her death; in fact, 42 percent of the children killed by their parents last year had previously been reported as victims of abuse. Given those grim statistics,

some experts argue that courts should be quicker to permanently remove children from parents who have proven abusive in the past. But others say the system should do more to help such parents curb their violent tendencies and turn their lives around. "We make it easier to pick up the phone and report our neighbors for violence and abuse," says David Wolfe, professor of psychology and psychiatry at the University of Western Ontario, "than we do for parents to call in and request help for themselves."

The cases like Susan Smith's, though rare, are somehow more disturbing, since there were few apparent hints that her boys might be in jeopardy. Smith's skill at concocting a story that could seize the nation's sympathy is even more chilling. But that, too, fits a familiar pattern, says Fox—and it reminds him of a black joke that criminologists share: "How do you tell the difference between the sociopathic killer and the innocent person? The sociopath has a better story."

QUESTIONS ABOUT THE READING

1. According to the article, most parental killing of children is the culmination of a long pattern of violent maltreatment. Are the psychological patterns described in the article consistent with characteristics of abusers described in your text? If not, what differences do you see?

2. Your text emphasizes the importance of looking at maltreatment of children from an ecological perspective, including factors associated with the child, the community, and the larger society, as well as the abuser. Are any of the first three factors considered in the article? Do you think additional analysis along these lines would be useful?

3. According to the article, some experts advocate permanent removal of children from abusive parents, while others argue for treatment to help them stop their abusive behavior. What approach do the authors of your text appear to favor?

ANSWER KEY FOR CHAPTER 8

Note: Numbers in parentheses refer to pages in the textbook where answers can be found.

CHAPTER 8 REVIEW

Learning Objectives for Section I
1. (page 305)
2. (305)
3. (305-306)

Important Terms for Section II
1. gross motor (page 306)
2. fine motor (306)
3. preference (309)

Learning Objectives for Section II
1. (pages 307-308)
2. (308)
3. (308-309)
4. (309-310)
5. (310-311)
6. (311-312)

Learning Objectives for Section III
1. (page 312)
2. (313)
3. (313)
4. (313-315)
5. (315-316)
6. (316-321)

Important Terms for Section IV
1. transitional (page 322)
2. wetting (324)

Learning Objectives for Section IV
1. (pages 321-322)
2. (323)
3. (324)
4. (324)
5. (324-325)

Important Terms for Section V
1. abuse (page 325)

2. battered child (325)
3. sexual abuse (325)
4. neglect (325)
5. nonorganic (325)
6. failure (325)

Learning Objectives for Section V
1. (page 325)
2. (326-327)
3. (327)
4. (328)
5. (328-330)
6. (330-333)

CHAPTER 8 QUIZ

Matching—Numbers
1. 7 (page 324)
2. 3 (315)
3. 6 (316)
4. 13 (317)
5. 40 (317)
6. 17 (310)
7. 46 (305)
8. 30 (328)
9. 4 (307, 308)
10. 5 (308)

Multiple-Choice
1. a (pages 305-306)
2. c (307)
3. b (307)
4. c (310)
5. c (311)
6. b (313)
7. d (313)
8. d (316)
9. c (316-317)
10. c (318)
11. d (319, 321)
12. b (321-322)
13. a (324)
14. d (325)
15. b (326)
16. b (326)

17. d (327)
18. c (327)
19. a (329)
20. a (330-331)

True or False?

1. T (page 305)
2. T (306)
3. F—Five-year-old girls are better at catching balls and other tasks involving small muscle coordination. (308)
4. T (309)
5. F—Adults should let children draw what they like without imposing suggestions; pressure to portray reality leads children to move away from a concern with form and design and often to lose interest in art. (311)
6. F—In early childhood the lungs are not yet fully developed. (312)
7. F—Deaths caused by illness are relatively rare in childhood compared with such deaths in adulthood. (313)
8. T (313)
9. F—Children suffer fewer injuries in day care centers than at home. (314)
10. F—Baby teeth affect jaw development, and lifelong dental habits may be set in early childhood. (315)

11. F—Prolonged thumb-sucking seems to be merely a habit and is most effectively treated with a dental appliance. (316)
12. T (316)
13. T (318)
14. F—Moderate lead poisoning can be treated with medication. (321)
15. T (324-325)
16. T (325)
17. F—More than 90 percent of child abusers are not psychotic; and far from being malicious, they often hate themselves for what they do but cannot control themselves. (326)
18. T (327)
19. F—Child abuse rates in low-income neighborhoods vary greatly, depending on such factors as community cohesion and social supports. (328)
20. T (328)
21. T (329)
22. F—Many abused children are resilient; according to one analysis, only one-third grow up to abuse their own children. (330)
23. F—Any extreme change in a young child's behavior can be a sign of sexual abuse. (331-332)

COGNITIVE DEVELOPMENT IN EARLY CHILDHOOD

OVERVIEW

Chapter 9 focuses on the rapid development of cognitive skills during the preschool years. In this chapter, the authors:

- Explore how young children think and remember

- Report research showing that young children are more intellectually competent than psychologists once believed

- Trace the development of language in early childhood

- Discuss the assessment of intelligence in early childhood

- Examine factors—including the personality, parents, preschool, kindergarten, and television—that influence cognitive development

CHAPTER 9 REVIEW

Section I Aspects of Cognitive Development

FRAMEWORK FOR SECTION I

A. Cognitive Concepts Studied by Piaget and Subsequent Researchers
 1. Concepts Identified by Piaget: Typical Advances of Early Childhood
  a. The Symbolic Function: The Use of Symbols to Represent Specific Objects
   (1) Significance of the Symbolic Function
   (2) Indications of the Symbolic Function
  b. Understanding Identities
  c. Understanding Cause and Effect
  d. Putting Oneself in Another's Place: Empathy
  e. Ability to Classify
  f. Understanding Numbers
 2. Piaget's Preoperational Stage: Limitations of Thought
  a. Centration
  b. Confusing Appearance with Reality
  c. Irreversibility
  d. Focus on States Rather Than on Transformations
  e. Transductive Reasoning
  f. Egocentrism
   (1) Studying Egocentrism
  g. Animism
 3. Can Cognitive Abilities Be Accelerated through Training?
 4. Assessing Piaget's Theory
  a. Piaget's Underestimation of Children's Abilities
  b. Other Criticisms
  c. Piaget's Contributions, Theoretical and Practical
B. Language in Early Childhood
 1. Words, Sentences, and Grammar
  a. Linguistic Advances
  b. Linguistic Immaturity
 2. Pragmatics: The Development of Social Speech
 3. Private Speech
 4. Delayed Language Development
  a. Causes of Delayed Language Development
  b. Implications of Delayed Language Development
 5. Development of Literacy
 6. Practical Applications of Research on Language Development
C. Development of Memory: The Child as a Processor of Information
 1. Recognition and Recall
  a. The Importance of General Knowledge
  b. Mastery Motivation, Study Activities, and Strategies
 2. Childhood Memories
  a. Implicit and Explicit Memories
  b. Three Types of Memory
   (1) Generic Memory
   (2) Episodic Memory
   (3) Autobiographical Memory
 3. Influences on Children's Memory
  a. Language
  b. Social Interaction
  c. Unusual Activities
  d. Personal Involvement
D. Development of Intelligence
 1. Assessing Intelligence by Traditional Psychometric Measures
  a. What Do Scores on Intelligence Tests Mean?
  b. Stanford-Binet Intelligence Scale
  c. Wechsler Preschool and Primary Scale of Intelligence (WPPSI-R)
 2. Assessing Intelligence By Finding the "Zone of Proximal Development" (ZPD)

IMPORTANT TERMS FOR SECTION I

Completion: Fill in the blanks to complete the definitions of key terms for this section of Chapter 9.

1. _____: Ability, described by Piaget, to use mental representation, shown in language, symbolic play, and deferred imitation.

2. **symbol:** In Piaget's terminology, a personal mental representation of a(n) _____ experience.

3. _____ **imitation:** Ability to observe an action and imitate it after time.

4. **symbolic play:** Play in which a(n) _____ stands for something else.

5. **preoperational stage:** In Piaget's theory, the second major period of cognitive development (approximately age 2 to age 7), in which children are able to think in _____ but are limited by their inability to use _____.

6. _____: In Piaget's terminology, thinking about one aspect of a situation while neglecting others.

7. _____: In Piaget's terminology, to think simultaneously about several aspects of a situation.

8. **conservation:** Piaget's term for awareness that two stimuli which are equal (in length, weight, or amount, for example) remain equal in the face of _____ alteration, so long as nothing has been added to or taken away from either stimulus.

9. _____: Failure to understand that an operation or action can go two or more ways.

10. **transduction:** In Piaget's terminology, a child's method of thinking about two or more experiences without relying on abstract _____.

11. _____: As used by Piaget, a child's inability to consider another person's point of view.

12. **animism:** Tendency to attribute _____ to objects that are not _____.

13. **theory of mind:** Understanding of mental _____.

14. _____: Process by which a child absorbs the meaning of a new word after hearing it only once or twice in conversation.

15. **pragmatics:** The practical use of _____.

16. _____ **speech:** Speech intended to be understood by a listener.

17. _____ **speech:** Talking aloud to oneself with no intent to communicate with anyone else.

18. _____: The ability to read and write.

19. _____: Ability to correctly identify a stimulus as something previously known; compare *recall*.

20. _____: Ability to reproduce material from memory; compare *recognition*.

21. _____ **memory:** Memory that relies on a script.

22. _____: General outline of a familiar, repeated event.

23. _____ **memory:** Memory of an event that happened once, at a specific time or place.

24. _____ **memory:** Memory of specific events in one's own life.

25. **standardized norm:** Standard obtained from the scores of a large, _____ sample of children of the same age who took a test while it was being developed.

26. _____: Degree to which a test measures the abilities it claims to measure.

27. _____: Degree to which a test yields reasonably consistent results time after time.

28. **Stanford-Binet Intelligence Scale:** The first individual childhood intelligence test to be developed; measures practical judgment, memory, and _____ orientation.

29. **Wechsler Preschool and Primary Scale of Intelligence (WPPSI-R):** Individual childhood (ages 3 to 7) intelligence test that yields separate verbal and _____ scores as well as a combined score.

30. _____ (abbreviated ____): Vygotsky's term for the level at which children can almost perform a task on their own.

LEARNING OBJECTIVES FOR SECTION I

After reading and reviewing this section of Chapter 9, you should be able to do the following.

1. Name at least six cognitive advances of early to middle childhood and explain their significance.

2. Define the symbolic function, name three ways in which young children display it, and give an example of each.

3. Define and give an example of each of the following achievements: understanding of identities, understanding of cause and effect, empathy, ability to classify, and understanding of numbers.

4. Summarize what Piaget observed to be the chief difference between children's intellectual abilities in early childhood and middle childhood.

5. Give examples of each of the following limitations Piaget observed in preoperational thought: centration, confusing appearance with reality, irreversibility, focus on states rather than on transformations, transductive reasoning, egocentrism, and animism.

6. Explain under what circumstances cognitive abilities can be accelerated through training.

7. Evaluate Piaget's theory—its shortcomings and contributions—and explain why he may have underestimated children's thought processes.

8.   Discuss recent findings about children's
     ability to distinguish fantasy from reality, to
     intentionally deceive, to recognize false
     beliefs, and to be aware of mental activity.

9.   List advances in, and limitations on,
     linguistic ability in early childhood.

10. Identify factors influencing young children's
     ability to communicate through speech.

11. Compare three views of the function and
     value of private speech, state which view
     seems to be supported by research, and point
     out practical implications.

12. List seven types of private speech, and give
     an example of each type.

13. Discuss causes and implications of delayed
     language development.

14. Identify three factors that can foster the
     development of literacy.

15. Give at least three practical suggestions for
     encouraging language development.

16. Distinguish between recognition and recall,
     tell which is more difficult for young
     children, and name three factors influencing
     how well young children recall.

17. Give three possible reasons for infantile amnesia, and explain the difference between implicit and explicit memory.

18. Distinguish among generic memory, episodic memory, and autobiographical memory, and state at least two functions of autobiographical memory.

19. Identify five important factors that influence young children's ability to remember.

20. Explain why and how intelligence tests are standardized, and the importance of validity and reliability.

21. Explain a common misconception about the meaning of intelligence test scores.

22. Explain why psychometric tests are more reliable for 4-year-olds than for infants.

23. Name and describe two psychometric intelligence tests used with young children.

24. Explain how Vygotsky's concept of the zone of proximal development can be used in assessing young children's intellectual potential.

Section II Influences on Cognitive Development

FRAMEWORK FOR SECTION II

A. How Does Personality Influence Cognitive Development?
B. How Do Parents Influence Cognitive Development?
   1. Providing an Environment for Learning
   2. Scaffolding: How Parents Teach Children
   3. The Quality of Parenting

IMPORTANT TERM FOR SECTION II

Completion: Fill in the blank to complete the definition of the key term for this section of Chapter 9.

1. _____: Temporary support given a child to do a task.

LEARNING OBJECTIVES FOR SECTION II

After reading and reviewing this section of Chapter 9, you should be able to do the following.

1. Briefly discuss the relationship between young children's social-emotional and cognitive functioning.

2. Discuss how parents and the home environment influence young children's cognitive development, and explain the value of scaffolding as a teaching technique.

Section III The Widening Environment

FRAMEWORK FOR SECTION III

A. Preschool
   1. How Good Preschools Foster Development
   2. How Academically Oriented Should Preschool Be?
B. Kindergarten
   1. How Much Like "Real" School Should Kindergarten Be?
   2. Predicting Future School Success
C. Compensatory Preschool Programs for Disadvantaged Children
   1. Project Head Start
   2. Long-Term Benefits of Compensatory Preschool Education
D. Educational Television

IMPORTANT TERM FOR SECTION III

Completion: Fill in the blank to complete the definition of the key term for this section of Chapter 9.

1. **Project** _____: Compensatory preschool educational program begun in 1965.

LEARNING OBJECTIVES FOR SECTION III

After reading and reviewing this section of Chapter 9, you should be able to do the following.

1. State at least two ways in which a good preschool can foster children's development.

2. Summarize research on the value of an academic emphasis in preschool.

3. Give examples of cultural differences in goals for, and methods of, preschool education in the United States, Japan, and China.

4. Give pros and cons of full-day kindergarten.

5. Name two fairly reliable predictors of future school achievement that can be observed in kindergarten.

6. State the goals of compensatory preschool programs, and assess the short-term and long-term benefits of Project Head Start and other compensatory programs.

7. Discuss outcomes of watching Sesame Street, and list suggestions for guiding children's television viewing.

CHAPTER 9 QUIZ

Matching—Terms and Situations: Match each of the situations described in the left-hand column with the applicable term in the right-hand column.

1. Sherry knows that all babies have mothers. She knows that Stacy is a baby. Therefore, she concludes that Stacy has a mother. ___

2. Andy saw his parents leave for the hospital and saw them bring his baby brother home for the first time. He thinks that they went to the hospital and picked out a baby. ___

3. Scott puts on a lion costume for Halloween. His baby sister cries when she sees him. "Don't worry; I'm still Scott," he says. ___

4. Amy is sitting in the back seat of the family car; she is wearing sandals. Her father is driving. "Look, Daddy," says Amy, "I have a sore on my toe." Her father replies, "I can't see it right now—I'll look at it later." "Why can't you see it?" asks Amy. ___

5. Billy knows that robins, ducks, and blue jays have wings. He knows that robins, ducks, and blue jays are birds. Therefore he assumes that all birds have wings. ___

6. Ann and her older sister Maria are having lunch. Their mother pours a mug of soup for each. Although the two portions are equal, Maria's mug is taller and narrower than Ann's. "She got more," Ann complains. "Hers is bigger." ___

7. Charles wore his raincoat to preschool one day. It rained. The next day he refused to wear his raincoat. "I don't want it to rain," he explained. ___

8. Rita sees her mother working at a computer. The next day, while playing "office," she "types" on a toy typewriter. ___

9. Jo breaks a ball of clay into two pieces. "Now I have more clay," she says. Her older sister smiles: "If you put it back together, it'll be the same as before." But Jo insists: "No, it's more." ___

10. On Mother's Day, Emmett picks a flower and gives it to a neighbor woman. "Why did you do that?" asks his mother. "Because she doesn't have any children," he replies. ___

a. deferred imitation

b. understanding of identities

c. empathy

d. egocentrism

e. centration

f. irreversibility

g. focus on states rather than transformation

h. transduction

i. induction

j. deduction

Multiple-Choice: Circle the choice that best completes or answers each item.

1. The symbolic function is characterized by
   a. sensory cues
   b. mental representations
   c. abstract thinking
   d. all of the above

2. *All but which* of the following are manifestations of the symbolic function?
   a. language
   b. deferred imitation
   c. invisible imitation
   d. symbolic play

3. Ten beads are arranged in a row. Whether they are counted from left to right or from right to left, there are 10 beads. This is an example of which principle?
    a. 1-to-1
    b. stable-order
    c. order-irrelevance
    d. cardinality

4. According to Piaget, children at the preoperational stage tend to
    a. conserve
    b. decenter
    c. centrate
    d. focus on transformations rather than states

5. *All but which* of the following are limitations of preoperational thought identified by Piaget?
    a. egocentrism
    b. animism
    c. irreversibility
    d. selective memory

6. Transductive reasoning involves
    a. deduction
    b. induction
    c. logic
    d. none of the above

7. Ten beads are arranged in a circle. If they are rearranged in a row, they will be the same 10 beads. This is an example of the principle of
    a. identity
    b. reversibility
    c. compensation
    d. abstraction

8. Research indicates that Piaget underestimated preoperational children's ability to
    a. distinguish between appearance and reality
    b. distinguish between real and imagined events
    c. both a and b
    d. neither a nor b

9. Overregularization of linguistic rules is a sign of
    a. development of social speech
    b. too much correction by adults
    c. linguistic progress
    d. an academic preschool background

10. Children begin to develop the ability to converse at about age
    a. 2 1/2
    b. 3
    c. 4
    d. 5

11. Which of the following viewed private speech as inappropriate for young children?
    a. Watson
    b. Piaget
    c. Vygotsky
    d. Kohlberg

12. Children with delayed language development
    a. have below-average intelligence
    b. come from homes where they do not get enough linguistic input
    c. have parents who use complex speech with them
    d. need to hear a word more often than other children before they can understand it

13. To best encourage young children's language development, adults should
    a. engage in simple conversations with them, using common words
    b. talk about personal topics, food, and table manners
    c. talk about things the adults are interested in
    d. encourage imaginative play

14. Recent research suggests that the most important factor in young children's ability to recall is
    a. general knowledge
    b. memory strategies
    c. mastery motivation
    d. intelligence

15. Memory without awareness is called
    a.   implicit
    b.   explicit
    c.   generic
    d.   none of the above; memory is not possible without awareness

16. Episodic memories
    a.   rarely become part of autobiographical memory
    b.   are long-lasting even in 2-year-olds
    c.   are better retained by boys than by girls
    d.   are best retained when talked about

17. Young children best remember things they
    a.   see
    b.   do for the first time
    c.   have done once or twice before
    d.   do frequently

18. Which of the following statements about performance on intelligence tests is true?
    a.   Because intelligence is inborn, an individual's IQ is fairly stable; thus test performance, in general, has remained approximately constant.
    b.   Experience and other factors can contribute to a rise or fall in IQ; but, on the average, test performance has remained approximately constant.
    c.   Experience and other factors can contribute to a rise or fall in IQ; test performance, in general, has improved in recent years.
    d.   Experience and other factors can contribute to a rise or fall in IQ; test performance, in general, has declined in recent years.

19. The revised version of the Stanford-Binet Intelligence Scale, prepared in 1985, primarily emphasizes
    a.   IQ as an overall measure of intelligence
    b.   verbal items
    c.   nonverbal items
    d.   patterns and levels of cognitive development

20. The zone of proximal development is the level at which children can
    a.   perform a task easily on their own
    b.   perform a task on their own, but with difficulty
    c.   perform a task with some guidance
    d.   not perform a task at all

21. Which of the following appears to be true of the relationship between socioeconomic status and a child's IQ?
    a.   Socioeconomic status is the most important factor in IQ.
    b.   Socioeconomic status is the least important factor in IQ.
    c.   Socioeconomic status bears little relationship to IQ.
    d.   Socioeconomic status is one of several social and family risk factors that affect IQ.

22. In which country is academic instruction in preschool most highly valued?
    a.   United States
    b.   Japan
    c.   China
    d.   All of the above place an equally high value on academic instruction.

23. The "age effect" means that
    a.   children learn more easily at an earlier age; therefore, most children benefit from an academically oriented preschool experience
    b.   the youngest children in a kindergarten class do poorly in comparison with the oldest children
    c.   children who are close to age 6 when they enter kindergarten tend to be bored in school and do poorly in comparison with younger children
    d.   younger preschoolers in compensatory programs do better than older ones

24. High school students from deprived backgrounds who participated in Project Head Start are more likely than youngsters from similar backgrounds who did not participate to
   a. show permanent gains in IQ
   b. stay in school
   c. do as well in school as average middle-class children
   d. all of the above

25. A typical preschooler watches how many hours of television per day?
   a. less than 2
   b. 2 to 3
   c. about 5
   d. 6 or more

True or False? In the blank following each item, write T (for *true*) or F (for *false*). In the space below each item, if the statement is false, rewrite it to make it true.

1. Symbolic thought depends on sensory cues. ___

2. During the preoperational stage, it is common for a child to believe that growth since infancy has made him or her a different person. ___

3. Not until age 7 or 8 can children classify items using two criteria. ___

4. According to Piaget, children at the preoperational stage do not understand that water poured from a pitcher into a glass can be restored to its original state by pouring it back into the pitcher. ___

5. Egocentrism, for Piaget, means selfishness. ___

6. When a child is on the verge of grasping a new concept, training may accelerate that process. ___

7. Preschool children realize that thought is continuous. ___

8. Children age 4 to 5 can use prepositions. ___

9. Recent research has confirmed Piaget's view that most preschool speech is egocentric. ___

10. The most sociable children tend to use private speech the most. ____

11. A preschooler who cannot speak clearly is likely to be unpopular. ____

12. A young child recalls items better when they are related to each other. ____

13. Autobiographical memory typically begins before 3 years of age. ____

14. In court cases concerning charges of child abuse, preschoolers tend to be less reliable witnesses than older children. ____

15. The Stanford-Binet Intelligence Scale and the Wechsler Preschool and Primary Scale of Intelligence are group tests often administered in early childhood. ____

16. Children whose parents help them with a task they haven't quite mastered tend to become overly dependent on parental support. ____

17. Children who attend academically oriented preschools tend to excel throughout their school careers. ____

18. The most important behavioral predictor of future school achievement is attentiveness.
____

19. Project Head Start is a compensatory preschool program for poor minority children. ____

20. The neediest children in Project Head Start make the greatest short-term intellectual gains. ____

21. Sesame Street, though intended as an educational program, seems to have only entertainment value. ____

TOPICS FOR THOUGHT AND DISCUSSION

1. Piaget apparently underestimated children's thought processes because he overestimated their language abilities. Have you ever given an incorrect answer to a question you could have answered correctly if the question had been phrased more simply? Does this sort of experience suggest that adults should speak to young children only in words they can understand? How does this idea square with findings, reported in your text, that children develop best linguistically through exposure to unfamiliar words?

2. According to your text, the most popular children are most likely to use private speech. Can you suggest reasons why that might be true?

3. According to your text, the cause[s] of delayed language development are unclear. On the basis of the information given, can you suggest any new hypotheses or avenues of research on this topic?

4. Some people believe that it is beneficial to develop young children's memory by encouraging them to memorize poems and other literary passages. On the basis of the information in Chapter 9 of your text, how would you react to such a practice? What suggestions would you make for helping to develop young children's memory?

5. In view of the information presented in Box 9-2 in your text, what legal safeguards can you suggest to help ensure the accuracy of children's testimony in court cases involving charges of abuse?

6. Developers of IQ tests have had to raise norms because of a general improvement in scores, apparently due (at least in part) to environmental influences such as preschool, educational television, and better-educated parents. Might such influences help account for recent findings that young children are more intellectually competent than Piaget's observations would suggest?

7. Parents are sometimes advised not to help school children with homework so as to promote independence and responsibility. Does this advice appear to be inconsistent with the findings about scaffolding presented in your text? Do you think the age of the child might make a difference?

8. On the basis of the arguments and research presented in your text, what is your attitude toward academically oriented preschool and full-day kindergarten programs for disadvantaged children? For middle-class children?

9. On the basis of the information presented in your text, would you favor an expansion of the Head Start program, as the authors seem to? Why or why not?

CHAPTER 9 READING

INTRODUCTION

Shirley Jackson was a novelist and short-story writer whose best-known work, "The Lottery," is one of the most famous stories ever written. If you have encountered "The Lottery" in anthologies, you know that it is both mystifying and terrifying. The following story, "Charles," written in 1948, is in a much lighter vein, though it too has an element of mystery.

CHARLES

by Shirley Jackson

The day my son Laurie started kindergarten he renounced corduroy overalls with bibs and began wearing blue jeans with a belt; I watched him go off the first morning with the older girl next door, seeing clearly that an era of my life was ended, my sweet-voiced nursery-school tot replaced by a long-trousered, swaggering character who forgot to stop at the corner and wave good-bye to me.

He came home the same way, the front door slamming open, his cap on the floor, and the voice suddenly become raucous shouting, "Isn't anybody here?"

At lunch he spoke insolently to his father, spilled his baby sister's milk, and remarked that his teacher said we were not to take the name of the Lord in vain.

"How was school today?" I asked, elaborately casual.

"All right," he said.

"Did you learn anything?" his father asked.

Laurie regarded his father coldly. "I didn't learn nothing," he said.

"Anything," I said. "Didn't learn anything."

"The teacher spanked a boy, though," Laurie said, addressing his bread and butter. "For being fresh," he added, with his mouth full.

"What did he do?" I asked. "Who was it?"

Laurie thought. "It was Charles," he said. "He was fresh. The teacher spanked him and made him stand in a corner. He was awfully fresh."

"What did he do?" I asked again, but Laurie slid off his chair, took a cookie, and left, while his father was still saying, "See here, young man."

The next day Laurie remarked at lunch, as soon as he sat down, "Well, Charles was bad again today." He grinned enormously and said, "Today Charles hit the teacher."

"Good heavens," I said, mindful of the Lord's name. "I suppose he got spanked again?"

"He sure did," Laurie said. "Look up," he said to his father.

"What?" his father said, looking up.

"Look down," Laurie said. "Look at my thumb. Gee, you're dumb." He began to laugh insanely.

"Why did Charles hit the teacher?" I asked quickly.

"Because she tried to make him color with red crayons," Laurie said. "Charles wanted to color with green crayons so he hit the teacher and she spanked him and said nobody play with Charles but everybody did."

The third day—it was Wednesday of the first week—Charles bounced a see-saw on to the head of a little girl and made her bleed, and the teacher made him stay inside all during recess. Thursday Charles had to stand in a corner during story-time because he kept pounding his feet on the floor. Friday Charles was deprived of blackboard privileges because he threw chalk.

On Saturday I remarked to my husband, "Do you think kindergarten is too unsettling for Laurie? All his toughness, and bad grammar, and this Charles boy sounds like such a bad influence."

"It'll be all right," my husband said reassuringly. "Bound to be people like Charles in the world. Might as well meet them now as later."

On Monday Laurie came home late, full of news. "Charles," he shouted as he came up the hill; I was waiting anxiously on the front steps. "Charles," Laurie yelled all the way up the hill, "Charles was bad again."

"Come right in," I said, as soon as he came close enough. "Lunch is waiting."

"You know what Charles did?" he demanded, following me through the door. "Charles yelled so in school they sent a boy in from first grade to tell the teacher she had to make Charles keep quiet, and so Charles had to stay after school. And so all the children stayed to watch him."

"What did he do?" I asked.

"He just sat there," Laurie said, climbing into his chair at the table. "Hi, Pop, y'old dust mop."

"Charles had to stay after school today," I told my husband. "Everyone stayed with him."

"What does this Charles look like?" my husband asked Laurie. "What's his other name?"

"He's bigger than me," Laurie said. "And he doesn't have any rubbers and he doesn't ever wear a jacket."

Monday night was the first Parent-Teachers meeting, and only the fact that the baby had a cold kept me from going; I wanted passionately to meet Charles's mother. On Tuesday Laurie remarked suddenly, "Our teacher had a friend come to see her in school today."

"Charles's mother?" my husband and I asked simultaneously.

"Naaah," Laurie said scornfully. "It was a man who came and made us do exercises, we had to touch our toes. Look." He climbed down from his chair and squatted down and touched his toes. "Like this," he said. He got solemnly back into his chair and said, picking up his fork, "Charles didn't even do exercises."

"That's fine," I said heartily. "Didn't Charles want to do exercises?"

"Naaah," Laurie said. "Charles was so fresh to the teacher's friend he wasn't let do exercises."

"Fresh again?" I said.

"He kicked the teacher's friend," Laurie said. "The teacher's friend told Charles to touch his toes like I just did and Charles kicked him."

"What are they going to do about Charles, do you suppose?" Laurie's father asked him.

Laurie shrugged elaborately. "Throw him out of school, I guess," he said.

Wednesday and Thursday were routine; Charles yelled during story hour and hit a boy in the stomach and made him cry. On Friday Charles stayed after school again and so did all the other children.

With the third week of kindergarten Charles was an institution in our family; the baby was being a Charles when she cried all afternoon; Laurie did a Charles when he filled his wagon full of mud and pulled it through the kitchen; even my husband, when he caught his elbow in the telephone cord and pulled telephone, ashtray, and a bowl of flowers off the table, said, after the first minute, "Looks like Charles."

During the third and fourth weeks it looked like a reformation in Charles; Laurie reported grimly at lunch on Thursday of the third week, "Charles was so good today the teacher gave him an apple."

"What?" I said, and my husband added warily, "You mean Charles?"

"Charles," Laurie said. "He gave the crayons around and he picked up the books afterward and the teacher said he was her helper."

"What happened?" I asked incredulously.

"He was her helper, that's all," Laurie said, and shrugged.

"Can this be true, about Charles?" I asked my husband that night. "Can something like this happen?"

"Wait and see," my husband said cynically. "When you've got a Charles to deal with, this may mean he's only plotting."

He seemed to be wrong. For over a week Charles was the teacher's helper; each day he handed things out and he picked things up; no one had to stay after school.

"The P.T.A. meeting's next week again," I told my husband one evening. "I'm going to find Charles's mother there."

"Ask her what happened to Charles," my husband said. "I'd like to know."

"I'd like to know myself," I said.

On Friday of that week things were back to normal. "You know what Charles did today?" Laurie demanded at the lunch table, in a voice slightly awed. "He told a little girl to say a word and she said it and the teacher washed her mouth out with soap and Charles laughed."

"What word?" his father asked unwisely, and Laurie said, "I'll have to whisper it to you, it's so bad." He got down off his chair and went around to his father. His father bent his head down and Laurie whispered joyfully. His father's eyes widened.

"Did Charles tell the little girl to say that?" he asked respectfully.

"She said it twice," Laurie said. "Charles told her to say it twice."

"What happened to Charles?" my husband asked.

"Nothing," Laurie said. "He was passing out the crayons."

Monday morning Charles abandoned the little girl and said the evil word himself three or four times, getting his mouth washed out with soap each time. He also threw chalk.

My husband came to the door with me that evening as I set out for the P.T.A. meeting. "Invite her over for a cup of tea after the meeting," he said. "I want to get a look at her."

"If only she's there," I said prayerfully.

"She'll be there," my husband said. "I don't see how they could hold a P.T.A. meeting without Charles's mother."

At the meeting I sat restlessly, scanning each comfortable matronly face, trying to determine which one hid the secret of Charles. None of them looked to me haggard enough. No one stood up in the meeting and apologized for the way her son had been acting. No one mentioned Charles.

After the meeting I identified and sought out Laurie's kindergarten teacher. She had a plate with a cup of tea and a piece of chocolate cake; I had a plate with a cup of tea and a piece of marshmallow cake. We maneuvered up to one another cautiously, and smiled.

"I've been so anxious to meet you," I said. "I'm Laurie's mother."

"We're all so interested in Laurie," she said.

"Well, he certainly likes kindergarten," I said. "He talks about it all the time."

"We had a little trouble adjusting, the first week or so," she said primly, "but now he's a fine little helper. With occasional lapses, of course."

"Laurie usually adjusts very quickly," I said. "I suppose this time it's Charles's influence."

"Charles?"

"Yes," I said, laughing, "you must have your hands full in that kindergarten, with Charles."

"Charles?" she said. "We don't have any Charles in the kindergarten."

QUESTIONS ABOUT THE READING

1. Did the ending of the story surprise you? If not, at what point did you begin to guess "Charles's" identity? Why do you think Laurie's parents failed to figure it out?

2. Are Laurie's constant descriptions of "Charles's" activities examples of the symbolic function? If so, in what way? Why did Laurie (according to his teacher) become better behaved about the same time that Laurie told his parents "Charles" did?

3. According to Piaget, a boy of kindergarten age normally has an understanding of his own identity. Research also suggests that young children understand the difference between fantasy and reality. Did Laurie exhibit a lack in these areas? Do you think Laurie believed that it was "Charles" who was doing the things Laurie described? If not, why do you think Laurie attributed those actions to "Charles"?

4. This classic story was written more than 40 years ago, before the changes in the kindergarten curriculum and format that are described in Chapter 9 of your text. Did you notice any elements of the story that "date" it? On the basis of Laurie's descriptions of what went on in kindergarten, what sorts of things did he seem to be learning there? Do those things seem to be important?

ANSWER KEY FOR CHAPTER 9

Note: Numbers in parentheses refer to pages in the textbook where answers can be found.

CHAPTER 9 REVIEW

Important Terms for Section I

1. symbolic function (page 340)
2. sensory (340)
3. deferred (341)
4. object (341)
5. symbols, logic (343)
6. centrate (343)
7. decenter (343)
8. perceptual (343)
9. irreversibility (346)
10. logic (346)
11. egocentrism (346)
12. life, alive (347)
13. processes (349)
14. fast mapping (352)
15. language (353)
16. social (353)
17. private (354)
18. literacy (357)
19. recognition (359)
20. recall (359)

21. generic (360)
22. script (360)
23. episodic (361)
24. autobiographical (361)
25. representative (365)
26. validity (365)
27. reliability (365)
28. spatial (365)
29. performance (366)
30. zone of proximal development (ZPD) (366)

Learning Objectives for Section I

1. (pages 339-342)
2. (340-341)
3. (341-342)
4. (342-343)
5. (343-348)
6. (348)
7. (348-349)
8. (350-351)
9. (350-353)
10. (353-354)
11. (354-355)
12. (355)
13. (356-357)
14. (357-358)
15. (358)
16. (359-360)
17. (360)
18. (360-361)
19. (361-364)
20. (364-365)
21. (365)
22. (365)
23. (365-366)
24. (366)

Important Term for Section II

1. scaffolding (page 367)

Learning Objectives for Section II

1. (pages 366-367)
2. (367-369)
3. (370)

Important Term for Section III

1. Head Start (page 372)

Learning Objectives for Section III

1. (page 369)
2. (369)
3. (370)
4. (371)
5. (371-372)
6. (372-374)
7. (374-375)

CHAPTER 9 QUIZ

Matching—Terms and Situations

1. j (page 346)
2. g (344, 346)
3. b (339, 341)
4. d (346-347)
5. i (346)
6. e (343, 344)
7. h (344, 346)
8. a (341)
9. f (344, 346)
10. c (340, 341-342)

Multiple-Choice

1. b (page 340)
2. c (340-341)
3. c (342)
4. c (343)
5. d (344, 346-348)
6. d (344, 346)
7. b (348)
8. b (350)
9. c (352)
10. a (353)
11. a (354)
12. d (356)
13. d (357-358)
14. c (359)
15. a (360)
16. d (361-363)
17. b (363-364)
18. c (365)
19. d (365)
20. c (366)
21. d (367-368)
22. c (370)
23. b (371)

24. b (373)
25. b (375)

True or False?

1.   F—Symbolic thought is independent of sensory cues. (pages 339, 340)
2.   F—By the preoperational stage, children have developed an understanding of identity. (341)
3.   F—Many 4-year-olds can classify by 2 criteria. (342)
4.   T (344, 346)
5.   F—Egocentrism is not selfishness but self-centered understanding, according to Piaget. (346)
6.   T (348)
7.   F—Preschool children seem to believe that thought starts and stops. (351)
8.   T (352)
9.   F—Recent research shows that children's speech is quite social from an early age. (353-354)
10. T (354)

11. F—Comprehension is more important than clear speech in determining a preschooler's popularity. (356)
12. T (359)
13. F—Autobiographical memory rarely begins before age 3. (361)
14. T (363)
15. F—The Stanford-Binet and the Wechsler are individual tests. (365-366)
16. F—Scaffolding, or temporary support, can help children master a task; the more finely tuned the help, the better a child does. (367)
17. F—Children who attend academically oriented preschools may excel during the early years of school but tend to lose their advantage later. (369)
18. T (372)
19. F—Project Head Start is for low-income children, regardless of race or ethnic origin. (372)
20. T (373)
21. F—Viewers of Sesame Street develop larger vocabularies and improve in cognitive skills. (374)

PERSONALITY AND SOCIAL DEVELOPMENT IN EARLY CHILDHOOD

OVERVIEW

Chapter 10 traces several strands of personality development in early childhood. In this chapter, the authors:

- Discuss the development of young children's sense of self, feelings about the self, and gender identity, and how gender differences come about

- Assess the influence of child-rearing styles and practices on personality development in early childhood

- Explain how altruism, aggression, and fearfulness develop

- Describe relationships with siblings and peers

- Describe several types of play and how gender affects play

CHAPTER 10 REVIEW

Section I Important Personality Developments in Early Childhood

FRAMEWORK FOR SECTION I

A. Self-Understanding
   1. A Neo-Piagetian Progression
B. The Emerging Self-Concept
   1. The Early Sense of Self
   2. Measures and Characteristics of Self-Esteem
   3. Initiative versus Guilt
   4. Sources of Self-Esteem
C. Emotional Growth
   1. Understanding of Simultaneous Emotions
   2. Emergence of Emotions Directed toward the Self
D. Identification of Self: Gender Identity
   1. Explanations for Gender Identity
     a. Social-Learning Theory: Observing and Imitating Models
      (1) How Identification Occurs
      (2) Effects of Identification
      (3) Evaluating Social-Learning Theory
     b. Cognitive-Developmental Theory: Mental Processes
      (1) Gender Identity and Gender Constancy
     c. Gender-Schema Theory: A "Cognitive-Social" Approach
      (1) Evaluating the Cognitive Theories
   2. How Gender Affects Development
     a. How Different Are Girls and Boys?
     b. Attitudes toward Gender Differences
     c. Gender Roles and Gender-Typing
     d. Gender Stereotypes
     e. Androgyny
   3. How Gender Differences Come About
     a. Biological Influences
     b. Family Influences
     c. Media Influences
     d. Cultural Influences

IMPORTANT TERMS FOR SECTION I

Completion: Fill in the blanks to complete the definitions of key terms for this section of Chapter 10.

1. **self-_____:** What people believe about who they are; sense of self.
2. **self-_____:** One aspect of the sense of self; cluster of characteristics considered important in describing oneself.
3. **_____ self:** The self one would like to be.
4. **_____ self:** The self one actually is.
5. **self-_____:** The judgment people make about their own worth.
6. **_____ versus _____:** Third of Erikson's psychosocial crises, in which the child must balance the desire to pursue goals with the moral reservations that prevent carrying them out; successful resolution leads to the virtue of purpose.
7. **_____:** Process by which a person acquires the characteristics of another person or group.
8. **_____:** What it means psychologically to be male or female.
9. **_____ differences:** Actual biological differences between the sexes.
10. **_____ differences:** Psychological or behavioral differences between the sexes.
11. **_____:** Awareness of one's own sex.
12. **_____:** Behaviors and attitudes a culture deems appropriate for males and females.
13. **gender _____, or gender _____:** Awareness that one will always be male or female.

14. **gender-_____ theory:** Theory that children socialize themselves in their gender roles by developing a concept of what it means to be male or female in a particular culture.

15. **gender-_____:** Pattern of behavior organized around gender.

16. _____: Process by which a person learns a gender role.

17. _____: Exaggerated generalizations about male or female behavior.

18. _____: Having some characteristics considered typical of males and other characteristics considered typical of females.

LEARNING OBJECTIVES FOR SECTION I

After reading and reviewing this section of Chapter 10, you should be able to do the following.

1. Name two steps in self-definition that occur between ages 4 and 6, according to neo-Piagetian theory.

2. Trace the emergence of the sense of self from infancy through early childhood.

3. Name two categories of traits describing children with high and low self-esteem, and identify the chief source of self-esteem in early childhood.

4. Identify the conflict involved in Erikson's third crisis—initiative versus guilt—and summarize the outcome of a successful or unsuccessful resolution of that crisis.

5. Identify two dimensions of emotion, and describe five levels of understanding of simultaneous emotions that children typically undergo between ages 4 and 12.

6. Describe four levels of understanding of emotions directed toward the self that children typically undergo between ages 4 and 8.

7. Summarize and evaluate explanations for the development of identification in general and gender identity in particular, according to the social-learning, cognitive-developmental, and gender-schema theories.

8. Assess the extent of physical, cognitive, and personality differences between boys and girls.

9. Explain the importance of gender roles and gender-typing and the danger of gender stereotypes, and list at least four suggestions by Sandra Bem for raising children without gender stereotypes.

10. Describe an androgynous person.

11. Assess the evidence for biological influences on behavioral differences between the sexes, and explain why biology fails to fully explain these differences.

12. Discuss the influence of parents (especially fathers) on gender-typing.

13. Discuss the influence of television on gender-stereotyping.

14. Assess cultural influences on gender roles.

Section II Child-Rearing Practices

FRAMEWORK FOR SECTION II

A. How Child-Rearing Practices Affect Personality Development
   1. Parents' Styles and Children's Competence: Baumrind's Research
      a. Three Kinds of Parenting Styles
      b. Evaluating Baumrind's Work
      c. Why Is Authoritative Child Rearing Special?

2. "Poisonous Pedagogy" and Adult
    Personality: Research Based on Miller's
    Concept
3. Love and Maturity
B. Discipline
    1. Internalization
    2. Reinforcement and Punishment
        a. Reinforcements
        b. "Rewarding" with Punishment
        c. When Does Punishment Work?
        d. The Dangers of Punishment

IMPORTANT TERMS FOR SECTION II

Completion: Fill in the blanks to complete the
definitions of key terms for this section of
Chapter 10.

1. _____ **parents:** In Baumrind's
    terminology, parents whose primary child-
    rearing values are based on control and
    obedience.

2. _____ **parents:** In Baumrind's
    terminology, parents whose primary child-
    rearing values are self-expression and self-
    regulation.

3. _____ **parents:** In Baumrind's
    terminology, parents whose primary child-
    rearing values blend respect for the child's
    individuality with a desire to instill social
    values in the child.

4. **discipline:** The process of socialization, of
    teaching children behavior, character, and
    self-_____.

5. **socialization:** The process by which children
    acquire habits, skills, values, and motives
    that will enable them to become productive,
    law-abiding members of _____.

6. **internalization:** End result of socialization,
    when children take on the values and
    attitudes of society as their _____.

7. **behavior _____:** Therapeutic approach
    using principles of learning theory to
    encourage desired behaviors or to eliminate
    undesired ones; also called *behavior therapy*.

LEARNING OBJECTIVES FOR SECTION II

After reading and reviewing this section of
Chapter 10, you should be able to do the
following.

1. Compare and evaluate authoritarian,
    permissive, and authoritative styles of
    parenting as identified by Baumrind.

2. Discuss Miller's concept of "poisonous
    pedagogy" and its relationship to
    psychological adjustment in adulthood; name
    at least six "poisonous" child-rearing
    practices and at least six associated
    personality characteristics of adult children.

3. Compare the long-term effects of specific
    child-rearing practices with the effect of
    loving treatment.

4. Discuss the connection between discipline and socialization; name two methods by which parents socialize children, and identity three steps necessary for internalization to occur.

5. Compare Scarr's, Baumrind's, and Jackson's views on "good-enough" parenting.

6. Compare the effectiveness of reinforcement and punishment.

7. Differentiate between internal and external rewards, giving an example of each.

8. List and explain four factors that influence the effectiveness of punishment, and cite at least three dangers of harsh punishment.

Section III Specific Developmental Issues

FRAMEWORK FOR SECTION III

A. Altruism, or Prosocial Behavior
   1. Origins of Prosocial Behavior
      a. The Child
      b. The Family
      c. The School
      d. The Culture
B. Aggression
   1. The Rise and Decline of Aggression
   2. Triggers of Aggression
      a. Reinforcement
      b. Frustration and Imitation
      c. Effects of Televised Violence
   3. Reducing Aggression
C. Fearfulness
   1. What Do Children Fear, and Why?
   2. Preventing and Treating Fears

IMPORTANT TERMS FOR SECTION III

Completion: Fill in the blanks to complete the definitions of key terms for this section of Chapter 10.

1. **altruism, or prosocial behavior:** Acing out of concern for another person with no expectation of _____; selflessness.

2. _____ **behavior:** Hostile actions intended to hurt somebody or to establish dominance.

3. **systematic** _____: Gradual exposure to a feared object for the purpose of overcoming the fear.

LEARNING OBJECTIVES FOR SECTION III

After reading and reviewing this section of Chapter 10, you should be able to do the following.

1. Identify origins of prosocial behavior in the child, the family, the school, and the culture.

2. Distinguish between instrumental and hostile aggression, and trace the rise and decline of aggression in early childhood.

3. Discuss four factors that can trigger aggression, and identify successful and unsuccessful techniques for reducing it.

4. Discuss sources of young children's fears, and identify methods of prevention and treatment.

Section IV The Widening World: Relationships with Other Children

FRAMEWORK FOR SECTION IV

A. The Only Child
B. Brothers and Sisters
C. Friendships and Peer Relationships
   1. Behavior Patterns That Affect Choice of Playmates and Friends
   2. Family Ties and Popularity with Peers
   3. How Adults Can Help Children Make Friends

LEARNING OBJECTIVES FOR SECTION IV

After reading and reviewing this section of Chapter 10, you should be able to do the following.

1. Compare research in the United States and China on characteristics of only children, and discuss implications of China's "one-child" policy.

2. Describe typical sibling interactions in early childhood and how those interactions influence other relationships.

3. Identify important features of early friendships, and cite behavior patterns that affect the choice of playmates and friends.

4. Discuss how family relationships influence popularity, and suggest ways adults can help unpopular children make friends.

Section V Children's Play

FRAMEWORK FOR SECTION V

A. Play as the "Business" of Early Childhood
B. Concepts of Play
   1. Social and Nonsocial Play
      a. Influence of Day Care
      b. Is Solitary Play Always Less Mature Than Group Play?
   2. Cognitive Play
   3. Imaginative Play
C. How Gender Affects Play

IMPORTANT TERM FOR SECTION V

Completion: Fill in the blank to complete the definition of the key term for this section of Chapter 10.

1. _____ **play:** Play involving imaginary situations; also called *fantasy play*, *dramatic play*, or *pretend play*.

LEARNING OBJECTIVES FOR SECTION V

After reading and reviewing this section of Chapter 10, you should be able to do the following.

1. Name six types of social and nonsocial play identified by Mildred Parten; summarize research on the types of play that occur in day care centers, and on the value of nonsocial play.

2. Name four types of cognitive play identified by Piaget, and explain the significance of imaginative play.

3. Discuss how gender influences children's play.

CHAPTER 10 QUIZ

Matching—Who's Who: Match each name in the left-hand column with the appropriate description from the right-hand column.

1. Jerome Kagan ___
2. Lawrence Kohlberg ___
3. Erik Erikson ___
4. Sandra Bem ___
5. Alice Miller ___
6. Sandra Scarr ___
7. Albert Bandura ___
8. Mildred Parten ___
9. Diana Baumrind ___
10. Sigmund Freud ___
11. Jacquelyn Faye Jackson ___

a. originated gender-schema theory
b. linked "poisonous pedagogy" with adult personality problems
c. described how children identify with models
d. identified styles of parenting
e. described gender identity as the result of repression of the wish to possess the parent of the other sex and identification with the "aggressor" parent
f. linked gender identity with cognitive development
g. identified classic model for development of social play
h. studied frustration and imitation as triggers for aggression
i. defends "good enough" parenting
j. theorized that children need to balance initiative and guilt
k. advocates intervention to promote beneficial development

Multiple-Choice: Circle the choice that best completes or answers each item.

1. According to neo-Piagetian thinkers, the ability to link two aspects of the self generally occurs at about age(s)
   a. 2 to 3
   b. 4
   c. 5 to 6
   d. 7

2. The sequence of early development of the self-concept is
   a. self-recognition; self-awareness; self-definition; real and ideal self
   b. self-awareness; self-recognition; self-definition; real and ideal self
   c. real and ideal self; self-awareness; self-definition; self-recognition
   d. self-definition; self-awareness; self-recognition; real and ideal self

3. Unsuccessful resolution of the crisis of initiative versus guilt may cause
   a. impotence
   b. inhibition
   c. intolerance
   d. any of the above

4. Successful resolution of the crisis of initiative versus guilt leads to the virtue of
   a. will
   b. self-control
   c. purpose
   d. spontaneity

5. Which of the following is *not* strongly correlated with self-esteem in early childhood?
   a. child's sense of own competence or skills
   b. acceptance and social support from parents
   c. acceptance and social support from teachers
   d. acceptance and social support from peers

6. "I'm happy about moving to Connecticut, but I'm lonesome for Grandma and Grandpa," says Daniel. Daniel is probably at which level of understanding of simultaneous emotions?
    a. 1
    b. 2
    c. 3
    d. 4

7. At Level 3 in Harter's progression of understanding of emotions directed toward the self, children
    a. have internalized standards for pride and shame
    b. are aware of parents' being proud or ashamed but not of having those feelings themselves
    c. are unaware of pride or shame, whether an action is observed or not
    d. are aware of pride or shame, but only if an action is observed

8. Gender differences are
    a. biological differences between the sexes
    b. psychological differences between the sexes
    c. behaviors and attitudes deemed appropriate for males and females
    d. all of the above

9. According to social-learning theory, a boy is most likely to identify with a father who is
    a. powerful
    b. nurturant
    c. competent
    d. all of the above

10. According to Kohlberg, gender identity is typically acquired at about age
    a. 2 to 3
    b. 4 to 5
    c. 6 to 7
    d. 8 to 9

11. According to Bem, parents can raise children without gender stereotypes by following *all but which* of the following suggestions?
    a. exposing children to nontraditional occupations
    b. giving them nonstereotyped gifts
    c. monitoring their reading and television viewing
    d. deemphasizing anatomical differences

12. Research on sex and gender differences has found that
    a. aside from anatomy, young boys and girls are more alike than different
    b. girls are more vulnerable than boys
    c. boys excel in computation and understanding of mathematical concepts
    d. girls have superior verbal ability from early childhood on

13. Gender roles include
    a. interests
    b. skills
    c. both a and b
    d. neither a nor b

14. According to Bem, an androgynous personality is
    a. predominantly "masculine"
    b. predominantly "feminine"
    c. another name for schizophrenic
    d. the healthiest type

15. A typical child, by the time of graduation from high school, is estimated to have watched approximately how many hours of television?
    a. 250
    b. 2500
    c. 25,000
    d. 250,000

16. Baumrind's research suggests that the most effective style of parenting is
    a. authoritarian
    b. permissive
    c. authoritative
    d. All of the above are equally effective.

17. According to Miller, "poisonous pedagogy"
    a. is practiced both consciously and unconsciously
    b. is particularly harmful in lower-class families
    c. is most influential when practiced by mothers
    d. has negative short-run consequences but little correlation with adult personality

18. Inductive techniques of socialization include *all but which* of the following?
    a. setting firm limits
    b. reasoning with a child
    c. logical consequences
    d. generalizing about children's behavior

19. Punishment is more effective when it
    a. is consistent
    b. takes place after a child has done something wrong
    c. is accompanied by a detailed explanation
    d. all of the above

20. The upbringing of Europeans who risked their lives to save Jews during World War II emphasized
    a. fairness
    b. obedience
    c. self-reliance
    d. all of the above

21. In general, aggressive preschoolers are
    a. unsociable
    b. the least competent
    c. behaving normally
    d. likely to be just as aggressive at age 8

22. According to social-learning theory and research, *all but which* of the following statements about aggression in young children are true?
    a. A frustrated child is more likely to act aggressively than a contented one.
    b. Children who have seen an aggressive adult are more likely to act aggressively.
    c. Televised violence tends to promote aggression.
    d. Spanking is generally an effective way to curb aggression.

23. The most common fears of children age 3 to 6 include *all but which* of the following?
    a. dogs
    b. thunderstorms
    c. death
    d. doctors

24. An effective way to help young children overcome fears is
    a. ignoring their fears
    b. explaining why their fears are unreasonable
    c. encouraging expression of fears
    d. removing a feared object

25. As compared with children who have siblings, children without siblings tend to be
    a. more self-centered
    b. more achievement-oriented
    c. less sociable
    d. less cooperative

26. Which of the following is more important to 4-year-olds than to 7-year-olds in choosing friends?
    a. physical characteristics
    b. affection
    c. support
    d. common activities

27. According to Parten, which of the following shows the most advancement toward social play?
    a. building a block tower alongside another child who is building a block tower
    b. playing with a truck near other children who are building a block tower
    c. watching other children build a block tower
    d. talking to children who are building a block tower

28. According to research done since 1970, which of the following statements about preschool children's play is *not* true?
    a. Some children's play is more social than others'.
    b. Social play seems to have decreased since the 1920s.
    c. Middle-class children tend to play more socially than less advantaged children.
    d. Nonsocial, or solitary, play is a sign of immaturity.

29. A 3-year-old pushing a toy train and saying "choo-choo" is engaged in what kind of play?
    a. functional
    b. imaginative
    c. constructive
    d. associative

30. Which of the following statements about children's play is true?
    a. Children who watch a lot of television play more imaginatively than children who watch little television.
    b. About one-third of kindergartners' play is imaginative
    c. Children in day care centers with same-age grouping play more sociably than other children.
    d. Sex segregation in free play typically does not occur until middle childhood.

True or False? In the blank following each item, write T (for *true*) or F (for *false*). In the space below each item, if the statement is false, rewrite it to make it true.

1. Young children's self-definition focuses on observable, or external, aspects of the self. ___

2. Children do not develop a sense of self-esteem until middle childhood. ___

3. Erikson's crisis of initiative versus guilt reflects a split between the childlike and adult parts of the personality. ___

4. Four-year-olds typically do not understand that they can have contradictory emotions at the same time. ___

5. According to social-learning theory, when a young boy identifies with a major league baseball player, he believes he can hit a ball the way that player does. ___

6. Research shows that children become gender-typed by imitating their parents. ___

7. Kohlberg suggested that gender constancy follows the establishment of gender differences in behavior. ___

8. Gender-schema theory holds that gender-typing can be deliberately modified. ___

9. Preschool boys show more spatial ability than preschool girls. ___

10. Bright children are the quickest to become gender-typed. ___

11. According to Bem, an androgynous personality displays more typically "masculine" traits than typically "feminine" traits. ___

12. Studies suggest that biological influences are the chief factor in gender differences. ___

13. Parents, especially fathers, tend to gender-socialize boys more strongly than girls. ___

14. Social-learning theory would predict that children who watch television a great deal will become more gender-stereotyped than children who rarely watch. ___

15. A criticism of Baumrind's work on styles of parenting is that it does not take into account how children affect parents. ___

16. Children of easygoing, loving parents tend to behave less morally while growing up than children of stricter parents. ___

17. Sandra Scarr maintains that developmentalists have overemphasized the influence of parenting on children's development. ___

18. It is best to let children reflect on their actions before punishing them. ___

19. Middle-class children tend to be more altruistic than poor children. ___

20. A toddler who grabs a toy from another child is displaying hostile aggression. ___

21. After age 6 or 7, children become more aggressive. ___

22. The effects of televised violence seen by 8-year-olds can endure through the teenage years. ___

23. Childhood fears are best treated by ignoring them. ___

24. Early sibling interactions are primarily competitive. ___

25. Young children's relationships with other children tend to reflect their relationships with their parents. ___

26. Children who frequently play by themselves are likely to be unpopular. ___

27. Children who engage in a great deal of imaginary play tend to be moody loners. ___

TOPICS FOR THOUGHT AND DISCUSSION

1. On the basis of the discussions in your text, can you suggest ways adults can foster emotional growth and a positive self-concept in a young child?

2. Which of the theories discussed in Chapter 10 of your text seems to best explain the acquisition of gender identity and gender roles? Why? Do you think that selecting elements from more than one theory would produce a more complete or more satisfactory explanation?

3. On the basis of Chapter 10, which appears to have a stronger influence on gender differences—biology or experience?

4. If television can help abolish gender stereotypes, should such programming be designed? If so, how? What aspects of male and female personality should be portrayed?

5. Were you surprised that children of permissive parents tend to be less exploratory than children of authoritarian

parents? Does the authors' explanation (page 397 in your text) make sense to you? Why or why not?

6. According to Miller, parents who engage in "poisonous pedagogy" do it for both conscious and unconscious reasons—often because they themselves were damaged in this way. Therefore, she says, it is important to break the generation-to-generation cycle. Can you suggest ways to do this?

7. Since aggression tends to decline after early childhood, should parents of young children simply let it take its course? How would authoritarian, permissive, and authoritative parents be likely to answer this question?

8. Research suggests that violent television programs promote or reinforce aggressive behavior, even years later. If this is so, should violence be banned from children's programs? From programs aired at times when children are likely to see them?

9. Discrepancies between Parten's findings and more recent studies of children's play have been explained as a possible result of environmental and social class differences between the groups of children studied. Could such differences help explain why some of Piaget's findings (discussed in Chapter 9) have not held up in recent research?

CHAPTER 10 READING

INTRODUCTION

How much should parents intervene in children's development? How can parents best help children to learn, to become competent, to pursue their interests and abilities? When are praise and encouragement helpful? Can they be harmful?

Naomi Aldort, founder and director of the seminar program "Raising Our Children, Raising Ourselves," argues that the best thing parents can do for children is to get out of their way and let them be themselves. At the time she wrote this article, which is reprinted from the Summer 1994 issue of *Mothering* magazine, Aldort was 44 years old and lived with her husband, Harvey, age 53, and their children, Yonaton, age 8, Lennon, age 3½, and Oliver, age 6 months, on Lopez Island, Washington.

GETTING OUT OF THE WAY

by Naomi Aldort

My husband and I are often complimented on our two boys' behavior and demeanor. People think

that we discipline them. We don't. It is *ourselves* we discipline.

We provide our boys with their needs, protection, and exposure to life's possibilities. We do not, however, meddle in their play, their learning, their creativity, or any other form of growth. We love, hug, feed, share, listen, respond, and participate when asked. Yet, we keep our children free of insult and manipulation resulting from "helpful" comments and ideas—influences to which children are so sensitive in their state of dependency.

Parental Self-Discipline

This type of discipline is not easy. Not only does our society not support it, but the temptation to break "the rules" lives within us. The drive to intervene in children's activities is rooted in our upbringing and reinforced in the current culture.

For me, the most difficult challenge to overcome has been the narcissistic impulse to show off my children. One day, when our oldest child was two years old, he played a smooth scale on the piano. I was amazed, yet held fast to my rule and stayed out of his way. Free to play out of his own love and interest, and not to gratify me, he went on improving his scale with tremendous joy and concentration for quite some time. Not until my husband came home did I fall into the trap. Unable to wait for a repeat performance in its own time, I covertly tried to direct our son to the piano to do his "trick."

Untrained in doing for the sake of pleasing, he was not fooled. He sensed the hoax and refused to play. Several weeks passed before he again immersed himself in the scale. This child loves to do things for others, enjoys helping and service; yet, when he does something out of *self-interest*, that is how it must remain.

Although the self-discipline required of a parent is often challenging, it becomes second nature with time and experience. For me, this type of discipline developed gradually, beginning with descriptive acknowledgment[1] seven years ago and culminating in unadulterated staying-out-of-the-way four years later. My best allies have been my realizations as a mother and educator, Daniel Greenberg's book *Free at Last*, and discussions with Jean Liedloff, author of *The Continuum Concept*, about letting children be themselves.

At first, I thought that commenting, acknowledging, and praising children for their achievements express love and build self-esteem. In time, I realized that these well-intended interventions do just the opposite: *they foster dependency on external validation and undermine the children's trust in themselves*. Children who are subjected to endless commentary, acknowledgment, and praise eventually learn to do things not for their own sake, but to please others. Gratifying others soon becomes their primary motivation, replacing impulses stemming from the authentic self and leading to its loss.

Contrary to common belief, children feel *more* loved and self-assured when we do *not* intervene in their activities. Not only do they remain secure in our love and support when we refrain from intervening, but they need us to protect them from these intrusions, which can interfere with their progress, self-reliance, and emotional well-being.

When we intervene with praise, wants, advice, and rewards, doubts sneak in and shake loose our children's trust in themselves and in us. Sensitive and smart, they perceive that we have an agenda, that we are manipulating them toward some preferred or "improved" end result. This awareness gets them thinking: "Perhaps what I am trying to achieve is wrong—I can't trust myself to know or choose" or "Mom and Dad have an agenda that I must fulfill if I am to have their approval and their love."

Gradually, a shift occurs. Children who were once doing for the sake of personal pleasure or understanding begin doing for the sake of pleasing. No longer do they trust in their actions, and no longer do they trust us, for we are not really on their side. Along with the shift to pleasing us comes the *fear of not pleasing us.* Emotional and intellectual dependency, low self-esteem, and lack of self-confidence invariably follow.

Even when we intervene with casual commentary on our children's imaginative play, doubts sneak in. What children are experiencing inwardly at these times is so often remote from our "educated" guesses that bewilderment soon turns to self-denial and self-doubt. Moreover, children perceive the phony and patronizing remarks for what they are, and may conclude that it is OK to be insincere and pretentious.

From Praising to Observing

It is difficult to stop dishing out praise. For one thing, we are hooked on our conditioning as well as on the "hard sell" of the holy cow called Praise. For another, we are easily misled: the praised-for-every-achievement child seems like a happy, successful, highly self-esteemed child. In reality, such a child has shifted to the pleasing mode, driven to success not by personal curiosity or delight, but by the desire to oblige us and live up to our expectations. As educator John Holt has said of children, "They are afraid, above all else, of failing, of disappointing or displeasing the many anxious adults around them, whose limitless hopes and expectations for them hang over their heads like a cloud."[2] In short, the esteem we notice is not *self*-esteem, for the self has been lost in the early years of this type of conditioning. The happiness we see is not pleasure, but rather *relief* that another pleasing act has been accomplished, securing parental approval (aka emotional survival) and concealing a feeling of deep loss.

Children, too, can be fooled into believing that these pleasing behaviors originate within and have everything to do with who they are. The ultimate deception comes when children grow up to become seemingly accomplished and happy adults. Psychoanalyst Alice Miller, in her book *The Drama of the Gifted Child*, gives voice to the lamentable conviction that arises: "Without these achievements, these gifts, I could never be loved.... Without these qualities, which I have, a person is completely worthless." Miller goes on to explain why achievement based on pleasing denies self-understanding and, in so doing, leads to depression, feelings of never enough, and other emotional disturbances in often the most successful people.[3]

To follow one's own drummer, a person needs to exercise the muscles of free choice and self-learning *from the start*. The difficulty we have in trusting our children's ability to flex these muscles stems from our own experience of not having been trusted. Trusting is, simply, not natural to us. Only as we make a concerted effort to get out—and stay out—of our children's way do we discover the wonderful truth: the magic is already in our children, ready to unfold in its own way and its own time.

Nearly every child comes to life equipped with a self that is capable of blooming to capacity. Unhindered in its growth, this self will lead the child to skills and knowledge and, in the process, self-actualization.

We have no right to attempt to control the direction of this growth. Instead of training our children through various forms of intervention to fit our vision for them, we need to train ourselves to respect nature's creation and to safeguard its full, authentic bloom.

Indeed, the end result we are looking for—an able, highly self-esteemed, creative, curious, and responsible human being—is already observable in a two-year-old child.[4] Allowed to put these gifts to use in a self-directed, self-trusting way, the youngster will develop capabilities while enhancing these desirable qualities. Maturation will then come as an authentic expression of the self, rather than as an appeasement to domination.

Getting out of the way gives us an opportunity to become curious observers. At the same time, it frees us of power struggles and initiates an approach to parenthood that is infinitely more enjoyable and fulfilling. I know of no more interesting, engaging, fascinating, and glorious "entertainment" in life than watching children unfold freely.

Notes

1.   Adele Faber and Elaine Mazlish, *How to Talk So Kids Will Listen and Listen So Kids Will Talk* (New York: Avon, 1980), pp. 171-200.
2.   John Holt, *How Children Fail* (New York: Pitman Publishing, 1964), p. xiii.
3.   Alice Miller, *The Drama of the Gifted Child* (New York: Basic Books, 1983), p. 104.
4.   Daniel Greenberg, *A Paradigm Shift in Education*. An audiocassette available from The Sudbury Valley School Press in Framingham, MA.

QUESTIONS ABOUT THE READING

1.   Which of the three parenting styles identified by Diana Baumrind—authoritarian, permissive, or authoritative—does Aldort's philosophy of parenting most closely resemble? How do you think Baumrind would respond to this article? How might Sandra Scarr respond? Jacquelyn Faye Jackson?

2.   Aldort argues that praising children for their achievements, or even commenting casually, is counterproductive because it makes children dependent on external validation. Do you agree or disagree? What evidence does Aldort give to support this argument? (Note: the question of internal versus external motivation is discussed in Chapter 12 of your text.)

3.   Aldort seems to assumes that children, like flowers, contain within themselves everything they need to flower and reach their "full, authentic bloom." Do you think the authors of your text would agree or disagree? Can you find specific passages, in Chapter 10 or other chapters, which are consistent or inconsistent with Aldort's point of view?

4.   One of Aldort's major concerns is the development of self-esteem. How does her treatment of this topic square with the research findings reported on pages 382 to 384 of your text?

5.   Aldort cites the work of the psychoanalyst Alice Miller in support of her argument that achievement directed toward pleasing adults denies self-understanding and can lead to emotional disturbance. Do Harrington's findings on Miller's concept of "poisonous pedagogy" (as presented in Tables 10-2 to 10-4 in your text) seem to support Aldort's position?

6. The psychoanalyst Erik Erikson's third crisis of personality development, *initiative versus guilt*, revolves around a balancing of personal motivations and the desire for social approval. What do you think would be Aldort's view of this idea?

7. Aldort claims to have achieved good results with her children by following her "rules" of parental self-discipline. Given the children's ages, what questions would you like to ask—and have answered—about their development as they get older?

ANSWER KEY FOR CHAPTER 10

Note: Numbers in parentheses refer to pages in the textbook where answers can be found.

CHAPTER 10 REVIEW

Important Terms for Section I

1. concept (page 381)
2. definition (382)
3. ideal (382)
4. real (382)
5. esteem (382)
6. initiative, guilt (383)
7. identification (386)
8. gender (386)
9. sex (386)
10. gender (386)
11. gender identity (386)
12. gender roles (386)
13. constancy, conservation (389)
14. schema (389)
15. schema (389)
16. gender-typing (392)
17. gender sterotypes (393)
18. androgynous (393)

Learning Objectives for Section I

1. (page 381)
2. (381-382)
3. (382, 384)
4. (383-384)
5. (384-385)
6. (385-386)
7. (387-391)
8. (391-392)
9. (390, 392-393)
10. (393)
11. (393-394)
12. (394)

13. (394-395)
14. (395)

Important Terms for Section II

1. authoritarian (page 396)
2. permissive (396)
3. authoritative (396)
4. control (401)
5. society (401)
6. own (401)
7. modification (404)

Learning Objectives for Section II

1. (pages 396-398)
2. (398-400)
3. (400-401)
4. (401-404)
5. (402-403)
6. (404-405)
7. (404)
8. (404-405)

Important Terms for Section III

1. reward (page 405)
2. aggressive (407)
3. desensitization (413)

Learning Objectives for Section III

1. (pages 405-407)
2. (407-408)
3. (408-411)
4. (411-413)

Learning Objectives for Section IV

1. (pages 413, 414-415)
2. (413-416)
3. (416-417)
4. (417-419)

Important Term for Section V

1. imaginative (page 421)

Learning Objectives for Section V

1. (pages 420-421)
2. (421-423)
3. (423)

CHAPTER 10 QUIZ

Matching—Who's Who

1. c (page 387)
2. f (389)
3. j (383)
4. a (389)
5. b (398)
6. i (402)
7. h (409)
8. g (420)
9. d (396)
10. e (387)
11. k (403)

Multiple-Choice

1. c (page 381)
2. b (382)
3. d (384)
4. c (383, 384)
5. a (384)
6. d (385)
7. d (386)
8. b (386)
9. d (388)
10. a (389)
11. d (390)
12. a (391-392)
13. c (392)
14. d (393)
15. c (394)
16. c (396-398)
17. c (398-400)
18. d (403)
19. a (404-405)
20. a (406)
21. c (408)
22. d (408-411)
23. c (411-412)

24. c (412-413)
25. b (413, 414-415)
26. a (416)
27. a (420)
28. d (420-421)
29. b (421-423)
30. b (423)

True or False?

1. T (pages 381, 382)
2. F—Although young children do not express a sense of self-esteem in words, their behavior shows it. (382)
3. T (383-384)
4. T (384-385)
5. T (387)
6. F—When children are tested on masculinity and femininity, they are no more like their parents than like a random set of parents, and no more like the same-sex parent than like the other parent. (388-389)
7. F—Kohlberg suggested that gender constancy precedes gender differences. (389)
8. T (390)
9. F—Gender differences in spatial ability do not show up until after age 10 or 11. (391)
10. T (392)
11. F—An androgynous personality contains a balanced combination of the typical characteristics of both sexes. (393)
12. F—Studies are inconclusive but suggest that both biology and environment play a role. (393-394)
13. T (394)
14. T (395)
15. T (397)
16. T (401)
17. T (402)
18. F—The less time between an action and its punishment, the better. (404-405)
19. F—Socioeconomic status is not a factor in prosocial behavior. (405)
20. F—A toddler who grabs a toy from another child is displaying instrumental, not hostile, aggression. (407-408)
21. F—After age 6 or 7, children become less aggressive. (408)
22. T (410)

23. F—Childhood fears are best treated by reassurance, by encouraging expression of the fear, and by gradual exposure to the feared object. (413)
24. F—Early sibling interactions are primarily prosocial, not competitive. (415-416)
25. T (417-418)

26. F—Some kinds of nonsocial play are associated with social competence and popularity. (421)
27. F—Children who play imaginatively tend to play happily and to be cooperative and popular. (422-423)

PHYSICAL DEVELOPMENT AND HEALTH IN MIDDLE CHILDHOOD

OVERVIEW

Chapter 11 follows a child's physical growth and development during the elementary school years. In this chapter, the authors:

- Point out factors that influence height and weight in middle childhood

- Outline nutritional requirements and discuss their relationship to growth and development

- Discuss childhood obesity, its possible causes, and treatment

- Describe gender differences in motor skills for boys and girls, and discuss the importance of organized sports and rough-and-tumble play

- Identify health and safety concerns and present recommendations for improving children's health and fitness

- Explain how children's understanding of health and illness develops and how cultural attitudes affect health care

CHAPTER 11 REVIEW

Section I   Growth during the School Years

FRAMEWORK FOR SECTION I

A. Height and Weight
1. Variations in Growth: Norms and Ethnic Considerations
2. Abnormal Growth
B. Nutrition and Growth
1. Specific Nutritional Requirements
2. Malnutrition
a. Effects of Malnutrition
b. Effects of Intervention
3. Obesity
a. What Is Obesity, and How Common Is It?
b. What Causes Obesity?
c. Treating Childhood Obesity

IMPORTANT TERM FOR SECTION I

Completion: Fill in the blank to complete the definition of the key term for this section of Chapter 11.

1. **obesity:** Overweight condition marked by a skin-fold measurement in the _____ percentile (thicker than the skin fold of _____ percent of children of the same age and sex).

LEARNING OBJECTIVES FOR SECTION I

After reading and reviewing this section of Chapter 11, you should be able to do the following.

1. Summarize the growth patterns of boys and girls in middle childhood and their average changes in height and weight.

2. Identify factors that account for ethnic variations in growth.

3. State considerations in treating children whose growth is below normal.

4. Outline nutritional needs during middle childhood.

5. Describe effects of malnutrition and intervention on personality and behavior.

6. Identify trends in the prevalence of obesity, list four possible causes of this condition, and evaluate various treatments.

Section II Motor Development

FRAMEWORK FOR SECTION II

A. Motor Skills in Middle Childhood
    1. Gender Differences
B. Physical Play in Middle Childhood
    1. Organized Sports
    2. Rough-and-Tumble Play

LEARNING OBJECTIVES FOR SECTION III

After reading and reviewing this section of Chapter 11, you should be able to do the following.

1. Summarize gender differences in the development of motor skills from age 6 to age 12, and suggest appropriate physical activities for boys and girls.

2. Discuss the role of organized sports and rough-and-tumble play in school children's development.

Section III Health and Safety

FRAMEWORK FOR SECTION III

A. Health Concerns
    1. Acute Conditions
    2. Chronic Conditions
        a. Effects on Daily Life
        b. Cultural and Ethnic Factors
        c. Specific Chronic Conditions
            (1) Vision and Hearing Disorders
            (2) Asthma
            (3) Stuttering
            (4) Tics
    3. Dental Health and Dental Problems
B. Safety Concerns: Accidental Injuries
    1. Which Children Are Most Likely to Be Hurt?
    2. How Are Children Most Likely to Be Hurt?

IMPORTANT TERMS FOR SECTION III

Completion: Fill in the blanks to complete the definitions of key terms for this section of Chapter 11.

1. **acute medical conditions:** Medical conditions that last for a _____ time.

2. **chronic medical conditions:** Illnesses or impairments that persist for at least _____.

3. **asthma:** A chronic respiratory disease characterized by sudden attacks of coughing, wheezing, and difficulty in _____.

4. **stuttering:** Involuntary _____ or prolongation of syllables.

5. **tics:** Involuntary, repetitive muscular movements; also called _____ movement disorder.

LEARNING OBJECTIVES FOR SECTION III

After reading and reviewing this section of Chapter 11, you should be able to do the following.

1. Explain why today's schoolchildren are less healthy than children of the previous generation and what can be done to improve their health and fitness.

2. Summarize the prevalence of various acute and chronic medical conditions in middle childhood, and explain how a chronic condition can affect everyday life.

3. Describe cognitive changes in children's understanding of health and illness, and specifically of causes of AIDS.

4. Identify cultural and ethnic factors in the prevalence of chronic illness, and give two examples of how cultural attitudes affect health care.

5. Describe normal changes in vision in middle childhood and summarize the incidence of vision and hearing problems.

6. Summarize causes, incidence, and treatments for asthma, stuttering, and tics.

7. Assess the current state of dental health and dental care among school-age children, and suggest a way to deal with children's fear of going to the dentist.

8. Tell why accidental injury is a great concern in middle childhood; point out which children are at the greatest risk and where, and how accidents can be prevented.

CHAPTER 11 QUIZ

Matching—Numbers: Match each of the items in the left-hand column with the correct number in the right-hand column.

1.   Height (in inches) of average 9-year-old boy or girl ___

2.   Average number of calories (in hundreds) needed daily in middle childhood ___

3.   Percentile of skin-fold measurement indicating obesity ___

4.   Percentile of skin-fold measurement indicating superobesity ___

5.   Age at which first molars typically erupt ___

6.   Age at which second molars typically erupt ___

7.   Approximate percentage of prepubertal children who stutter ___

8.   Age at which typical child can balance on one foot without looking ___

9.   Age at which typical child can grip with 12 pounds of pressure ___

10. Age at which typical child can do a 3-foot standing high jump ___

6
7
8
10
12
13
24
53
85
95

Multiple-Choice: Circle the choice that best completes or answers each item.

1.   The average annual weight gain (in pounds) in middle childhood is
     a.   1 to 2
     b.   3 to 4
     c.   5 to 8
     d.   9 to 12

2.   Girls generally begin their growth spurt at about age
     a.   9
     b.   10 to 12
     c.   13 or 14
     d.   15

3.   Which of the following statements about physical development in middle childhood is *not* true?
     a.   Girls retain more fatty tissue than boys.
     b.   Risk of accidental injury decreases.
     c.   Colds and sore throats are prevalent.
     d.   Motor abilities improve.

4.   Eight-year-olds tend to be tallest in which of the following parts of the world?
     a.   southeast Asia
     b.   Oceania
     c.   South America
     d.   eastern Australia

5.   Synthetic growth-hormone therapy has *all but which* of the following drawbacks?
     a.   side effects
     b.   uncertainty about safety
     c.   uncertainty about long-term effects
     d.   possibility of negating its own effects by delaying puberty

6.   Children who were malnourished during infancy tend to be passive and unsociable because
     a.   as infants, they were too weak to attract the mother's attention
     b.   their mothers do not care about them
     c.   they have learned not to depend on other people
     d.   they have too little sugar in their diet

7. *All but which* of the following have been advanced as possible causes of obesity?
   a. genetic predisposition
   b. late weaning during infancy
   c. watching television
   d. being in a low socioeconomic group

8. Differences between prepubescent boys' and girls' motor abilities appear to be due chiefly to differences in
   a. strength
   b. endurance
   c. interest and motivation
   d. expectations and participation

9. Rough-and-tumble play
   a. is at least 25 percent of schoolchildren's free play
   b. serves social as well as physical purposes
   c. occurs mainly in societies that emphasize fighting and hunting
   d. is more typical among older children than younger ones

10. About what percentage of American children under age 18 have a chronic medical condition?
    a. 5
    b. 10
    c. 20
    d. 30

11. Egocentric explanations for illness
    a. are abnormal in children older than 7
    b. can be a defense against feelings of helplessness
    c. make children superstitious about germs
    d. make children more vulnerable to AIDS

12. Which child is most likely to have a severe chronic medical condition?
    a. white
    b. African American
    c. Latino
    d. none of the above; no significant differences among these groups have been reported

13. Which child is *least* likely to have a visual problem or hearing loss?
    a. white
    b. African American
    c. Latino
    d. none of the above; no significant differences among these groups have been reported

14. Which child is most likely to have asthma?
    a. white
    b. African American
    c. Latino
    d. none of the above; no significant differences among these groups have been reported

15. Effective treatment for stuttering includes
    a. breathing with upper chest muscles
    b. speaking rapidly
    c. computerized voice monitoring
    d. none of the above; there is no known effective method to treat stuttering

16. Tics
    a. become more frequent during sleep
    b. sometimes last less than a year
    c. signify mental retardation
    d. are almost always emotionally caused

17. The improvement in American schoolchildren's dental health can be attributed largely to
    a. improved eating habits
    b. less fear of the dentist than in early childhood
    c. fluoridated drinking water and toothpaste
    d. all of the above

18. The leading cause of disability and death in children over 1 year of age is
    a. heart disease
    b. obesity
    c. injury
    d. viral infection

19. Most childhood accidents occur in
    a.   automobiles or the home
    b.   school
    c.   team or individual sports
    d.   playgrounds

True or False? In the blank following each item, write T (for *true*) or F (for *false*). In the space below each item, if the statement is false, rewrite it to make it true.

1.   White children are usually bigger than African American children of the same age and sex. ___

2.   Overweight children tend to mature late. ___

3.   Sugar makes children hyperactive. ___

4.   Effects of malnutrition are irreversible. ___

5.   Obesity is more common in the western United States than in the northeast or midwest. ___

6.   Behavior modification has been somewhat effective in treating obesity. ___

7.   Prepubescent boys and girls who take part in similar activities show similar abilities. ___

8. Competitive team sports promote fitness in school-aged children. ___

9. The prevalence of chronic medical conditions in middle childhood has increased in the past several years. ___

10. Children with chronic medical conditions tend to have problems in school. ___

11. In some cultures, illness is seen as punishment for transgression. ___

12. Children under 6 years old tend to be nearsighted. ___

13. Stuttering is more common in girls than in boys. ___

14. Childhood tics may be a symptom of neurological disorder. ___

15. Tooth decay can be prevented by the use of adhesive sealants on chewing surfaces. ___

16. Boys at all ages have higher accident rates than girls. ___

17. Children with siblings are more likely to be injured than children who have no siblings. ___

18. Children are more likely to have bicycle accidents when using their bikes for play than for transportation. ___

TOPICS FOR THOUGHT AND DISCUSSION

1. What are the dangers of judging health and screening for abnormalities on the basis of average figures for physical growth? What specific problems might arise—for example, with respect to diagnosing malnutrition or deciding on the advisability of administering growth hormones?

2. Why do you think magical explanations for illness sometimes last well into childhood? Might there be a conflict between children's cognitive development and their emotional needs?

3. The authors of your text suggest that youngsters who, in early childhood, adjust well to going to the dentist become more resistant to dental visits in middle childhood because they are modeling their parents' behavior. Does this seem to you to be a likely explanation? If not, can you suggest another explanation?

4. The authors of your text say that competitive sports may not be the best way to promote fitness in schoolchildren and that the children who are most fit already tend to be the ones who engage in such sports. Given the emphasis on competitive athletics in American society, can you suggest ways to promote interest in noncompetitive sports for everyone?

5. According to Box 11-3 in your text, many cultures hold beliefs in nonmedical causes for illness or disability, and such beliefs can result in failure to take steps that might improve the condition or help deal with it realistically. Yet, as the authors point out, the American medical establishment also is governed by a belief system that may not be acceptable to members of some cultures. Can you suggest guidelines for health professionals who have to deal with such cultural conflicts?

CHAPTER 11 READING

INTRODUCTION

The subtitle of Lew Golan's autobiography, *Reading Between the Lips*, is *A Totally Deaf Man Makes It in the Mainstream*. And, indeed, Lew (born Ira) Golan has been successful by any standard. Golan has been a copy editor on the sports desk of the *Chicago Sun-Times*, an advertising copywriter, an editor of academic books, a marketing executive (senior vice-president and director of creative services at Frankel & Company in Chicago), and a television writer, as well as a father and grandfather. He has lived for most of his adult life in Highland Park, Illinois, on Chicago's North Shore, and in Israel. He currently resides in Tel Aviv with his hearing wife, Barbara.

In *Reading Between the Lips* (to quote the forward by Henry Kisor, book editor of the *Sun-Times*, who is also deaf), Golan "shows that total deafness ... is not an impenetrable barrier to making it in a hearing world .... he paints an upbeat picture of what it's like to be separated from others by a sound barrier—and how he usually manages to get through, over, or around the barrier in one way or another."

Golan also speaks candidly and forcefully on the current controversy over "mainstreaming" deaf children. On one side are those who advocate teaching all deaf children sign language—which, Golan argues, inevitably segregates them from hearing people, not only in school but throughout life, and prevents them from succeeding in the larger society. On the other side are "oralists," who advocate oral communication by speaking and lipreading for those children who can master it, as Golan did.

According to your text, about 15 percent of children under 18 are estimated to be affected by deafness or hearing loss. In Golan's case, this chronic condition was the result of an acute illness: spinal meningitis, the effects of which are better understood today than when Golan was stricken with it. In this excerpt, condensed from the first two chapters of *Reading Between the Lips*, Golan tells how he became deaf at age 6, how he learned to read lips, and what school arrangements his parents made for him.

EXCERPTS FROM "READING BETWEEN THE LIPS"

by Lew Golan

Other Than That, Mrs. Lincoln . . .

February 14, 1940, was like most winter days on Chicago's south Side: murky and chilly and windy. In the first-grade classroom at Horseman Elementary, we opened the valentine box to determine the winner of the annual popularity contest.

I was more interested in the trays of heart-shaped sugar cookies. Even at the age of six, I already had an enviable reputation for pigging out on sweets.

So when I told my teacher that I wasn't feeling well, she was neither surprised nor alarmed. She telephoned my mother to let her know I was coming home, made sure I had buckled the ear flaps of my Charles Lindbergh fleece-lined leather hat under my chin, and sent me out into a biting wind.

Six blocks later I pushed open the front door.

"What's wrong, Ira?"

"I don't feel so good. My head hurts."

My mother felt my forehead. It was burning. "Lie down on the couch. I'll call the doctor."

The doctor was a family friend who lived a couple of blocks up the street.

A few minutes later he was taking my pulse and temperature.

"It's probably the flu, Lil. There's a lot of it going around. He's running a high fever. Give him aspirin and orange juice, and keep him off his feet. Don't worry about it."

I went to sleep on the couch. It was early afternoon.

Some hours later, I woke up to find my mother's hand on my forehead. My father was standing behind her.

My mother's lips moved, but no sounds came from her mouth.

"Hey, mom, why aren't you talking out loud?"

My temperature was 105 and climbing. I couldn't hear anything.

The doctor recommended a specialist. My parents bundled me up and drove me over to the hospital.

My temperature went up to 106. I went into a coma.

The diagnosis: spinal meningitis.

In 1940 there was little, if anything, you could do for spinal meningitis. It was fatal in 95 percent of the cases. Of the five percent who survived, most were left crippled in one way or another.

After several days, my fever broke. I came out of the coma.

The doctors found that I had a 100 percent loss of hearing in both ears and that the loss was apparently permanent.

Other than that, they said, I was fine.

Other than that, Mrs. Lincoln, how did you like the play?

Today, as a parent and grandparent, my perspective of that event is very different from my state of mind at the time.

Today, I can empathize with my parents.

I can imagine the shock and despair they must have felt when it hit them that their little boy would never hear again.

They must have been tormented by painful questions: What will happen to him now? How will he communicate with people? Will he be able to have friends? How will he get through school? How will he earn a living? Will he be able to marry and raise a family?

On the other hand, there was another perspective: *mine.*

How did *I* feel when I woke up from a nap on the couch and discovered that I couldn't hear anything?

How did *I* respond to the shock of my sudden loss?

Uh . . . what shock?

I was six years old. What did I know about life? To me, despair was something you felt when the White Sox blew a three-run lead in the late innings.

I didn't have the faintest idea of the difficulties that lay ahead for a deaf person. And what I didn't know didn't worry me.

I felt no panic, no fear—unlike the way I'm sure I would have felt if I had suddenly become blind. I felt no sense of disorientation. I didn't get upset or cry.

Something was different, yes; something was missing, yes.

But I accepted it the way I accepted that nine-year-old Joe was bigger than six-year-old me and always got dibs on everything.

It may not have been fair. It may have had its bad moments.

But that's the way it was.

It didn't occur to me to ask "Why me?"

After I came out of the coma, I remained in the hospital for a few weeks. My health improved, but the prognosis didn't.

The doctors concluded that my auditory nerves were irreversibly destroyed. They told my parents that I would be totally deaf for the rest of my life.

They were half right. I have no hearing at all.

But the doctors were wrong about the physical description of my deafness. Half a century later, I found out that there was probably nothing the matter with my auditory nerves.

As with most other people who lose their hearing from spinal meningitis, the problem is in the cochlea—a snail-shaped tube in the inner ear.

Normally, sound waves cause the eardrum to vibrate. Then the vibrations are transmitted to the fluid-filled cochlea and converted to waves, which move thousands of tiny hair cells. The swaying hair cells convert the fluid waves to electrical impulses, which the auditory nerves transmit to the brain.

But my high fever destroyed the hair cells, severing a link in the hearing process. So you could say that I became deaf because of premature baldness.

Winter melted way, and spring bloomed. I came home from the hospital and spent another few weeks regaining my strength.

In the meantime, the Great Debate raged between the oralists and the signers.

Should I be placed in a school for the deaf and be taught to communicate through sign language?

Or should I stay in the hearing world and learn to communicate solely by speaking and speechreading?

Proponents of the two camps pulled my parents back and forth.

Those in favor of sign language said it would enable me to communicate quickly and accurately without the frustrations and misunderstandings that bedevil those who try to read lips.

They said it would enable me to get a complete education in a school for the deaf without missing any of what my teachers or classmates were saying.

They said it would let me feel comfortable in a community of other people like me, without the problems and tension of trying to fit into a foreign environment.

But, said the oralists: while sign language would give me the freedom to fly with other deaf people, it would ground me in the hearing world.

My options—academic, social and vocational—would be limited by dependence on sign language, since most people do not sign.

Furthermore, the hearing world had been my world for six years. My family and friends were all hearing. The environment was not foreign to me.

In the end my parents decided to go the oral way, and I never learned a word of sign language.

Considering the circumstances, it seems to have been an easy decision for my parents.

I had been talking for four years before I lost my hearing, and I did not lose the ability to speak.

Also, I had been reading and writing for at least three years. By the time I was six, I was reading the morning *Tribune* and the afternoon *Daily News*.

I don't know whether the term "language skills" existed in those days, but I had them.

And my intelligence was quite a bit above average.

What all this means is that I was old enough to have acquired a very good foundation for communicating—yet I was still young enough to adapt quickly and easily to the nuisance of deafness.

I was very, very lucky.

But what about someone who is born deaf, or becomes deaf before mastering spoken language?

In *Seeing Voices*, Oliver Sacks emphasized over and over again how difficult it is for a prelingually deaf child to learn to speak:

> The essential point is this: that profoundly deaf people show no native disposition whatever to speak. Speaking is an ability that must be taught to them and is a labor of years....
> ...her mother devoted hours every day to an intensive one-to-one tuition of speech—a grueling business that lasted twelve years....
> ...years of the most intensive and arduous training, with one teacher working with one pupil....
> Teaching of speech is arduous and occupies dozens of hours a week....
> ...poses great difficulties, and which may require thousands of hours of individual tuition to achieve....

It unquestionably is extremely difficult, and takes long hours of dedicated effort by the child and her parents and her teachers. Incredible amounts of work and patience are required to teach speech and speechreading to prelingually deaf children.

Nevertheless, did Sacks mention that prelingually deaf children *are* learning to speak—and that some rely on speech alone?

No.

Did Sacks mention that for many prelingually deaf children, learning to speak has been well worth all that time and effort?

No.

Did he mention the indisputable advantages of being able to speak?

No.

Did he give any encouragement to those parents who have been indomitable in the face of adversity—helping their children learn to speak so they will be able to participate as fully as possible in the hearing world?

No.

One of the most cherished shibboleths of ASL militants and their supporters involves the motivation of parents.

Hearing parents, they claim, want their deaf child to speak and speechread because of an egotistical desire for the child to be like themselves, instead of choosing what is best for the child.

Those who parrot this line cannot swallow the idea that most parents who choose speaking and speechreading as the primary mode of communication for their child are acting in what they honestly believe are the best interests of the child.

So they try to send the parents on a guilt trip—ascribing ulterior motives to the parents' sincere efforts to give their child the best preparation for a happy, fulfilling and successful life.

This shrill rhetoric does nothing to help parents make a rational, informed decision in regard to their deaf child.

There are some good reasons for certain children to learn sign language—but this is not one of them.

Filling In the _ _ _ _ _ _ _ _

By the time the doctors okayed my return to school after several weeks of recuperating at home, it was almost time for school to be out for summer vacation.

So my parents made arrangements for Mrs. Kinsella to teach me lipreading (which today is called, more accurately, speechreading). Every Tuesday and Thursday morning during July and August, I went to Mrs. Kinsella's home on the southwest side for a one-hour lesson.

Speechreading turned out to have some factors in common with swimming.

First of all: some people are natural swimmers, and some people are natural lipreaders. (Some people are both, but my swimming coach at the University of Chicago assured me that I wasn't among them.)

Second, the basics are very simple. There really isn't much to learn about how to swim or how to read lips.

Finally, knowing the mechanics of swimming does not make you a swimmer. Although "I know how to swim" has a connotation of "I can swim," these statements are not literally the same.

You can learn everything there is to know about swimming by reading books and watching demonstrations—you can "know" how to swim—but you won't have the ability to swim until you go into the water and start practicing.

And once you can swim, the only way to improve your ability is by keeping at it. The more you swim, the better you might get.

It's the same with speechreading. The "how to" (what little there is of it) is just the starting point. The rest of it you learn the hard way, through experience.

For a couple of hours a week during the summer of that watershed year, I learned "how" to read lips.

After that, I was on my own to sink or swim.

Some people try to belittle speechreading by claiming that it's impossible to understand more than 40 percent of what someone says. This is a patently false claim.

The English language has about 40 different sounds; they are called phonemes. About 16 of these (40 percent) are more or less clearly lipreadable without ambiguity.

But there's another vital factor in speechreading: *context*.

Phonemes are embedded in words, words are embedded in phrases, phrases are embedded in sentences, and sentences are embedded in the context of a specific conversation in a specific language (which has specific grammatical structure) with a specific person in a specific situation about a specific subject.

Even if only 40 percent of the individual phonemes are unambiguously lipreadable *by themselves*, the multiple contexts and my own general knowledge and other factors such as body language and facial expressions enable me to read between the lips and fill in the blanks—so that I can understand most or all of what the speaker is saying, not just 40 percent as the naysayers claim.

It's similar to the way in which hearing people know whether a spoken word is "there," "their" or "they're." For example:

There are three books on the table.
Their books are on the table.
They're on the table.

When the first word is spoken, you may not know which one it is. But after the rest of the sentence provides the context, you easily fill in the blanks retroactively and automatically.

At any given moment, I may be getting anywhere between 100 percent and zero percent of the words someone is saying. But the actual percentage is irrelevant.

The important thing is not what proportion of the spoken words I understand—but whether I get the message.

I made Mrs. Kinsella's task relatively easy. For a six-year-old, I had an extraordinary vocabulary. And I instinctively picked up clues that enabled me to read between the lips.

But what if I had been born deaf, or was too young to talk (let alone have an adequate vocabulary when I became deaf)?

Then it would have been more difficult for me to reach the level of communication on which my life has been based.

The prelingually deaf must learn to make sounds they never heard and to put them together to form words they never knew.

At the same time, they must learn to recognize these sounds and words visually. Both the chicken and the egg have to come at virtually the same time.

It's difficult, but it's possible.

Prelingually deaf children who learn to speak and speechread despite formidable obstacles . . . and their teachers and parents who make it possible . . . are admirable, gutsy, persistent people.

Back to 1940 and Mrs. Kinsella: her regular job was teaching deaf and hard-of-hearing students in a public elementary school.

Parker Elementary School, on the southwest side, was one of three Chicago public schools which, in addition to having regular classes for hearing children, also had a separate class in each grade for oral hearing-impaired children.

These classes had fewer students than did the regular classes.

Although most of the students were hard of hearing, there were also a few deaf students who could speak and read lips.

When the oralists convinced my parents not to send me to a school for the deaf, they suggested that I go to Parker. They felt that the small classes in a regular public school environment would ease my readjustment to the hearing world.

At the time, it probably sounded like a good idea for me to go there. For a six-year-old deaf student who wanted to go the oral route rather than use sign language, it offered what today would be called a supportive environment.

But in retrospect, it was probably a mistake. The last thing I needed was to have things made easier for me.

My parents read a never-ending flow of books and magazines—partly because there was no TV then, but mostly because they enjoyed reading. It was a natural part of our home life.

Partly as a result of the example set by my parents, I became both an early reader and an early user of the dictionary. I was incorrigibly curious, and I wallowed in the inexhaustible reservoirs of information contained in the printed word.

In particular, I was hooked on the dictionary. Whenever I was confronted by a word I didn't know, I had to look it up right away. Then I would continue leafing through the dictionary simply for the pleasure of learning new words.

Considering this background, it shouldn't be surprising that I was on a fast track during my elementary school years.

By reading the textbooks and looking up unknown words in the dictionary, I was able to grasp the material fairly easily.

So, in subjects such as math and science and history, the classroom sessions often added little or nothing to what I had already learned from my homework.

With books, I was in my natural element.

Besides, reading permitted me to learn as fast as I wanted. I didn't have to wait while the teacher explained something to classmates who weren't able to get it the first time around.

In the early 1940s, Parker had no formal enrichment programs for overachievers. My teachers winged it, giving me assignments from higher grades to keep me busy. In fourth grade, for example, I was getting eighth-grade English assignments.

I was no genius; I simply happened to be a bright kid in a relatively unchallenging environment.

The teachers at Parker were trained to deal with students whose communication problems got in the way of their education. My teachers' problem was that, partly because of my heavy reading, I didn't have a problem.

So they solved their problem by having me skip five semesters; I finished seven grades in five years.

Although my parents were, to some extent, mainstreaming me by having me go to a regular public school in which most of the students had normal hearing, they may have been overly cautious when they put me in the special classes.

Today, there are several degrees of educational mainstreaming. They are differentiated by how much time a student spends actually integrated in regular classes with hearing children, and how much time (if any) in classes for deaf and hard-of-hearing children taught by a trained teacher of the deaf.

In 1940, the oral route meant either special classes for most of the day at Parker, or full integration at Horseman.

Although it eventually became apparent that I didn't need the special classes, they decided to let me finish elementary school there rather than change schools again. At the rate I was going, I'd be out of there soon enough.

Then I went into full integration at the University of Chicago High School, where my brother was a student.

The integration of deaf children with hearing children does not necessarily mean social acceptance.

There is a feeling that even if such integration is educationally successful, the human cost can sometimes be high.

The lack of acceptance by hearing children can mean a lonely, frustrated childhood, which can lead to a negative self-image.

This is one of the main reasons why some people advocate that deaf children be taught in special classes with other deaf children, using sign language in and out of the classroom.

They say it will help deaf children thrive emotionally—because the children will be able to relax and understand everything that is said, thereby feeling good about themselves.

Again, it all depends on the child and the circumstances.

I know that I, for one, certainly did *not* have anything like the miserable, lonely childhood that pro-signers like to impute to oral children in a hearing environment.

Growing up in a typical middle-class family in a typical Chicago neighborhood, I led a fairly enjoyable life with my family and my friends—all of whom were hearing.

It's true, however, that every summer I was made to feel quite inferior for unendurable months.

Joe DiMaggio and the New York Yankee dynasty had a truly phenomenal talent for doing just that to baseball fans (hearing and deaf alike) in less-fortunate American League cities.

QUESTIONS ABOUT THE READING

1. Did Golan help you to imagine how the world might seem to someone without hearing?

2. Do you agree with Golan that deaf children who are capable of learning speechreading should do so? What counter-arguments do you think a proponent of sign language would make?

3. In addition to being deaf, Golan is intellectually gifted (a topic discussed in Chapter 12 of your text). To what extent do you think his experience, and the arguments he makes about education and communication for deaf children, apply to those less gifted than he?

ANSWER KEY FOR CHAPTER 11

Note: Numbers in parentheses refer to pages in the textbook where answers can be found.

CHAPTER 11 REVIEW

Important Term for Section I
1. 85th, 85 (page 435)

Learning Objectives for Section I
1. (page 431)
2. (432)
3. (432-433)
4. (433-434)
5. (434-435)
6. (435-438)

Learning Objectives for Section II
1. (pages 438-440)
2. (440-442)

Important Terms for Section III
1. long (page 443)
2. 3 months (443)
3. breathing (448)
4. repetition (448)
5. stereotyped (449)

Learning Objectives for Section III
1. (page 441)
2. (442-445)
3. (444)
4. (445-447)
5. (448)
6. (448-449)

7. (449-451)
8. (451-453)

CHAPTER 11 QUIZ

Matching-Numbers
1. 53 (page 431)
2. 24 (433)
3. 85 (435, 436)
4. 95 (436)
5. 6 (449)
6. 13 (449)
7. 10 (449)
8. 7 (440)
9. 8 (440)
10. 12 (440)

Multiple-Choice
1. c (page 431)
2. b (431)
3. b (451)
4. d (432)
5. a (432-433)
6. a (434)
7. b (436-437)
8. c (438-439)
9. b (442)
10. d (443)
11. b (444)
12. d (446)
13. b (448)
14. b (448)
15. c (449)
16. b (449)
17. c (449)

18. c (451)
19. a (452)

True or False?

1. F—African American children are usually somewhat bigger than white children of the same age and sex. (page 432)
2. F—Overweight children tend to mature early. (432)
3. F—Recent research suggests that sugar does not adversely affect children's behavior or mood. (434)
4. F—Dietary supplements can offset poor outcomes of malnutrition. (435)
5. F—Obesity is more common in the northeast and midwest. (436)
6. T (437)
7. T (439)
8. F—Competitive team sports do not promote fitness but are engaged in by the children who already are most fit. (441)
9. T (443)
10. F—Most children with chronic conditions do not have problems in school. (445)
11. T (447)
12. F—Children under 6 tend to be farsighted. (448)
13. F—Stuttering is 3 times more common in boys than in girls. (448)
14. T (449)
15. T (449-450)
16. F—Boys have higher accident rates than girls except at age 1. (451)
17. T (451)
18. F—Accident rates and severity are similar when bicycles are used for transportation and for play. (391-392)

COGNITIVE DEVELOPMENT IN MIDDLE CHILDHOOD

OVERVIEW

Chapter 12 focuses on a number of important issues concerning cognitive development in middle childhood. In this chapter the authors:

- Look at the cognitive development of school-age children from the Piagetian, Vygotskian, information-processing, and psychometric perspectives

- Describe advances in moral development, memory, and language abilities

- Discuss controversies surrounding the design and use of IQ tests and bilingual education

- Examine the role that school plays in children's lives, influences on children's schooling, and how schools meet special needs

CHAPTER 12 REVIEW

Section I   Approaches to Cognitive Development

FRAMEWORK FOR SECTION I

A. Piagetian Approach: The Stage of Concrete Operations (About 7 to 11 Years)
   1. Conservation
       a. Testing Conservation
       b. Horizontal Décalage: Development of Different Types of Conservation
       c. Effects of Experience on Conservation
   2. Other Important Cognitive Abilities
       a. Seriation
       b. Transitive Inference
       c. Classification
   3. Social Implications of Cognitive Development
   4. Number and Mathematics
   5. Moral Development
       a. Piaget: Stages of Constraint and Cooperation
       b. Selman: Role-Taking Ability
B. Vygotskian Approach: The Impact of Social Interaction
   1. Social Interactions
   2. Scaffolding in Everyday Life
C. Information-Processing in Middle Childhood
   1. Memory Capacity
   2. Mnemonics: Strategies for Remembering
       a. Rehearsal
       b. Organization
       c. Elaboration
       d. External Aids
   3. Metamemory
D. Psychometric Approach: Measuring Individual Differences in Intelligence
   1. Psychometric Intelligence Tests for Schoolchildren
   2. Pros and Cons of Intelligence Testing
       a. Advantages of IQ Testing
       b. Problems with IQ Testing
   3. Implications of Intelligence Tests
       a. Cross-Cultural Testing
       b. Cultural Differences in IQ Test Scores

IMPORTANT TERMS FOR SECTION I

Completion: Fill in the blanks to complete the definitions of key terms for this section of Chapter 12.

1. **concrete operations:** Piaget's third stage of cognitive development, during which children develop the ability to think logically about the here and now, but not about _____.

2. **conservation:** Piaget's term for awareness that two stimuli which are equal (in length, weight, or amount, for example) remain equal in the face of perceptual _____ , so long as nothing has been added to or taken away from either stimulus.

3. **horizontal décalage:** In Piaget's terminology, the development of different types of _____ at different ages; thus, a child can _____ substance before weight, and substance and weight before volume.

4. **seriation:** Ability to order items along a _____.

5. _____ **inference:** Understanding of the relationship between two objects by knowing the relationship of each to a third object.

6. **class _____:** Understanding of the relationship between the whole and the part.

7. **morality of _____:** In Piaget's theory, the first stage of moral reasoning, in which a child thinks rigidly about moral concepts; also called heteronomous morality.

8. **morality of _____:** In Piaget's theory, the second stage of moral reasoning, in which a child has moral flexibility; also called autonomous morality.

9. **role-taking:** In _____'s terminology, assuming another person's point of view.

10. **scaffolding:** Temporary _____ given to a child to do a task.

11. **rehearsal:** Mnemonic strategy to keep an item in short-term memory through conscious _____.

12. _____: Mnemonic strategy of categorizing material in one's mind into related groupings to aid in remembering.

13. **elaboration:** Mnemonic strategy of linking items to be remembered by creating a(n) _____ about them or a visual image of them.

14. _____: Knowledge of the processes of memory.

15. **Wechsler Intelligence Scale for Children (WISC-III):** Individual intelligence test for children that includes _____ and _____ subtests.

16. _____ **Assessment Battery for Children (abbreviated ___):** Individual intelligence test for children.

17. _____-_____ **School Ability Test:** Group intelligence test for children.

18. _____ **tests:** Tests that measure children's basic capacity to learn, that is, their general intelligence.

19. _____ **tests:** Tests that assess how much children know in various subject areas.

LEARNING OBJECTIVES FOR SECTION I

After reading and reviewing this section of Chapter 12, you should be able to do the following.

1. List six improved capabilities children achieve in the stage of concrete operations, and state one important limitation of concrete operational thought.

2. Explain the concept of conservation and how it is tested.

3. Outline the sequence in which different types of conservation typically develop; cite factors that affect the age at which they develop; and discuss the effects of experience on conservation.

4. Explain how schoolchildren show an understanding of seriation, transitive inference, and class inclusion.

5. Explain the relationship between classification skills and gender stereotyping.

6. Trace the development of number skills in middle childhood, and cite evidence that mathematical concepts may be learned informally.

7. Explain the link between moral and cognitive development, and describe Piaget's two stages of moral reasoning in childhood.

8. Describe Selman's five stages of role-taking.

9. Give an example of how a teacher can use scaffolding to teach a skill.

10. Name three steps in the operation of memory (according to information processing theory) and state how memory capacity typically develops during middle childhood.

11. Identify four common mnemonic strategies and assess their use by school-age children.

12. Trace progress in schoolchildren's understanding of their own memory processes.

13. Name and briefly describe three commonly used intelligence tests for school-age children.

14. Distinguish between aptitude and achievement tests, and summarize the pros and cons of intelligence testing.

15. Discuss the problem of cultural bias in designing intelligence tests.

16. Assess factors affecting differences between intelligence test scores of white and African American children, and list suggestions for assessing ability more fairly.

17. Give reasons for the high achievement of Asian and Asian American schoolchildren.

18. List at least five ways to teach children thinking skills.

Section II Development of Language in Middle Childhood

FRAMEWORK FOR SECTION II

A. Grammar: The Structure of Language
B. Pragmatics: Language and Communication
C. Children's Humor
D. Development of Literacy
   1. Sociocultural Aspects of Literacy Development
   2. When Friends Write Together: Links between Cognitive and Emotional Domains
E. Bilingualism and Bilingual Education

IMPORTANT TERMS FOR SECTION II

Completion: Fill in the blanks to complete the definitions of key terms for this section of Chapter 12.

1. **syntax:** Way in which words are organized into phrases and _____.

2. _____: Knowledge of the communication process.

3. _____ **education:** Educational program in which children are taught in more than one language.

4. _____: Fluency in two languages.

5. _____: Process of changing one's speech to match the situation.

LEARNING OBJECTIVES FOR SECTION II

After reading and reviewing this section of Chapter 12, you should be able to do the following.

1. Trace the development of schoolchildren's use and understanding of grammar (including syntax).

2. Explain the significance of the development of metacommunication during middle childhood.

3. Summarize the relationship between humor and cognitive development.

4. Discuss and give examples of how social interaction fosters the growth of literacy.

5. Discuss the issues involved in the controversy over bilingual education.

Section III   The Child in School

FRAMEWORK FOR SECTION III

A. Recent Trends in Education
B. Influences on Children's Schooling
   1. The Child
      a. Temperament
      b. Emotional State
   2. The Parents
      a. Motivating Children
      b. Parental Beliefs
      c. Parental Involvement in School Activities
   3. The Teacher
   4. The Culture
C. Schoolchildren with Special Needs
   1. Mentally Retarded, Learning-Disabled, and Hyperactive Children
      a. Mental Retardation
      b. Learning Disabilities
      c. Hyperactivity and Attention Deficits
      d. Educating Children with Disabilities
   2. Gifted, Creative, and Talented Children
      a. Giftedness

(1) Defining and Identifying Giftedness

(2) The Lives of Gifted Children

   b. Educating Gifted Children

   c. Creativity

(1) Defining and Identifying Creativity

(2) Fostering Creativity

   d. Talent: Recognizing and Encouraging Talented Children

IMPORTANT TERMS FOR SECTION III

Completion: Fill in the blanks to complete the definitions of key terms for this section of Chapter 12.

1. _____ **prophecy:** Prediction of behavior, which biases people to act as though the prophecy were already true.

2. **mental** _____: Below-average cognitive functioning.

3. **dyslexia:** Difficulty in learning to _____.

4. _____ **(abbreviated ___):** Disorders that interfere with specific aspects of learning and school achievement.

5. **attention-deficit hyperactivity disorder (ADHD):** Syndrome characterized by inattention, impulsivity, and considerable activity at _____ times and places.

6. **mainstreaming:** Integration of disabled and nondisabled children in the same _____.

7. _____: Possession of one or more of the following: superior general intellect, superiority in a single domain (like mathematics or science), artistic talent, leadership ability, or creative thinking.

8. _____: Ability to see things in a new light, to see problems that others may fail to recognize, and to come up with new, unusual, and effective solutions.

9. **convergent thinking:** Thinking aimed at finding the one _____ answer to a problem.

10. _____ **thinking:** Creative thinking; the ability to discover new, unusual answers.

LEARNING OBJECTIVES FOR SECTION III

After reading and reviewing this section of Chapter 12, you should be able to do the following.

1. Summarize recent trends in American education.

2. Tell two ways a child's temperament can influence performance in school.

3. Discuss how a child's emotional state can influence school performance, and give a reason why this connection seems to be especially strong for girls.

4. Assess the relationship between parenting styles—authoritarian, permissive, and authoritative—and children's motivation to achieve in school.

5. Discuss how parental beliefs (which vary among cultures) and parents' involvement in school activities can affect children's achievement in school.

6. List at least six ways parents can help children achieve in school, and at least eight suggestions for helping children read better.

7. Cite findings about teachers' influence on students' success, and explain the role of the self-fulfilling prophecy.

8. Name at least six principles that have proven successful in educating children from minority cultures.

9. Discuss the incidence, causes, effects, prognosis, and treatment of mental retardation, learning disabilities, and hyperactivity.

10. Name six principles embodied in the Education for All Handicapped Children Act, and state pros and cons of mainstreaming students with disabilities.

11. Compare four ways of defining and identifying giftedness.

12. Summarize findings about the life success and social adjustment of gifted children.

14. Explain how creativity differs from academic intelligence, why it is difficult to identify, and how it can be fostered.

13. Compare two approaches to educating gifted children.

15. Identify three factors important in the development of talent, which have led to outstanding achievement.

CHAPTER 12 QUIZ

Matching—Who's Who: Match each name in the left-hand column with the appropriate description at the right.

1. Jean Piaget ___
2. Robert Selman ___
3. Howard Gardner ___
4. Lev Vygotsky ___
5. Robert Sternberg ___
6. Carol S. Chomsky ___
7. Anne Haas Dyson ___
8. Thomas Edison ___
9. Balamurati Krishna Ambati ___
10. Lewis Terman ___

a. held that higher cognitive functions result from internalization of learnings from social interaction
b. tested children's understanding of syntax
c. had dyslexia
d. identified the phenomenon of horizontal décalage
e. mastered calculus at age 4 and was a third-year premedical student at age 12
f. proposed the existence of seven separate "intelligences"
g. initiated a longitudinal study of gifted children
h. studied how children use writing to strengthen sociocultural connections
i. theorized that gifted children process novel tasks very efficiently
j. held that moral development is linked to role-taking

Multiple-Choice: Circle the choice that best completes or answers each item.

1. A child in Piaget's stage of concrete operations can do *all but which* of the following?
   a. understand time and space
   b. classify objects
   c. distinguish between reality and fantasy
   d. think hypothetically

2. Generally, the last type of conservation to develop is
   a. volume
   b. weight
   c. substance
   d. none of the above; they all develop at about the same time

3. According to Piaget, the factor that most strongly affects the development of conservation is
   a. intelligence
   b. maturation
   c. experience
   d. cultural background

4. "Jeremy is taller than Julia, and Julia is taller than me, so Jeremy is taller than me." This is an example of
   a. seriation
   b. transitive inference
   c. class inclusion
   d. horizontal décalage

5. Rita has just developed a new skill: First she counts the fingers on her left hand ("1-2-3-4-5"). When asked how many fingers she has on *both* hands, she begins counting the fingers on her right hand, going on with "6-7-8-9-10." Rita is probably about how old?
   a. 4 or 5
   b. 6 or 7
   c. 8 or 9
   d. 10 or 11

6. In Piaget's theory of moral reasoning, children reach the stage of morality of cooperation when they can
   a. think less egocentrically
   b. accept parental standards and rules
   c. judge an act by its consequences
   d. all of the above

7. In Selman's theory, reciprocal awareness typically develops at about what age?
   a. 3 to 4
   b. 5 to 7
   c. 8 to 10
   d. 11 to 13

8. According to Vygotsky's theory, children internalize
   a. what they have learned from adults
   b. self-developed values
   c. intuitive learning
   d. moral reasoning

9. Failure to remember can occur because of deficiencies in
   a. encoding
   b. storage
   c. retrieval
   d. any of the above

10. Which of the following is an external aid to memory?
    a. organization
    b. elaboration
    c. writing
    d. rehearsal

11. Which of the following statements about metamemory is true?
    a. Until age 6, children have virtually no awareness of how their memory works.
    b. Metamemory improves steadily from kindergarten through fifth grade.
    c. Metamemory improves only slightly before third grade, then takes a big jump between third and fifth grades.
    d. Metamemory does not begin to develop until age 10 or 11.

12. The most widely used individual intelligence test is the
    a. Wechsler Intelligence Scale for Children
    b. Stanford-Binet Intelligence Scale
    c. Otis-Lennon School Ability Test
    d. Kaufman Assessment Battery for Children

13. Which of the following statements about IQ tests is true?
    a. Despite standardization, the tests have little validity or reliability.
    b. Scores are poor predictors of achievement in school.
    c. Scores are more closely related to age than to amount of schooling.
    d. Because tests are timed, children who work slowly tend to do poorly.

14. Test developers have been unable to devise culture-free intelligence tests because
    a. tests require the use of language
    b. "common" experiences are affected by cultural values
    c. it is impossible to eliminate culture-linked content
    d. all of the above

15. Which of the following sentence constructions would a 6-year-old be most likely to use?
    a. "I knew that the teacher was going to call on me."
    b. "These cookies were baked yesterday."
    c. "If my father was here, he'd beat you up."
    d. "I have looked all over for my ball, and I can't find it."

16. Which fourth-grader(s) is (are) likely to write a story with fewer errors and more elaborate ideas and to concentrate better on the task?
    a. boy working alone
    b. girl working alone
    c. child working with friend
    d. child working with classmate who is not a friend

17. Which of the following is likely to do best in the early grades of school?
    a. Anne, who always does what the teacher tells her to do
    b. Barry, who fidgets in his seat
    c. Carol, who frequently raises her hand in class
    d. Doug, who frequently gets into fights on the playground

18. Which of the following parents is most likely to have a child who is a high achiever?
    a. Alice, who expects her daughter to do well in school and gives her extra allowance when she does
    b. Brenda, who expects her son to do well and praises him when he does
    c. Curt, who puts pressure on his son to do well but doesn't really expect him to
    d. David, who expects his daughter to do well and punishes her when she falls short

19. Experience with a successful early education program in Hawaii suggests that teachers can help children from minority cultures feel more comfortable and achieve more by doing *all but which* of the following?
    a. matching their own patterns and rhythms of speech to the students'
    b. relating new learnings to students' experience
    c. adjusting for culturally influenced cognitive styles
    d. teaching subject matter important in the students' cultures

20. About 85 percent of the retarded population are affected
    a. mildly
    b. moderately
    c. severely
    d. profoundly

21. About how many adults suffer from learning disabilities?
    a. 5,000 to 10,000
    b. 50,000 to 100,000
    c. 500,000 to 1 million
    d. 5 million to 10 million

22. The Education for All Handicapped Children Act requires placement of handicapped children, whenever possible, in
    a. residential programs
    b. special schools
    c. special classes
    d. mainstreamed classes

23. Identification of giftedness may be based on
    a. an IQ score of 130 or higher
    b. outstanding ability in a specific area like math or science
    c. creativity
    d. any of the above

24. Which of Gardner's "intelligences" is measured by traditional intelligence tests?
    a. musical
    b. spatial
    c. bodily-kinesthetic
    d. none of the above

25. Gifted children tend to have social and emotional problems if their IQs are higher than
    a. 130
    b. 150
    c. 180
    d. 200

26. Tests of creativity attempt to measure
    a. convergent thinking
    b. divergent thinking
    c. subjective thinking
    d. artistic talent

True or False? In the blank following each item, write T (for *true*) or F (for *false*). In the space below each item, if the statement is false, rewrite it to make it true.

1. According to Piaget, the ability to think abstractly develops in the stage of concrete operations, which coincides with middle childhood. ____

2. A team captain who lines up team members in order of height is showing sequential processing. ____

3. Gender stereotypes can be fostered by immature classification skills. ____

4. In Piaget's stage of morality of constraint, children give more weight to the consequences of an action than to the intent behind it. ____

5. When second-graders try to remember a list of items, they are more likely to categorize the information than to repeat it over and over. ___

6. Black Americans, on average, score 15 points lower on IQ tests than white Americans. ___

7. The ability to think is inborn and cannot be taught. ___

8. The explanation for the high achievement of Asian children is that they start out with a slight cognitive advantage. ___

9. Children's understanding of syntax continues to develop until the age of 9 or later. ___

10. Five-year-olds sometimes are unaware that when they do not understand directions they cannot do a job well. ___

11. Children who make up jokes and puns are generally seen by teachers as troublemakers. ___

12. Bilingual children tend to have trouble switching from one language to the other. ___

13. The "back to basics" trend in education was inspired by a drop in high school students' SAT scores during the mid-1970s. ___

14. Children who are highly empathetic tend to have good language skills. ___

15. Schoolchildren's achievement tends to match their parents' and teachers' expectations. ___

16. Children with learning disabilities tend to have below-average intelligence. ___

17. With proper guidance, a child can outgrow a learning disability such as dyslexia. ___

18. Hyperactivity tends to run in families.___

19. Advocates of enriching rather than accelerating gifted children's education believe that skipping grades exposes children to too much pressure. ___

20. Creativity and intelligence are highly correlated. ___

21. There is little or no evidence that tests of creativity, such as the Torrance Tests of Creative Thinking, are valid. ___

22. A study of high achievers done in Chicago found value in a "longitudinal" approach to the training of talent. ___

TOPICS FOR THOUGHT AND DISCUSSION

1. Piaget stressed maturation as the main factor in cognitive development. But findings reported in your text suggest that school and other cultural experience may play a more important role than Piaget suggested. Do such findings lend support to Vygotsky's approach? How do you think Vygotsky might explain the phenomenon of horizontal décalage?

2. According to your text, an experiment in which children were taught classification skills to overcome gender stereotyping supports cognitive-developmental theory about gender roles. How, specifically, does it do this?

3. What areas of agreement and disagreement do you find in the theories of moral development proposed by Piaget and Selman?

4. On the basis of your experience, does the hypothesis (reported in your text) that poor short-term memory may help explain young children's difficulty with conservation tasks seem probable? If not, can you suggest an alternative hypothesis?

5. Considering the pros and cons of intelligence testing, how much credence should be given to IQ scores, and to what uses, if any, should they be put? What is your reaction to the suggestions given in your text for dealing with possible problems of cultural bias? (Note that one of the suggested practices— separate norms for different racial or ethnic groups—has been outlawed by Congress with regard to aptitude tests used to screen applicants for employment.)

6. On the basis of the discussion in your text, which of the two approaches to bilingual education would you tend to favor? What additional information, if any, would you need to make up your mind?

7. Do you think that the "back to the basics" trend is likely to produce predominantly convergent or divergent thinkers?

8. Box 12-3 presents suggestions for helping children read better. Recalling Jim Trelease's recommendations about reading aloud to children (in Chapter 6 of this Study Guide), do you think that Trelease would approve of the suggestions in this box?

9. On the basis of the discussion in your text, what is your view of the advisability of mainstreaming retarded children? What additional information, if any, would you need to make a more definitive judgment?

10. The authors of your text adopt a definition of *giftedness* that includes artistic talent. The researchers who conducted the Chicago study of young achievers mentioned in your text seem to have defined *talent* more broadly, since the study included pianists, sculptors, athletes, mathematicians, and neurologists. How would you define *talent*? Is it simply a synonym for *giftedness*? How does it differ from creativity?

CHAPTER 12 READING

INTRODUCTION

Howard Gardner is a leader in modern educational theory and research. He is Professor of Education at Harvard University Graduate School of Education in Cambridge, Massachusetts, and Director of Project Zero, a research program investigating the development of knowledge, artistic ability, and creativity in young children. His extensive list of publications includes *Artful Scribbles: The Significance of Children's Drawings*; *Art, Mind, and Brain: A Cognitive Approach to Creativity*; *Frames of Mind: The Theory of Multiple Intelligences*; and *The Unschooled Mind*, all published by Basic Books.

One of the significant implications of Gardner's theory of multiple intelligences, which is mentioned briefly in Chapter 12 of your text, is to challenge the reliance of educators and psychologists on the IQ test as a measure of intelligence. The following interview, condensed from the April 1993 issue of *Educational Leadership*, deals with a broader question: How can children be educated so that they truly *understand* what they have learned and can apply it outside the classroom? The interviewer, Ron Brandt, is Executive Editor of the journal, which is published by the Association for Supervision and Curriculum Development.

ON TEACHING FOR UNDERSTANDING: A CONVERSATION WITH HOWARD GARDNER

by Ron Brandt

Would you say that most students don't really understand most of what they've been taught?

I'm afraid they don't. All the evidence I can find suggests that's the case. Most schools have fallen into a pattern of giving kids exercises and drills that result in their getting answers on tests that look like understanding. It's what I call the "correct answer compromise": students read a text, they take a test, and everybody agrees that if they say a certain thing it'll be counted as understanding.

But the findings of cognitive research over the past 20-30 years are really quite compelling: students do not *understand*, in the most basic sense of that term. That is, they lack the capacity to take knowledge learned in one setting and apply it appropriately in a different setting. Study after study has found that, by and large, even the best students in the best schools can't do that.

There's a famous example of Harvard graduates being asked, as they received their diploma, why the earth is warmer in the summer than in the winter. Out of 25 students, nearly all gave exactly the same answer that a 5-year-old would: the earth is closer to the sun in summer than in the winter. The fact is, it has nothing to do with that; it has to do with the tilt of the earth on its axis, which is either away or toward the sun, depending on what time of the year it is in a particular location.

In mathematics, the problem is that kids learn formulas by rote, and they learn to plug numbers into those formulas. As long as the problem is presented with the items in the right order, so to speak, everything is all right. But as soon as the problem is given another way requiring the students to understand what the formula refers to, to be able to use it flexibly, then the students fail.

In the social sciences, the problems are stereotypes and what I call "scripts"; that is, we learn a certain way of thinking about things when we're very young. These are very powerful stories, and they're very long-lived. They influence the way we understand and explain things. For example, there's the Star Wars script: the good guys look like you, the bad guys look different, the two gangs struggle, and in the end, the good guys win.

In your book The Unschooled Mind *(1991), you give a lot of attention to the research on the learning of very young children. Why?*

I think that humans have evolved to the point that 5-years-olds can figure out most things they need to know to survive. When I was writing my book, I happened to have a 5-year-old (my son Benjamin), so I didn't have a problem finding a subject for my research. And by and large when I asked him questions, he gave answers as good as anybody who wasn't an expert. He was able to understand a point, able to think about things, even to evaluate alternatives. He could come up with metaphors, examples, and so on.

So a 5-year-old mind is a terrific invention! It has theories: theories of mind, theories of matter, theories of life, theories of self.

That's the good news. On the other hand, the 5-year-old also develops many notions that are just wrong. For example, you have a heavy object in your hand and a light object in your hand. You drop them both at the same time, and the heavy one falls quicker. It's a very appealing idea—but it's dead wrong.

So you might say that the challenge of education is, on the one hand, to preserve the imagination and the questioning and the theoretical stance of a 5-year-old, but on the other hand—gradually but decisively—to replace those ideas that are not well-founded with theories, ideas, conceptions, stories, which are more accurate.

But that doesn't always happen.

Unfortunately, it seldom happens. As I argue in *The Unschooled Mind*, there are these engravings in the mind that are established early in life, and most of us never get rid of them. What school does is kind of pour powder over them so you can't see them. It makes kids look as if they have sophisticated understanding. But when the kids leave school, the understanding disappears, and the initial engravings are still there.

What can be done about it?

The best thing schools can do is come up with long-term regular procedures that gradually wear down those early engravings and that slowly construct better ones: more comprehensive theories, better explanations, less prejudiced views of the world.

In your book you suggest two models that could help schools make learning more authentic: children's museum-type programs and apprenticeships. Why those?

In an apprenticeship, you see a young person hanging around a very knowledgeable adult—an expert, someone who really knows what he or she is doing—watching that person, day after day, as he uses his knowledge. The master challenges his apprentice at the level the apprentice can handle. He doesn't give her something she could do six months ago; he doesn't give her tasks that are way too difficult. He's always calibrating the challenge for about where the student is. And I think that if you hang around an expert, not only will you develop requisite skills, you'll know when to use them and when not to use them.

But the point is for teachers and parents to think of themselves as masters and to challenge their apprentices. If the parent watches TV instead of reading, or the teacher reads one book a year—I'm told that's what the average teacher reads—that's the message the kids will get. But if the adults read and write and talk about current events, the kids will do it, too.

And children's museums?

They've grown dramatically in the last 25 years; there were just a handful in 1950-60, and now there are hundreds of them. They are places where kids can find things that interest them and explore these things at their own pace and in their own way. Frank Oppenheimer, who founded the Exploratorium in San Francisco, said, "Nobody flunks museums."

A good museum is a child-friendly place to learn. And many people, including me, have been fascinated as we've escorted kids whom we thought we knew to children's museums and discovered unexpected strengths or unexpected areas of confusion. Or discover[ed] that kids we thought of as being unable to learn were terrific learners, but in a very different type of environment. It broadens your notion of what kids are like, what they can do.

Of course, most teachers and principals don't have the resources, perhaps even the authority, to set up children's museum-like situations or establish apprenticeships.

The apprentice-master relationship is primarily a way of thinking. The master teacher thinks, "I'm not just passing on the contents of a textbook; I'm modeling a certain kind of knowledge and standards for making use of that knowledge in daily life." If you think of yourself like that, that's a revolutionary difference—and it doesn't cost a dime.

As for children's museums, many communities now have one. The problem is that it's considered a frill rather than an important means of education.

And even in communities that don't have a children's museum, educators can visit one in another city and watch what's going on, see how kids interact with stuff, observe the learning. I recommend that teachers visiting the San Jose Discovery Museum pretend to be 5-year-olds; regress to that age and see what it's like to learn about the world in those ways.

What about the way things are done in children's museums makes for authentic learning?

Well, take the Exploratorium in San Francisco. First of all, it's put together by people who know a lot about science. It's designed to reflect scientific knowledge that has been developed in the past couple of centuries—but there's nothing didactic or intimidating there at all.

Instead, there are the actual experiments that lead people to draw conclusions about science. So the kids themselves have the chance to be little scientists, to try experiments and see what happens. And the important thing is it doesn't matter the first or the second time they do something whether they have any idea as to what the "right" physical principle is; they're getting familiar with the phenomena in a way that fits their own tempo, learning style, profile of intelligences. They're getting a chance to test some of their own intuitive notions and see what about them is tenable and what is inadequate.

And if they spend more time there, they can read some of the material the museum provides or they can talk with one of the explainers who come around, or hang around with a teacher or parent who knows some things. So in that realistic environment they can enter into a discussion about the meaning of the things people have discovered in the sciences or the arts.

When you've encountered an idea in your own way and brought your own thinking to bear, the idea becomes much more a part of you. It isn't something that you read about from 3 o'clock to 3:15 and then forget; it's a part of your own experience. And if you're encouraged to take the lessons you learned in the Exploratorium and bring them home to your basement or your own room, or bring them to school—to what's going on in science class or art class—you then have what I call "resonance." The notion of resonance is that people are more likely to master concepts and understand potential implications of phenomena when they encounter them in different places. Children who have made bubbles or played with pendulums in children's museums will understand them more fully when they encounter them at school.

Let me ask, then, how these principles apply to what teachers do day-by-day with the kids in their classrooms?

The first question the teacher should ask is, "Why am I doing this? Do I believe it's important? Can I convey that to kids?" Not just because it's the next lesson, or because it comes from the textbook.

Then, the teachers need to figure out what's the very best way to introduce kids to this phenomenon: what's the generative idea, the puzzle, the thing that's really going to compel, maybe because it's surprising or intriguing.

Then it's important to provide what I call "multiple entry points." Kids don't all learn in the same way; they don't all find the same things interesting. In fact, based on my theory of multiple intelligences introduced in *Frames of Mind*, I'd say that you can approach almost any rich topic in a whole variety of ways.

We need to give kids a chance in school to enter the room by different windows, so to speak—but to be able to see the relationships among the different types of windows.

Another obvious implication, one that only a few people have begun to take seriously, is that we've got to do a lot fewer things in school. The greatest enemy of understanding is coverage. As long as you are determined to cover everything, you actually ensure that most kids are not going to understand. You've got to take enough time to get kids deeply involved in

something so they can think about it in lots of different ways and apply it—not just at school, but at home and on the street and so on.

Now, this is the most revolutionary idea in American education because most people can't abide the notion that we might leave out one decade of American history or one formula in math or one biological system. But that's crazy, because we now know that kids don't understand those things anyway. They forget them as soon as the test is over—because it hasn't been built into their brain, engraved in it. So since we know unambiguously that the way we do it now isn't working, we have to try something else.

You're really convinced of that?

Let me give you an example. Having written *The Unschooled Mind* and thinking that the ideas had a certain power, I tried out the theories on my graduate students studying cognitive development. At the beginning of the year, the middle of the year, [and] the end of the year, I gave all the students two tests. One was a conventional test of content knowledge: who was Piaget, what his theories were about; things like that. But the other was a test of understanding. I would give the students new situations that they hadn't seen before—articles out of the newspaper or phenomena that I just made up—and I would ask them to explain those phenomena.

Well, the results were very striking. Over the course of the term, the students' mastery of content zoomed up. Their understandings, on the other hand, were exactly the same; they didn't change at all. How humiliating! I could just see the headlines, "Harvard Professor of Well-Regarded Courses Documents That His Own Students Don't Understand."

Fortunately, it's a two-year program, so we're rewriting the course now; we're going to teach it very differently. So the message, I guess, is "Physician, heal thyself."

QUESTIONS ABOUT THE READING

1. Gardner suggests that 5-year-olds "can figure out most things they need to know to survive" but that some of their "theories" about the way things work are wrong. Is Gardner's description of the 5-year-old mind consistent with Piaget's? If not, in what

ways does it differ? Does the research Gardner summarizes suggest that Piaget may have been wrong in claiming that children's cognitive powers advance steadily during the school years?

2. According to Gardner, early, inaccurate ideas about the world become "engraved" on the mind and outlast school-learnings. How might Vygotsky explain this phenomenon? Do you think Vygotsky would agree with Gardner's suggestions for overcoming this problem?

3. Does Gardner's use of the term *scripts* to describe early, formulaic ways of thinking seem similar to or different from the use of the term *script* in Chapter 9 of your text (in the discussion of generic memory)?

4. If Gardner is right that much of what children learn in school soon fades away, is the usual emphasis on tested achievement misplaced? If so, what other means could be developed to discern whether children truly understand what they are learning?

5. Are Gardner's suggested educational methods consistent with some of those in Box 12-1 of your text, "Teaching Children To Think"?

6. Gardner, like Piaget, used his own child as a subject for his research. Thinking back to Chapter 1, what advantages and disadvantages do you see in such a research design?

ANSWER KEY FOR CHAPTER 12

Note: Numbers in parentheses refer to pages in the textbook where answers can be found.

CHAPTER 12 REVIEW

Important Terms for Section I
1. abstractions (page 459)
2. alteration (459)
3. conservation, conserve (460)
4. dimension (461)
5. transitive (461)
6. inclusion (462)
7. constraint (464)
8. cooperation (464)
9. Selman (464)
10. support (466)
11. repetition (467)
12. organization (468)
13. story (469)
14. metamemory (469)
15. verbal, performance (469)
16. Kaufman, K-ABC (470)
17. Otis-Lennon (470)
18. aptitude (470)

19. achievement (470)

Learning Objectives for Section I
1. (page 459)
2. (459-460)
3. (460-461)
4. (461-462)
5. (462)
6. (462-463)
7. (464, 465)
8. (464-465)
9. (466)
10. (467)
11. (467-469)
12. (469)
13. (469-470)
14. (470-471)
15. (471-473)
16. (473-476)
17. (474-475)
18. (472)

Important Terms for Section II
1. sentences (page 476)

2. metacommunication (477)
3. bilingual (480)
4. bilingualism (480)
5. code-switching (481)

Learning Objectives for Section II
1. (pages 476-477)
2. (477-478)
3. (478-479)
4. (479-480)
5. (480-481)

Important Terms for Section III
1. self-fulfilling (page 487)
2. retardation (490)
3. read (491)
4. learning disabilities (LDs) (491)
5. inappropriate (492)
6. classroom (494)
7. giftedness (496)
8. creativity (497)
9. "right" (497)
10. divergent (497)

Learning Objectives for Section III
1. (page 482)
2. (483)
3. (483)
4. (484)
5. (484-486)
6. (485)
7. (486-488)
8. (488-489)
9. (490-493)
10. (494-495)
11. (496)
12. (496-497)
13. (497)
14. (497-499)
15. (499-500)

CHAPTER 12 QUIZ

Matching-Who's Who
1. d (page 460)
2. j (464)
3. f (496)
4. a (465-466)

5. i (410)
6. b (477)
7. h (479)
8. c (491)
9. e (495)
10. g (496)

Multiple-Choice
1. d (page 459)
2. a (460)
3. b (461)
4. b (461)
5. b (463)
6. a (464, 465)
7. c (465)
8. a (466)
9. d (467)
10. c (469)
11. b (469)
12. a (469-470)
13. d (470-471)
14. c (472)
15. a (476-477)
16. c (480)
17. c (483)
18. b (484, 485)
19. d (489)
20. a (490)
21. d (492)
22. d (494)
23. d (496)
24. b (496)
25. c (497)
26. b (498)

True or False?
1. F—According to Piaget, the ability to think abstractly does not develop until adolescence. (page 459)
2. F—The captain is showing an understanding of seriation. (461)
3. T (462)
4. T (465)
5. F—Second-graders tend to use rehearsal spontaneously, but children ordinarily do not use organization spontaneously until age 10 or 11. (467-468)
6. T (473)

7. F—Research shows that children can be taught to think more effectively. (472)
8. F—Asian children show no early cognitive superiority; their superior performance seems to be related to educational and cultural differences. (474-475)
9. T (476-477)
10. T (477)
11. F—According to one study, children with a keen sense of humor tend to be competent in the classroom and to be seen positively by their teachers. (478-479)
12. F—Bilingual children tend to switch easily from one language to the other when the situation calls for it. (481)
13. T (482)
14. T (483)
15. T (485, 487)
16. F—Children with learning disabilities often have average or above average intelligence but have trouble processing sensory information. (491)
17. F—Learning disabilities are not outgrown, but people can learn to cope with them. (492-497)
18. T (493)
19. T (497)
20. F—Studies have found only modest correlations between creativity and intelligence. (497)
21. T (498)
22. T (499)

PERSONALITY AND SOCIAL DEVELOPMENT IN MIDDLE CHILDHOOD

OVERVIEW

Chapter 13 describes the rich, expanding social world of middle childhood and the personality changes a child experiences during these years. In this chapter, the authors:

- Discuss how self-concept and self-esteem develop during middle childhood

- Describe changes in parent-child relationships that occur during these years

- Assess the impact on children of parents' employment, of divorce and remarriage, of gay and lesbian parents, of poverty, and of other contextual factors

- Point out the importance of sibling relationships and their cultural context

- Describe the formation, composition, and effects of peer groups

- Examine the bases of popularity and friendship

- Describe common childhood emotional disturbances and their treatment

- Identify factors contributing to stress and resilience

CHAPTER 13 REVIEW

Section I   The Developing Self

FRAMEWORK FOR SECTION I

A. Developing a Self-Concept
B. Self-Esteem
   1. Industry and Self-Esteem
   2. Sources of Self-Esteem
      a. Self-Evaluations
      b. Emotional Growth
      c. Parenting Styles

IMPORTANT TERMS FOR SECTION I

Completion: Fill in the blanks to complete the definitions of key terms for this section of Chapter 13.

1. **self-_____:** Sense of self that guides one in deciding what to do in the future.

2. **self-_____:** The judgment people make about their personal worth.

3. **industry versus inferiority:** In Erikson's theory, the fourth crisis that children face; they must learn the _____ of their culture or risk developing feelings of inferiority.

4. **global self-_____:** Harter's term for self-esteem.

LEARNING OBJECTIVES FOR SECTION I

After reading and reviewing this section of Chapter 13, you should be able to do the following.

1. Explain the relationship between the development of representational systems and the development of the self-concept during middle childhood.

2. Describe personality characteristics of children with high and low self-esteem; and discuss Erikson's and Harter's views, along with research findings, on its sources.

3. State how emotional growth and parenting styles influence self-esteem.

Section II   The Child in the Family

FRAMEWORK FOR SECTION II

A. Parents and Children
   1. Relationships
   2. Issues
   3. Discipline
   4. Control and Coregulation
B. How Parents' Work Affects Children
   1. Mothers' Work
      a. The Mother's Psychological State
      b. Interactions in Working-Mother Families

c. Children's Reactions to Mothers' Work
d. The Ecological Context of the Family
2. Fathers' Work
3. Care for School-Age Children of Working Parents
C. Family Environment
1. Atmosphere
2. Structure
D. Children of Divorce
1. Children's Adjustment to Divorce
a. "Tasks" of Adjustment
2. Influences on Children's Adjustment to Divorce
a. Parenting Styles and Parents' Satisfaction
b. Remarriage of the Mother
c. Relationship with the Father
d. Accessibility of Both Parents
3. Long-Term Effects of Divorce on Children
E. One-Parent Families and Stepfamilies
1. Single-Parent Families
a. Effects on Children
b. Effects on Schooling
c. Long-Term Effects of the One-Parent Family
2. Stepfamilies
F. Cultural Context of the Family
1. Values and Behavior in Different Ethnic Groups
2. Poverty and Some of Its Effects on Children
3. When Families Move
4. Children of Gay and Lesbian Parents

IMPORTANT TERMS FOR SECTION II

Completion: Fill in the blanks to complete the definitions of key terms for this section of Chapter 13.

1. _____: Teaching intended to help children develop character, self-control, and moral behavior.

2. **coregulation:** _____ stage in the control of behavior in which parents exercise general

supervision and children exercise moment-to-moment self-regulation.

LEARNING OBJECTIVES FOR SECTION II

After reading and reviewing this section of Chapter 13, you should be able to do the following.

1. Rank the relative importance to school-age children of relationships with parents, peers, grandparents, and extended family.

2. Identify issues that arise between parents and school-age children and methods of discipline that parents typically use.

3. Describe how control of behavior gradually shifts from parent to child.

4. Describe how mothers' and fathers' employment affects children.

5. Identify four alternative forms of care for school-age children of working parents, and list at least six guidelines to determine when children are ready for self-care.

6. Describe effects of the atmosphere and structure of the home environment on children's behavior and adjustment.

7. Discuss how divorce affects children; list six "tasks" of adjustment; identify four factors that influence children's adjustment; and summarize research on long-term effects of divorce.

8. Summarize statistics on the prevalence of single-parent families, and identify effects of being raised in such a family.

9. Summarize findings on children's adjustment to life in a stepfamily.

10. Give three examples of adaptive strategies and goals of socialization in minority families.

11. Analyze effects of poverty and of frequent moves on children's well-being.

12. Briefly summarize research on social and personal development of children of gay and lesbian parents.

Section III Siblings, Peers, and Friends

FRAMEWORK FOR SECTION II

A. Brothers and Sisters
   1. How Siblings Help Each Other Develop
   2. Sibling Relationships in Cultural Context

B. The Peer Group
1. Formation of the Peer Group
2. Functions and Influence of the Peer Group
a. Positive Effects
b. Negative Effects: Conformity
3. Popularity
a. Individual Differences in Popularity
(1) The Popular Child
(2) The Unpopular Child
b. Influences on Popularity
(1) Cultural Influences
(2) Family Influences
(3) Helping Unpopular Children
4. How Can Interracial Peer Groups Be Encouraged?
C. Friendship
1. Why Are Friends Important?
2. Development of Children's Thinking about Friendship

IMPORTANT TERM FOR SECTION III

Completion: Fill in the blank to complete the definition of the key term for this section of Chapter 13.

1. _____: Negative attitudes toward certain groups.

LEARNING OBJECTIVES FOR SECTION II

After reading and reviewing this section of Chapter 13, you should be able to do the following.

1. Give one example of a direct way and one example of an indirect way in which school-age siblings influence each other, and name three benefits of sibling caretaking.

2. Explain how peer groups form, and discuss three positive effects and one negative effect of peer groups.

3. Describe some characteristics of popular and unpopular children, discuss influences on popularity, and suggest ways to help unpopular children gain social acceptance.

4. Briefly discuss effects of school integration in encouraging the formation of interracial peer groups.

5. Discuss the importance of friendships, and list and give examples of Selman's five stages of friendship.

Section IV   Mental Health in Childhood

FRAMEWORK FOR SECTION IV

A. Emotional Disturbances
1. Acting-Out Behavior
2. Separation Anxiety Disorder
3. Childhood Depression

B. Treatment Techniques
    1. Types of Therapy
    2. Effectiveness of Therapy
C. Stress and Resilience
    1. Sources of Stress
        a. Children's Fears
        b. Modern Pressures
    2. Coping with Stress: The Resilient Child

IMPORTANT TERMS FOR SECTION IV

Completion: Fill in the blanks to complete the definitions of key terms for this section of Chapter 13.

1. _____ **behavior:** Misbehavior (for example, lying or stealing) spurred by emotional difficulties.

2. **school _____:** Unrealistic fear of going to school; may be a form of separation anxiety disorder.

3. **separation anxiety disorder:** Condition lasting for at least 4 weeks that involves excessive anxiety concerning separation from people to whom a child is _____.

4. **childhood depression:** Affective disorder characterized by inability to have fun or to concentrate, and by an absence of normal emotional _____.

5. **individual psychotherapy:** Treatment technique in which a therapist generally helps a patient gain _____ into his or her personality and relationships and helps interpret feelings and behaviors.

6. **family therapy:** Treatment technique in which the whole family is treated together and is viewed as the _____.

7. **behavior therapy:** Treatment technique using principles of learning theory to alter behavior; also called *behavior* _____.

8. **drug therapy:** Administration of drugs to treat _____.

9. _____ **children:** Children who bounce back from unfortunate circumstances that would have a highly negative impact on the emotional development of most children.

LEARNING OBJECTIVES FOR SECTION III

After reading and reviewing this section of Chapter 13, you should be able to do the following.

1. Explain why acting-out behavior occurs, and state what forms it may take.

2. Describe symptoms and treatment of separation anxiety disorders, particularly school phobia.

3. List five symptoms of childhood depression.

4. Compare individual psychotherapy, family therapy, behavior therapy, and drug therapy.

5. List at least three sources of childhood stress and at least four typical childhood fears common to several cultures.

7. Name three sources of pressure on children in modern life.

6. Compare typical reactions to violence in early childhood, middle childhood, and adolescence.

8. Identify five factors that seem to contribute to resilience in children.

CHAPTER 13 QUIZ

Matching—Aspects of the Developing Self-Concept: Match each situation in the left-hand column with the most appropriate term in the right-hand column.

1. At the beginning of the school year, Mark's teacher asks the children in the class to tell something about themselves. When it is Mark's turn, he says, "I'm pretty good at sports, but I have trouble with spelling." ___

2. Caren and a friend are playing in Caren's room. Toys and books are piled everywhere. The girls want to play a game, but Caren cannot find it. "I'm not as orderly as I'd like to be," she says apologetically. ___

3. Gordon is making New Year's resolutions for a school assignment. "Be nice to my kid sister," he writes at the top of the list. ___

4. Jim is alone in the candy section of a supermarket. "No one's looking," he thinks, as he takes a piece of bubble gum and puts it in his pocket. "No, that's not right," he tells himself as he changes his mind and puts it back. ___

5. Dana is playing tennis. Trying to put away an overhead shot, she hits the ball into the net. "That's OK," she tells herself, "I can make the next one." ___

6. Tim and his buddies are hanging around a music store, which is having a sidewalk sale. While the clerk is distracted, some of the boys take cassettes out of a bin and put them in their pockets. Tim, seeing his friends do this, grabs a cassette even though he knows he shouldn't. ___

7. Jeremy comes home from school and finds a note from his mother: "Please remember to water the plants and clean up your room." Jeremy is tired and would rather watch television right away, but because of his mother's reminder, he does his chores first. ___

a. self-esteem
b. coregulation
c. self-evaluation in different domains
d. self-regulation
e. conformity
f. ideal self
g. real self

Multiple-Choice: Circle the choice that best completes or answers each item.

1. *All but which* of the following may be part of the self-concept?
   a. "I am a good athlete."
   b. "I am a hard worker."
   c. "I have trouble making friends."
   d. "I don't like Tracy."

2. The virtue that arises from successful resolution of Erikson's crisis of industry versus inferiority is
   a. productivity
   b. self-confidence
   c. competence
   d. industriousness

3. School-age children are different from younger children in that
   a. younger children have not yet developed a sense of self-esteem
   b. school-age children have an all-or-nothing opinion of themselves
   c. school-age children can express their self-judgments in words
   d. all of the above

4. According to Harter's research, the greatest contributor to self-esteem in middle childhood is
   a. regard by parents and classmates
   b. competence in schoolwork
   c. athletic skills
   d. good conduct

5. Parents of children with high self-esteem tend to use which parenting style?
   a. authoritarian
   b. permissive
   c. authoritative
   d. any of the above; no relationship has been found between parenting style and self-esteem

6. According to a review of family research, which of the following factors most strongly affects children's development?
   a. marital status of the parents
   b. number of parents in the home
   c. mother's employment
   d. atmosphere in the home

7. According to a survey of mostly middle-class fifth- and sixth-graders, the relationships that are most important to them are those with
   a. parents
   b. siblings
   c. peers
   d. grandparents

8. Which child is likely to receive the *least* social support from the extended family?
   a. white
   b. African American
   c. Latino
   d. none of the above; no significant ethnic or racial differences in extended family support have been found

9. About what proportion of married women with children under age 18 are in the work force?
   a. 30 percent
   b. 50 percent
   c. 70 percent
   d. 90 percent

10. In comparison with children of a full-time homemaker, school-age children of a working mother generally
    a. have lower self-esteem
    b. live in more structured homes
    c. are more dependent
    d. are more likely to be abused

11. Husbands of working mothers tend to be most involved with the child(ren) when
    a. there is only one child
    b. the mother works part-time
    c. the children are school-age
    d. the mother earns close to what the father does

12. About how many school-age "self-care children" of working parents are there in the United States today?
    a. fewer than 1 million
    b. 2 million
    c. 10 million
    d. 20 million

13. Which of the following statements about the effects of the family environment is most accurate, according to research?
    a. Children in two-parent homes are better-adjusted than those in one-parent homes.
    b. Children in one-parent homes are better adjusted than those in two-parent homes.
    c. Children in two-parent homes do better than those in one-parent homes if the parents have a good relationship.
    d. none of the above; no correlation has been found between children's adjustment and the number of parents in the home.

14. *All but which* of the following are emotional "tasks" that face children of divorce?
    a. acknowledging the reality of the divorce
    b. resuming customary pursuits
    c. resolving anger and self-blame
    d. being wary of intimate relationships

15. Which of the following statements about children's adjustment to divorce is true, according to research?
    a. Boys with authoritative parents usually have fewer behavior problems than those with authoritarian or permissive parents.
    b. Boys tend to have more adjustment problems than girls when their mothers remarry.
    c. Girls tend to have more behavior problems than boys when their mothers do not remarry.
    d. The best custody arrangement is generally with the parent of the same sex.

16. About what proportion of American children live in one-parent homes?
    a. nearly half
    b. 1 in 5
    c. 1 in 10
    d. 1 in 20

17. Which country has the lowest percentage of single-parent families?
    a. Australia
    b. France
    c. Japan
    d. Sweden

18. According to one large-scale study, which of the following factors has a more negative effect on school achievement?
    a. single-parent home
    b. low income
    c. Both have equally negative effects.
    d. Neither has a strongly negative effect.

19. Black parents living in poverty tend to use which disciplinary technique?
    a. physical punishment
    b. ignoring misbehavior
    c. praising good behavior
    d. reasoning and negotiating

20. The combination of siblings likely to quarrel most is
    a. two brothers
    b. two sisters
    c. a brother and sister
    d. none of the above; all quarrel equally

21. According to a Canadian study of fifth- and sixth-graders, *all but which* of the following are positive effects of the peer group?
    a. motivation to achieve
    b. sense of identity
    c. sense of belonging
    d. development of coregulation

22. In middle childhood, popular children tend to have *all but which* of the following?
    a. strong cognitive skills
    b. superior social skills
    c. strong interest in the other sex
    d. cooperative behavior

23. According to research, which of the following children is likely to be unpopular?
    a. Audrey, who is disciplined by physical punishment and threats
    b. Bonita, who is disciplined by reasoning
    c. Claudia, who is rarely disciplined
    d. none of the above; no relationship has been found between discipline and popularity

24. At which of Selman's levels of friendship would a child say, "He wouldn't let me watch television at his house, so he's not my friend anymore"?
    a. undifferentiated
    b. unilateral
    c. reciprocal
    d. mutual

25. Surveys have found that mental health problems of American 7- to 16-year-olds
    a. have decreased since the mid-1970s
    b. have increased about equally for boys and girls
    c. are greater for African American children than for white children of the same socioeconomic level
    d. center around fears, guilt, and bodily complaints

26. School-phobic children tend to be
    a. boys
    b. low achievers
    c. from close-knit families
    d. difficult to treat

27. Behavior modification is based on which theoretical perspective?
    a. psychoanalytic
    b. learning
    c. contextual
    d. cognitive

28. Fears of school-age children most often
    a. are different in different cultures
    b. center on wars and earthquakes
    c. concern things close to daily life
    d. lead to lasting insecurities

29. David Elkind has studied characteristics of which kind of child?
    a. resilient
    b. "hurried"
    c. maltreated
    d. school-phobic

True or False? In the blank following each item, write T (for *true*) or F (for *false*). In the space below each item, if the statement is false, rewrite it to make it true.

1. School-age children have trouble recognizing apparently contradictory aspects of themselves. ____

2. When 8- to 12-year-old children evaluate themselves, they give the most importance to physical appearance. ____

3. According to some research, school-age children spend only about half an hour a day interacting with their parents. ____

4. Issues between school-age children and their parents tend to center on schoolwork, friends, and chores. ___

5. Parents' approach to child rearing generally changes as children grow older. ___

6. Research has shown that children tend to be adversely affected by their mothers' employment. ___

7. Husbands of working mothers tend to be more involved in housework and child care than husbands of at-home mothers. ___

8. Self-care children generally live with poor single parents in urban neighborhoods. ___

9. Couples who share child care tend to have a more intimate relationship with each other than couples in which the mother does most of the child care. ___

10. Children often believe that they were responsible for their parents' divorce. ___

11. The final task children face, in their adjustment to divorce, is accepting its permanence. ___

12. Children whose parents have joint custody generally adjust to divorce better than those who are in sole custody of one parent. ___

13. A study of teenagers whose parents had divorced 10 years earlier found that the girls' long-term adjustment was better than the boys'. ___

14. Most divorced fathers who have custody of their children have remarried. ___

15. A stepfamily typically consists of a father, his children, and a stepmother. ___

16. Children generally take frequent moves in stride. ___

17. Children of gay and lesbian parents are likely to have psychological problems and to be sexually abused. ___

18. Younger siblings tend to be good at sensing other people's needs. ___

19. Elder siblings who take care of younger ones tend to resent them. ___

20. According to a Canadian study, the most common activity of fifth- and sixth-graders is watching television. ___

21. In China, popular children tend to be sensitive, quiet, and shy. ___

22. School integration has brought more acceptance of racial differences. ___

23. According to Selman, children at the undifferentiated level of friendship tend to think only of what they want from a relationship. ___

24. Ten-year-olds frequently make up stories about their exploits and lie to avoid punishment. ___

25. A child who exhibits school phobia should be allowed to stay home until the phobia subsides. ___

26. A good psychotherapist will show a child that feelings of hostility toward a parent are harmful. ___

27. In family therapy, the child whose problem causes the family to seek treatment is sometimes the healthiest member. ___

28. Drug therapy is treatment for drug addiction. ____

29. Therapy for specific problems tends to be more effective than therapy aimed at improving social adjustment in general. ____

30. School is a source of insecurity for many children. ____

31. Resilient children are likely to have at least one good relationship with a caring adult. ____

TOPICS FOR THOUGHT AND DISCUSSION

1. Which, in your experience, seems to be a more important source of children's self-esteem: what they think of themselves or what others think of them? What problems do you see in designing research to measure the separate impacts of these two factors? In view of this problem, how would you assess Harter's research design?

2. Harilyn Rousso, describing her own experience as a child with cerebral palsy, says that she learned to deny her disability so as not to accept society's definition of her as inferior. Is Rousso suggesting that her mother was wrong in trying to teach her to walk straighter? What specific suggestions would you give a parent for building the self-esteem of a child with a physical disability?

3. Some research suggests that a working woman who is satisfied with her life is likely to be a more effective parent, but a man who is deeply satisfied with his work may become so engrossed in it that he may tend to withdraw from family life. How might gender-typing (discussed in Chapter 10) help to explain this difference?

4. Siblings, the child's first "peer group," play an important role in the development of the self-concept. What differences, then, might you expect to find in the self-concept development of only children and of children with siblings?

5. The authors of your text state that some degree of conformity to group standards is healthy. Do you agree? Can you think of examples of healthy and unhealthy conformity that are not mentioned in your text?

6. The research on racial prejudice cited in your text is almost entirely from the 1960s and 1970s. Would you expect to find more or less prejudice among schoolchildren today? Why or why not?

7. Do you agree with David Elkind that children today are put under too much pressure to succeed and grow up too soon? Can you think of examples? As a parent, what might you do to avoid raising a "hurried child"?

CHAPTER 13 READING

INTRODUCTION

What happens to unpopular children when they grow up? For some, at least, the answer is a disturbing one—as this article, reprinted from *The Washington Post*, makes clear.

THE LEGACY OF REJECTION

by Don Oldenburg

When Joel Rifkin was a youngster, he suffered more than his share of rejection.

Accounts from neighbors following his arrest last month in New York portrayed the 34-year-old unemployed gardener as "quiet and shy." He never had girlfriends. He was always a loner. Former classmates from his school days in middle-class East Meadow, N.Y., where he still lived with his adoptive mother and sister, said Rifkin was taunted and ostracized by other students.

When police pulled over his pickup truck for a traffic violation on the night of June 28, they discovered a decomposing body in the back. Rifkin soon after confessed to strangling 17 prostitutes.

Not all children who are lonely on the playground grow up to become serial killers. Most don't. But researchers in child development are finding that children who experience continual rejection by other children often suffer serious psychological problems later in life.

"Our society underestimates the severity of this problem," says Gary W. Ladd, a professor of education[al] psychology at the University of Illinois at Champaign-Urbana. His research has contributed to psychology's recent refocusing on the plight of youngsters who struggle at making friends.

"The research shows that rejection during childhood is one of the best predictors of later-life difficulties," says Ladd. "These are kids who become delinquent, drop out of school, and (as adults) become alcoholics, have brushes with the law, commit suicide. . . . A lot of these children are emotionally very unhappy, lonely and depressed."

With the demographic growth in two-income and single-parent families today, more children are spending more time with their peers in preschool day-care centers and in before- and after-school programs.

Many child-development experts now believe close, regular contact with other children forms the primary context in which children acquire social skills for life. They learn how to interact successfully with their own age group. Playing with peers teaches them the standards of acceptable social behavior and the unwritten rules of social acceptance.

Trouble starts when a child is excluded, subjected to "peer rejection." For a variety of reasons, children who are rejected by their peers are avoided, mercilessly harassed and tormented, or simply ignored and isolated by other children. While such exclusion has long been known to be painful, only recently have researchers determined that it also denies admission to the developmental process that is important to achieving a psychologically healthy adulthood.

"The world of peers eventually becomes the world of fellow adults, so we're talking about an early version of the skills that become useful as adults," says psychologist John D. Coie. "If you miss out on them, they're difficult to pick up later."

Coie's research at Duke University has helped to establish that peer relations are more of an influential factor on child development than previously thought. Children dislike other children not because they dress differently, or because of their physical appearance, Coie has found, but because of how they "handle themselves" when interacting with other children. The bottom line is their behavior: Over-aggressiveness, anxiousness, even fearfulness about being with other children, can lead to peer-group exile.

Scientists are still trying to identify the values and styles of parenting that can set up a child for peer rejection. Early findings haven't produced any surprises: Warm and positive parenting tends to instill in a child a warm and positive perspective toward peers, while the opposite effect emerges from controlling or disagreeable or inconsistent parenting.

Of course, all children face some rejection. It's one of growing-up's hurtful adjustments, the sharp edge of the learning curve.

In fact, warns Stanley Greenspan, a child psychologist and professor of psychiatry at George Washington Medical School, children who don't take a few lumps might face a rough start in adulthood. But rejection over a long period is different—and no psychological plus. Almost half of the children rejected in the fifth grade continued to be rejected in every grade through the five years of one longitudinal study.

Status distinctions maintained by group perception don't change easily: Losers are seen as losers year after year, troublemakers as troublemakers, even if their behavior no longer warrants such labels. That label can also prove self-perpetuating, says Coie.

Teachers, Parents Can Help

Because peer rejection is a complex problem that can involve home influences, the rejected child's behavior, and dynamics of the peer group, researchers say there are no easy solutions.

For instance, changing the behavior of the rejected child may not be sufficient, they warn, if the group bias against the child doesn't also change.

"Parents have to be alert to some things," says Coie, who warns that it's easier to help younger children out of this problem than older ones.

"If the child is rarely talking about other kids, or he never plays with friends, or he comes home complaining about other kids behaving badly and it's always the other kids' fault, those are the signs something isn't going well with the peer group . . . . When you see a chronic pattern, parents may need to recognize that it may be something their child is doing and not just blame it on the other kids."

Greenspan believes teachers and school counselors are in the best position to make a difference. But the coauthor of *Playground Politics: Understanding the Emotional Life of Your School-Age Child* believes there are steps parents can take at home:

- Try to establish a relationship in which the parent and child can be more open and can learn from each other. "For a half hour a day, just hang out with the youngster," Greenspan advises. "See what comes out spontaneously. This establishes rapport."

- Once goodwill is established, "talk about the day-to-day events at school, who was nice and who was mean. Raise questions like, why does he think this clique of kids is pestering him? You become a little bit of a coach, helping him diagnose a situation."

- Guide the child in considering options. "Don't suggest them but help the child come up with his own. That 'way, you're developing a way of thinking and a way of coping rather than just giving solutions."

- Always try to empathize with how your child sees the world, even if you don't agree with it.

Bullies Also Likely to Face Problems

Withdrawn and submissive children aren't the only rejected youngsters missing out on the necessary "schooling" of day-to-day peer interaction. Ironically, the bully who inflicts pain on others is nearly as likely to be kept at arm's length by other children.

Several studies have found that from 40 to 50 percent of rejected children are highly aggressive. Rather than flinching in social circumstances, children who are rejected for being bullies commonly read other classmates' intentions as hostile and react aggressively. They solve problems using force. And they don't seem to be as aware that other children don't like them.

Researchers have tracked more negative results of peer rejection for aggressive children.

"Being aggressive and rejected seems to predict more conduct problems, such as an excessive use of violence, other kinds of antisocial behavior, and also depression and anxiety," says Coie.

"Kids who are nonaggressive and rejected seem to be more at risk for the psychological problems."

QUESTIONS ABOUT THE READING

1. The article states that rejection by peers "denies [a child] admission to the developmental process that is important to achieving a psychologically healthy adulthood." On the basis of your textbook's discussion of the functions and influence of the peer group, can you spell out more specifically what social skills an excluded child may not develop? Why do you think it is difficult to pick up those skills later?

2. Do you know anyone who was unpopular as a child and grew into a sociable, well-adjusted adult? If so, what factors do you think helped him or her overcome the effects of early rejection?

3. According to the article, what personality characteristics do rejected children tend to have? Are they similar to the characteristics of the unpopular child described in your text?

4. Both your text and the article identify parenting styles as contributing to rejection by peers. What other influences might play a part?

5. Both your text and the article suggest ways in which parents and other adults can help unpopular children. Are these suggestions similar or different? Which of them would you be most inclined to try if your child, or a child you know, was having trouble being accepted by peers?

ANSWER KEY FOR CHAPTER 13

Note: Numbers in parentheses refer to pages in the textbook where answers can be found.

CHAPTER 13 REVIEW

Important Terms for Section I

1. concept (page 507)
2. esteem (508)
3. skills (508)
4. worth (508)

Learning Objectives for Section I

1. (page 507)
2. (508-510)
3. (510-511)

Important Terms for Section II

1. discipline (page 513)
2. transitional (514)

Learning Objectives for Section II

1. (page 512)
2. (513-514)
3. (514)
4. (514-517)

5. (517, 518)
6. (518-520)
7. (520-523)
8. (523-525)
9. (525-526)
10. (526-527)
11. (527-528)
12. (528-529)

Important Term for Section III

1. prejudice (page 536)

Learning Objectives for Section III

1. (pages 529-530)
2. (530-533)
3. (533-536)
4. (536)
5. (537-538)

Important Terms for Section IV

1. acting-out (page 539)
2. phobia (540)
3. attached (540)
4. reactions (540)
5. insight (541)

6. client (541)
7. modification (541)
8. emotional disorders (541)
9. resilient (544)

Learning Objectives for Section IV

1. (pages 539-540)
2. (540)
3. (540)
4. (541-542)
5. (542-543)
6. (543)
7. (544)
8. (544-545)

CHAPTER 13 QUIZ

Matching-Aspects of the Developing Self-Concept

1. c (pages 507, 509)
2. g (508)
3. f (508)
4. d (514)
5. a (508)
6. e (532-533)
7. b (514)

Multiple-Choice

1. d (page 507)
2. c (508)
3. c (509)
4. a (509)
5. c (510)
6. d (511)
7. a (512)
8. a (512)
9. c (514)
10. b (515)
11. d (515)
12. b (517)
13. c (518-519)
14. d (520-521)
15. a (521)
16. b (523)
17. c (523-524)
18. b (524)
19. a (527)
20. a (529)
21. d (531)

22. c (533-534)
23. a (535)
24. b (537-538)
25. b (538-539)
26. c (540)
27. b (541)
28. c (542)
29. b (544)

True or False?

1. F—School-age children can make higher-order generalizations that include contradictory aspects of the self. (page 507)
2. T (509)
3. T (512)
4. T (513)
5. F—Although issues and disciplinary methods change as children get older, parents' basic approach to child rearing generally does not. (513-514)
6. F—Research has shown few adverse effects of mothers' employment. (514)
7. T (515)
8. F—Many self-care children are from well-educated, middle- to upper-class families in suburban or rural areas. (517)
9. T (519)
10. T (521)
11. F—The final task children face in their adjustment to divorce is achieving realistic hope about their own intimate relationships. (521)
12. F—Joint custody does not seem to help children adjust to divorce and may worsen the situation when the divorce has been bitter. (522)
13. T (522-523)
14. F—Six out of 10 custodial fathers are not married. (524)
15. F—A stepfamily is typically composed of a mother, her children, and a stepfather. (526)
16. F—Children who have moved 3 or more times are more at risk of emotional, behavioral, school, and health problems. (528)
17. F—Children of gay and lesbian parents are no more likely to have psychological problems or to be abused than children of heterosexuals. (528)

18. T (529)
19. F—When older siblings take care of younger ones, close bonds tend to form. (530).
20. F—The most common activities are conversation and "hanging out." (532)
21. T (534)
22. T (536)
23. T (537)
24. F—Children who continue to tell tall tales or lie frequently after the age of 6 or 7 may be acting out emotional problems. (539)
25. F—Children with school phobia should return to school as quickly (but gradually) as possible. (540)
26. F—A good psychotherapist will show acceptance of a child's feelings and of the child's right to have them. (541)
27. T (541)
28. F—Drug therapy is the treatment of emotional disorders with drugs. (541)
29. T (542)
30. T (542)
31. T (544)

PHYSICAL
DEVELOPMENT
AND HEALTH
IN ADOLESCENCE

OVERVIEW

Chapter 14 sketches the enormous physical changes that occur during adolescence. In this chapter, the authors:

● Discuss possible causes and effects of variations in timing of puberty

● Describe characteristic physical changes in males and females and psychological impacts of these changes

● Examine health issues and concerns, including causes, implications, prevention, and treatment of eating disorders, depression, drug abuse, sexually transmitted diseases, and abuse and neglect

● Describe trends and patterns in suicide among teenagers and suggest methods of prevention

CHAPTER 14 REVIEW

Section I Adolescence: A Developmental Transition

FRAMEWORK FOR SECTION I

A. Markers of Adolescence
B. Physical Changes
    1. Puberty
        a. The Timing of Puberty
        b. How Puberty Begins
        c. The Relationship between Stress and Puberty
    2. The Secular Trend
    3. The Adolescent Growth Spurt
    4. Primary Sex Characteristics
    5. Secondary Sex Characteristics
    6. Menarche
C. Psychological Issues Related to Physical Changes
    1. Effects of Early and Late Maturation
        a. Early and Late Maturation in Boys
        b. Early and Late Maturation in Girls
    2. Feelings about Menarche and Menstruation
    3. Feelings about Physical Appearance

IMPORTANT TERMS FOR INTRODUCTION AND SECTION I

Completion: Fill in the blanks to complete the definitions of key terms for this section of Chapter 14.

1. **adolescence:** Developmental transition period between childhood and _____.

2. **puberty:** Process that leads to sexual maturity and the ability to _____.

3. _____ **trend:** Trend noted by observing several generations; in child development, a trend toward earlier attainment of adult height and sexual maturity, which began about a century ago and appears to have ended in the United States.

4. **adolescent growth spurt:** Sharp increase in _____ and _____ that precedes sexual maturity.

5. _____ **sex characteristics:** Organs directly related to reproduction, which enlarge and mature in early adolescence; compare _____ sex characteristics.

6. _____ **sex characteristics:** Physiological signs of sexual maturation (such as breast development and growth of body hair) that do not involve the sex organs; compare _____ sex characteristics.

7. **menarche:** Girl's first _____.

LEARNING OBJECTIVES FOR SECTION I

After reading and reviewing this section of Chapter 14, you should be able to do the following.

1. Identify difficulties in precisely demarcating adolescence.

2. Tell what happens during puberty; state its duration and average age of onset in boys and girls; and discuss controversial research suggesting a relationship between stress and the timing of puberty.

3. List the typical sequence of physiological changes in adolescent girls and boys.

4. Define the secular trend and identify its most likely cause.

5. Describe the major physical changes that precede or signal sexual maturity: the adolescent growth spurt, changes in primary and secondary sex characteristics, and (for girls) menarche.

6. Compare psychological effects of early and late maturation in boys and in girls.

7. Discuss how adolescents feel about menarche, menstruation, and physical appearance.

Section II   Health Issues in Adolescence

FRAMEWORK FOR SECTION II

A. Health and Fitness
    1. Physical Activity—and Inactivity
    2. Other Health Concerns
    3. Health Care
B. Nutrition and Eating Disorders
    1. Adolescents' Nutritional Needs
    2. Obesity
        a. Consequences of Overweight
        b. Causes and Treatment of Overweight
    3. Anorexia Nervosa and Bulimia Nervosa
        a. Anorexia
        b. Bulimia
        c. Treatment for Anorexia and Bulimia
C. Depression
D. Use and Abuse of Drugs
    1. Current Trends in Drug Use
    2. Alcohol
    3. Marijuana
    4. Tobacco
E. Sexually Transmitted Diseases
    1. What Are STDs?
    2. Implications for Adolescents
F. Abuse and Neglect during Adolescence
G. Death in Adolescence
    1. Death Rates and Causes of Death
    2. Suicide among Adolescents
    3. What Society Can Do to Prevent Suicide

IMPORTANT TERMS FOR SECTION II

Completion: Fill in the blanks to complete the definitions of key terms for this section of Chapter 14.

1. **obesity:** Overweight condition involving a skinfold measurement in the _____ percentile.

2. _____ **nervosa:** Eating disorder, seen mostly in young women, characterized by self-starvation.

3. _____ nervosa: Eating disorder in which a person regularly eats huge quantities of food (binges) and then tries to nullify the effects by vomiting, purging, fasting, or excessive exercise.

4. **sexually transmitted diseases (STDs):** Diseases spread by sexual contact; also called _____ diseases.

LEARNING OBJECTIVES FOR SECTION II

After reading and reviewing this section of Chapter 14, you should be able to do the following.

1. Summarize health and fitness concerns about adolescents, particularly risks of athletic activity, dangers of inactivity, and the influence of poverty on access to health care.

2. List common nutritional deficiencies of adolescents.

3. Describe three common eating disorders—obesity, anorexia nervosa, and bulimia nervosa—and discuss their causes, effects, and treatment.

4. Give three reasons why adolescent girls are more at risk of depression than adolescent boys.

5. Identify trends, patterns, and consequences of drug use and abuse by adolescents, particularly with regard to alcohol, marijuana, and tobacco.

6. Identify symptoms, effects, and treatment of the most prevalent sexually transmitted diseases, discuss reasons for their high incidence among adolescents, and list suggestions for prevention.

7. Describe the nature and incidence of abuse and neglect of adolescents.

8. Name the three leading causes of death in adolescence, and differentiate death rates and causes by sex and race.

9. Identify trends and patterns of suicide among adolescents, and list suggestions for prevention.

CHAPTER 14 QUIZ

Matching—Health Issues: Match each term in the left-hand column with the appropriate description at the right.

1. Genital herpes simplex ___
2. Anorexia nervosa ___
3. AIDS ___
4. Alcohol ___
5. Chlamydia ___
6. Obesity ___
7. Trichomoniasis ___
8. Tobacco ___
9. Genital warts ___
10. Bulimia nervosa ___
11. Syphilis ___
12. Marijuana ___

a. eating disorder producing tooth decay and gastric irritation
b. failure of the immune system, caused by a virus transmitted through interpersonal exchanges of bodily fluids
c. drug used by nearly 9 out of 10 high school seniors
d. eating disorder associated with risk of life-threatening chronic conditions in adulthood
e. drug linked with lung cancer
f. eating disorder characterized by extreme thinness and distorted body image
g. most prevalent STD in the United States
h. small, painless growths
i. drug that can impede memory
j. STD that can lead to paralysis, convulsions, brain damage, and sometimes death
k. highly contagious, painful blisters with no known cure
l. second most common STD in the United States

Multiple-Choice: Circle the choice that best completes or answers each item.

1. Today the end of adolescence is
   a. no longer an important marker of development
   b. less clear-cut than before the twentieth century
   c. legally defined as age 18 in the United States for purposes of enlistment in the armed forces
   d. mainly a physiological phenomenon

2. Clitoridectomy is
   a. female sexual maturity
   b. male sexual maturity
   c. female genital mutilation
   d. male circumcision

3. The average age at which boys enter puberty is
   a. 10
   b. 12
   c. 13
   d. 14

4. During the past 100 years, the average age of sexual maturity in the United States
   a. has been dropping steadily
   b. has been dropping, but the trend has leveled off
   c. has been increasing
   d. has shown little or no change

5. The adolescent growth spurt often results in
   a. awkwardness
   b. disproportionate body parts
   c. nearsightedness
   d. all of the above

6. Which of the following are primary sex characteristics?
   a. pubic and underarm hair
   b. ovaries
   c. breasts
   d. all of the above

7. The first sign of puberty in girls is usually
   a. menstruation
   b. budding of the breasts
   c. underarm hair
   d. oily skin, leading to acne

8. According to some research, early-maturing girls are more likely than later-maturing girls to
   a. have a good body image
   b. be sociable and poised
   c. react positively to menarche
   d. have lower educational and occupational achievement as adults

9. The highest rate of injuries in high school sports is in
   a. football
   b. wrestling
   c. boys' soccer
   d. girls' cross-country running

10. The average teenage girl needs about how many calories per day?
    a. 1200
    b. 1500
    c. 1900
    d. 2200

11. About how many adolescents in the United States are obese?
    a. 1 in 5
    b. 1 in 10
    c. 1 in 20
    d. 1 in 50

12. The cause of anorexia nervosa is
    a. social pressure
    b. psychological disturbance
    c. physical disorder
    d. unknown

13. A sign of bulimia nervosa is
    a. loss of hair
    b. abnormal thinness
    c. eating very little
    d. each of the above

14. Who is most likely to suffer from depression?
    a. Aaron, who was cut from the football team
    b. Belinda, who has acne and experienced menarche the day she entered high school
    c. Cory, whose girlfriend just broke up with him
    d. any of the above

15. Overall, drug use among adolescents in the United States
    a. is more prevalent than ever before
    b. peaked during the 1960s and has declined ever since
    c. declined from 1979 to 1992 but then increased significantly
    d. increased during the late 1980s but decreased in the early 1990s

16. The leading cause of death among 15- to 24-year-old Americans is
    a. suicide
    b. homicide
    c. alcohol-related motor accidents
    d. drug overdoses

17. The most widely used illicit drug in the United States is
    a. hashish
    b. cocaine
    c. heroin
    d. marijuana

18. Which of the following statements about teenage smoking in the United States is true?
    a. Tobacco use has decreased continuously since the 1960s.
    b. More boys smoke than girls.
    c. Most smokers take their first puff in high school.
    d. Smokers become physically dependent on nicotine at about age 15.

19. Which of the following statements about the virus that causes AIDS is (are) true?
    a. It is always fatal.
    b. It has no known cure.
    c. Most victims worldwide are homosexual.
    d. all of the above

20. Which sexually transmitted disease has the following early symptoms: reddish-brown sores on the mouth or genitalia, and then a widespread skin rash?
    a. herpes
    b. gonorrhea
    c. syphilis
    d. AIDS

21. Physical abuse of teenagers is
    a. less common than abuse of younger children
    b. more common among girls than among boys
    c. more common among poor families than among middle-class ones
    d. more common among African Americans than among other groups

22. The leading cause of death of teenage black males is
    a. homicide
    b. suicide
    c. automobile accidents
    d. AIDS

23. About what percentage of high-achieving high school juniors and seniors say they have considered suicide?
    a. 5
    b. 15
    c. 30
    d. 50

True or False? In the blank following each item, write T (for *true*) or F (for *false*). In the space below each item, if the statement is false, rewrite it to make it true.

1. Among normal boys and girls, the time of onset of puberty varies by about 4 years. ___

2. Girls normally enter puberty about 2 years earlier than boys. ___

3. At puberty, the production of male and female hormones is triggered by the pituitary gland. ___

4. Some research suggests that girls who argue more with their mothers mature physically more rapidly than other girls. ___

5. The age at which youngsters reach adult height and sexual maturity is genetically determined. ___

6. The adolescent growth spurt begins earlier in girls than in boys.___

7. The principal sign of sexual maturity in boys is a nocturnal emission.___

8. The first menstruation means that a girl can become pregnant. ___

9. Early-maturing boys tend to have higher self-esteem than late maturers. ___

10. Most American girls today experience menarche negatively. ___

11. Most young teenagers are more concerned about their looks than any other aspect of themselves. ___

12. Adolescents from poor families are 3 times as likely as others to be in fair or poor health. ___

13. Anorexia nervosa is the most common eating disorder in the United States. ___

14. Antidepressant drugs can be used to treat anorexia and bulimia. ___

15. There is strong evidence of a hereditary influence on alcoholism.___

16. Use of marijuana first became common during the 1960s. ___

17. AIDS is caused by a bacterial infection. ___

18. Adolescents are more likely to be neglected than abused. ___

19. Girls are more likely to commit suicide than boys. ___

20. Most people who commit suicide have attempted it before. ___

TOPICS FOR THOUGHT AND DISCUSSION

1. Some research suggests that stress, perhaps caused by family conflict or other factors, may bring on early sexual maturation. Can you suggest a hypothesis other than those presented in your text to explain such findings? Can you suggest ways to confirm the conclusions of this research and to test various explanations?

2. The causes of both anorexia and bulimia are unknown. How might you design further experiments to test hypotheses about the causes of these disorders?

3. Can you suggest reasons why use of some drugs by adolescents has begun to increase after a 13-year decline?

4. Why are the health risks discussed in this chapter—eating disorders, drugs, and sexually transmitted diseases—particularly important in adolescence?

5. Your text, in Box 14-3, cites an example of a therapist who asked a pregnant teenager contemplating suicide to rank her options. Considering both the proper role of a psychotherapist and the other suggestions for preventing suicide given in the box, what should the therapist have done if the girl had ranked suicide as her best option?

CHAPTER 14 READING

INTRODUCTION

According to your text, suicide is one of the leading cause of death among teenagers. What percentage of young people who take their own lives, or try to, are gay or lesbian? Do the pressures of living as a homosexual in a predominantly heterosexual society contribute to higher suicide rates? Are gay and lesbian adolescents more likely to be under such pressures when they come out of the closet?

This article, reprinted from the 1995 issue of *Health & Human Development Research/Penn State*, reports on research that explored these and related questions. Anthony R. D'Augelli, a professor of human development at Pennsylvania State University, conducted the study in collaboration with Scott Hershberger, an assistant professor of psychology at the University of Minnesota, and Neil Pilkington, a doctoral student in clinical psychology at McGill University in Montreal. The research was supported by the Center for the Study of Child and Adolescent Development at Penn State and by a doctoral fellowship from the Social Sciences and Humanities Research Council of Canada.

SUICIDE AND INTOLERANCE

by Judith Maloney

As many as 30 percent of young suicides each year are gay and lesbian adolescents. Up to one-third of gay and lesbian adolescents try to take their own lives.

Reading these estimates in a 1989 federally funded report, Anthony D'Augelli, a Penn State professor of human development, thought they were perhaps too high.

Still, in conversations with young people here and around the country, he had heard their despair as they struggled to understand their sexual identities in the face of rejection from society, peers, and family. If open about their sexual orientation, they risked not just rejection, D'Augelli had learned, but persistent verbal attacks as well as physical abuse—from their peers and sometimes even from parents and teachers.

To what extent, he began to wonder, did this type of victimization jeopardize their mental health and adjustment, and could it be linked to suicidal patterns? To answer these questions, he decided to undertake a study of his own—"probably the first," he says, "that looks at the victimization issues in detail for young people, rather than for the general gay and lesbian population."

Studying young gay and lesbian people is problematic: They often are reluctant to identify themselves as gay, lesbian, or bisexual except in protected settings, like support groups in community centers; such centers are concentrated in metropolitan areas, giving researchers little or no access to rural subjects; and studies are necessarily limited to people who are "self-identifying"—that is, who have reached a certain level of conscious awareness of their sexual identities.

For D'Augelli's study, 194 15- to 21-year-olds in 14 lesbian and gay community centers in as many cities answered lengthy questionnaires—in confidential, adult-supervised group meetings—about their sexual orientation, social openness, level of disclosure within the family, experiences of victimization, and mental health problems. D'Augelli wanted to see how responses in different areas correlated: For example, were those who were more open about their sexual orientation more, or less, likely to be victimized?

The study divided victimization into three escalating levels: verbal abuse, including insults and threats of physical violence; minimal physical attack, including having objects thrown at one and being spat upon; and physical assault, including being punched or kicked, or being sexually assaulted. More than three-quarters of the participants (83 percent) said they had experienced at least one form of victimization. Verbal insults were reported by 80 percent of the youths; 33 percent said objects had been thrown at them and 13 percent had been spat upon; and 18 percent said they had been punched, kicked, or beaten because of their sexual orientation. About one-fifth, or 22 percent, reported at least one sexual assault.

The adolescents often allowed the abuse to go unreported. Some cited fear or embarrassment as their reason for keeping silent ("I was afraid of more harassment," one respondent wrote). Others described feelings of helplessness ("Authorities don't recognize bias crimes against gays"). Few in the study characterized their families as safe havens: Only 11 percent said that all their family members knew their sexual orientation and were supportive of them; 36 percent said they had been verbally abused, and 10 percent physically assaulted, by family members because of their sexual identities.

"When gay and lesbian kids tell their families about themselves," D'Augelli says, "they become more prone to being hurt."

D'Augelli tested for mental health problems among the study participants in a number of ways: As a measure of self-esteem, the subjects indicated agreement or disagreement with statements like, "At times I feel I'm no good at all." Participants rated their levels of distress about 12 concerns including anxiety, depression, and excessive drug use. They also filled out a brief inventory, designed to detect anxiety and other psychiatric symptoms. And they were asked about current suicidal thoughts ("Do you have thoughts about killing yourself?" rated on a four-point scale), and past suicide attempts—how many they had made, and methods used.

D'Augelli found much evidence of mental distress, with more than 50 percent of his subjects reporting that they were "very troubled" by depression and anxiety. About the same percentage said they had received professional counseling. The suicide attempt rates were even higher than those estimated by the 1989 federal report: Of the 194 youths participating in D'Augelli's study, 42 percent said they had made a suicide attempt, most of these by drug overdose; and 24 percent said they had made two or more attempts.

The results, D'Augelli says, reflect some complicated issues about openness. Those in the study who were less open about their sexuality, both with peers and with family members, reported more suicidal thoughts, suggesting that secrecy, and its accompanying feelings of shame and alienation, has a cost. Yet those more open about their sexuality—though they reported fewer suicidal thoughts—experienced greater victimization, which had significant negative effects on their mental health.

Although the study could not conclusively prove that victimization causes suicidal patterns, D'Augelli says its findings of mental health problems and suicide potential warrant concern and further study of this population. Even as society at large, he says, sends more messages of tolerance to gay, lesbian, and bisexual adolescents, and encourages them to be open at earlier ages, studies like his show that in their own private worlds of family and school they often continue to find themselves under attack.

QUESTIONS ABOUT THE READING

1. The article explains that studying young gays and lesbians is problematic because of the difficulty of identifying them. Thinking back to the discussion of research methods in Chapter 1, do you see any other possible problems with the type of research reported here?

2. In general, do the study participants tend to fit the profile given in your text of teenagers who are prone to suicide? If so, in what ways specifically?

3. The study had mixed findings about the effects on mental health of openly admitting a homosexual orientation. On the basis of the findings given here, would you have any advice for a gay or lesbian teenager who was considering whether to come out of the closet?

4. What steps can or should society take to reduce the risk of suicide among homosexual youth?

ANSWER KEY FOR CHAPTER 14

Note: Numbers in parentheses refer to pages in the textbook where answers can be found.

CHAPTER 14 REVIEW

Important Terms for Introduction and Section I

1.   adulthood (page 553)
2.   reproduce (555)
3.   secular (558)
4.   height, weight (558)
5.   primary, secondary (559)
6.   secondary, primary (559)
7.   menstruation (560)

Learning Objectives for Section I

1.   (pages 553-555)
2.   (555-558)
3.   (556)
4.   (558)
5.   (558-560)
6.   (561-562)
7.   (562-563)

Important Terms for Section II

1.   85th (page 566)
2.   anorexia (568)
3.   bulimia (569)
4.   venereal (574)

Learning Objectives for Section II

1.   (pages 563-566)
2.   (566)
3.   (566-570)
4.   (570)
5.   (570-574)
6.   (574-578)
7.   (578-579)
8.   (580)
9.   (580-582)

CHAPTER 14 QUIZ

Matching-Health Issues

1.   k (pages 574-575, 577)
2.   f (568)
3.   b (575)
4.   c (571-572)
5.   g (574, 577)
6.   d (566)
7.   l (574, 577)
8.   e (574)
9.   h (577)
10. a (569)
11. j (578)
12. i (573)

Multiple-Choice

1.   b (page 553)
2.   c (555)
3.   b (556)
4.   b (558)
5.   d (558-559)
6.   b (559)
7.   b (559)
8.   d (562)
9.   d (564)
10. d (566)
11. a (566)
12. d (568)
13. a (569)
14. b (570)
15. c (571)
16. c (572)
17. d (573)
18. d (574)
19. b (575-576)
20. c (578)
21. c (579)
22. a (580)
23. c (581-582)

True or False?

1.   F—Among normal boys and girls, the time of onset of puberty varies by 6 to 7 years. (page 556)
2.   T (556)
3.   T (556)
4.   T (557)
5.   F—The age at which youngsters reach adult height and sexual maturity has been

dropping, apparently as a result of higher living standards, though the leveling of this trend suggests some genetic limits. (558)

6. T (558)
7. F—The principal sign of sexual maturity in boys is presence of sperm in the urine. (559)
8. F—Early menstrual periods usually do not include ovulation; many girls cannot conceive for 12 to 18 months after their first menstruation. (560)
9. T (561)
10. F—Most American girls today take menarche in stride. (563)
11. T (563)
12. T (565)
13. F—Obesity is the most common eating disorder in the United States. (566)
14. T (570)
15. T (572)
16. F—Marijuana has been used all over the world for centuries but has become popular with the American middle class only since the 1960s. (573)
17. F—AIDS is caused by a viral infection. (575, 578)
18. T (579)
19. F—Boys are more likely to commit suicide. (580)
20. F—Ten to 40 percent of people who commit suicide have attempted it before. (582)

COGNITIVE DEVELOPMENT IN ADOLESCENCE

OVERVIEW

Chapter 15 examines progress in adolescents' cognitive development. In this chapter, the authors:

- Describe the dramatic changes in cognitive functioning that accompany the achievement of abstract and hypothetical thinking

- Identify immature thought processes and behaviors that appear in adolescence

- Explore the effects of cognitive development and cultural differences on moral reasoning

- Distinguish among three aspects of intelligence, which are useful in different kinds of situations

- Discuss effects of the transition to secondary school and summarize trends in high school education

- Examine influences on achievement in high school, and analyze the "dropout" phenomenon—who drops out, why, and with what consequences

- Outline stages in, and influences on, vocational planning

CHAPTER 15 REVIEW

Section I   Aspects of Cognitive Development

FRAMEWORK FOR SECTION I

A.   Cognition
1.   Cognitive Maturity: Piaget's Stage of Formal Operations
a.   The Nature of Formal Operations
(1)   Seeing New Possibilities
(2)   The Pendulum Problem
b.   What Brings About Cognitive Maturity?
c.   Assessing Cognitive Development: Limitations of Piaget's Theory
2.   Typical Characteristics of Adolescents' Thought
a.   Finding Fault with Authority Figures
b.   Argumentativeness
c.   Indecisiveness
d.   Apparent Hypocrisy
e.   Self-Consciousness
f.   Self-Centeredness
B.   Moral Development
1.   Kohlberg's Theory: Levels of Moral Reasoning
a.   Kohlberg's Moral Dilemmas
b.   Kohlberg's Levels and Stages
c.   Adolescent Moral Thinking
d.   How Do Adolescents at Different Levels React to Kohlberg's Dilemmas?
e.   Level I: Preconventional Morality
f.   Level II: Morality of Conventional Role Conformity
g.   Level III: Morality of Autonomous Moral Principles
h.   Evaluating Kohlberg's Theory
i.   Cross-Cultural Validity
j.   Validity for Females
k.   The Role of Experience
2.   The Influence of Social Context on Moral Development
a.   Gender Differences in Moral Development
b.   Family Influences on Moral Development
C.   Sternberg's Triarchic Theory of Intelligence
1.   Three Students
2.   Three Aspects of Intelligence
3.   How These Three Aspects of Intelligence Operate in Everyday Life
4.   The Triarchic Abilities Test

IMPORTANT TERMS FOR SECTION I

Completion: Fill in the blanks to complete the definitions of key terms for this section of Chapter 15.

1.   **formal operations:** In Piaget's terminology, the final stage of cognitive development, characterized by the ability to think

_____.

2.   _____: Observer who exists only in the mind of an adolescent and is as concerned with the adolescent's thoughts and behaviors as the adolescent is.

3.   **personal** _____: Conviction, typical in adolescence, that one is special, unique, and not subject to the rules that govern the rest of the world.

4.   **preconventional morality:** Kohlberg's first level of moral reasoning, in which the emphasis is on external control, obedience to the rules and standards of others, and the desire to avoid _____.

5.   **morality of conventional role conformity:** Second level in Kohlberg's theory of moral reasoning, in which children want to please other people and in which they have _____ the standards of authority figures.

6.   **morality of** _____: Third level of Kohlberg's theory of moral reasoning, in which people follow internally held moral principles and decide between conflicting moral standards.

7.   _____ **theory of intelligence:** Sternberg's theory describing three types of

intelligence: componental (analytic ability), experiential (insight and creativity), and contextual (practical knowledge).

LEARNING OBJECTIVES FOR SECTION I

After reading and reviewing this section of Chapter 15, you should be able to do the following.

1. Describe the capabilities characteristic of Piaget's stage of formal operations, particularly as illustrated by the pendulum problem.

2. Identify conditions that foster the achievement of cognitive maturity.

3. Cite some limitations of Piaget's theory.

4. Describe six immature thought processes or behaviors typical of adolescents, according to Elkind, and summarize research on the validity of his concept of the personal fable.

5. Identify and describe Kohlberg's three levels and six stages of moral reasoning, and give a typical answer to a moral dilemma at each stage.

6. Explain where and how most adolescents fit into Kohlberg's levels of moral reasoning, and give examples of reactions to a moral dilemma by persons at the preconventional, conventional, and postconventional levels.

7. Cite three criticisms of Kohlberg's theory.

8. Summarize recent research on gender differences in moral thinking, and identify five levels of the "ethic of care."

9. Discuss how interaction with parents can influence moral development.

10. Point out differences between the Chinese system of morality and Kohlberg's system.

11. Cite characteristics of, and influences on, a group of moral exemplars.

12. Define the three aspects of intelligence, according to Sternberg's triarchic theory; explain how they operate in everyday life, and how they can be tested.

Section II   Secondary School

FRAMEWORK FOR SECTION II

A. The Transition to Junior High or High School
    1. Patterns of Transition

    2. Effects of the Transition
       a. Gender-Related Correlates
       b. School-Related Correlates
       c. Home-Related Correlates
B. High School Today
    1. What Makes a High School Good?
C. Home Influences on Achievement in High School
    1. Parents' Interest
    2. Relationships with Parents
    3. Parenting Styles
    4. Socioeconomic Status
D. Dropping Out of School
    1. Who Drops Out?
    2. Why Do They Drop Out?
    3. What Happens to Dropouts?
    4. How Can Dropping Out Be Prevented?

LEARNING OBJECTIVES FOR SECTION II

After reading and reviewing this section of Chapter 15, you should be able to do the following.

1. Cite three factors that may make the transition from elementary school to junior high more stressful than going from elementary school directly to high school.

2. Summarize recent trends in high school education.

3. List at least four characteristics of a good high school and two practices that are harmful to low-achieving students.

4. Discuss four aspects of the home environment that influence achievement in high school.

5. Give arguments for and against part-time work for adolescents.

6. Cite ethnic, gender, and socioeconomic differences in high school dropout rates; discuss factors that influence students to drop out; summarize consequences of dropping out; and briefly describe a successful dropout prevention program.

Section III   Developing a Career

FRAMEWORK FOR SECTION III

A. Stages in Vocational Planning
B. Influences on Vocational Planning
    1. Societal Aids in the Transition from School to Work
    2. How Do Parents Affect Vocational Plans?
    3. How Does Gender Affect Vocational Plans?

LEARNING OBJECTIVES FOR SECTION III

After reading and reviewing this section of Chapter 15, you should be able to do the following.

1. Outline three classic stages in vocational planning.

2. Discuss the problems of noncollege-bound youth in making the transition from school to work.

3. Summarize the influences of parents and gender on adolescents' vocational planning.

CHAPTER 15 QUIZ

Matching—Numbers: Match each item in the left-hand column with the appropriate number from the right-hand column. (Note: Decimals have been rounded up or down to the nearest whole number.)

1. Percentage of Americans 25 and older who are high school graduates ___   3
2. Number of aspects of intelligence in Sternberg's triarchic theory ___   6
3. High school dropout rate (percent) for white Americans ___   9
4. Percentage of Upward Bound graduates who go on to 4-year colleges ___   14
5. High school dropout rate (percent) for Hispanic Americans ___   27
6. Percentage of American high school students who do not finish college ___   35
7. Percentage of male high school dropouts who were looking for work in 1987 ___   75
8. High school dropout rate (percent) for African Americans ___   77
9. Number of stages in Kohlberg's theory of moral development ___   80

Multiple-Choice: Circle the choice that best completes or answers each item.

1. An adolescent who can think abstractly, imagine possibilities, and test hypotheses is in Piaget's stage of
    a. concrete operations
    b. scientific operations
    c. logical operations
    d. formal operations

2. A successful solution of the pendulum problem depends upon
    a. careful observation
    b. trial and error
    c. inductive reasoning
    d. varying one factor at a time

3. Piaget's definition of cognitive maturity has been criticized for failure to consider
    a. nonscientific aspects of intelligence
    b. women's perspective
    c. cultural factors
    d. socioeconomic factors

4. Although Frank, aged 17, knows that drinking and driving is dangerous, he does it anyway. When his mother remonstrates, he tells her, "Get off my back, Mom—I'll be OK!" In Elkind's terminology, this is an example of
    a. argumentativeness
    b. the personal fable
    c. finding fault with authority figures
    d. apparent hypocrisy

5. According to Kohlberg, people indicate their level of moral development by
    a. their response to a moral dilemma
    b. the length of time they spend thinking about a moral dilemma
    c. the reasoning behind their response to a moral dilemma
    d. the kinds of moral dilemmas they consider

6. According to Kohlberg, a person's level of moral reasoning is related to
    a. training by parents
    b. education
    c. cognitive level
    d. emotional maturity

7. In Kohlberg's third stage, *maintaining mutual relations*, children obey rules because they want to
   a. avoid punishment
   b. be rewarded
   c. do their duty
   d. please and help others

8. Most adolescents are at which of Kohlberg's levels of moral development?
   a. preconventional
   b. conventional
   c. postconventional
   d. unconventional

9. *All but which* of the following have contributed to doubts about Kohlberg's theory?
   a. Research has failed to confirm his proposed sequence of stages.
   b. Men tend to score higher than women.
   c. People from nonwestern cultures score lower than westerners.
   d. The link between hypothetical and actual behavior is not clear.

10. When adolescents were administered the "Ethic of Care Interview,"
    a. younger teenagers scored higher than older ones
    b. girls scored higher than boys
    c. boys scored higher than girls
    d. none of the above; no significant age or gender correlations were found

11. Parents can best foster adolescents' moral development by
    a. letting them work out ethical dilemmas on their own
    b. asking clarifying questions
    c. giving advice
    d. lecturing

12. In Sternberg's triarchic theory, the componential element of intelligence is
    a. insightful
    b. practical
    c. analytical
    d. creative

13. Research on the transition to junior high school has found that
    a. girls find it especially stressful because they enter puberty earlier
    b. boys find it especially stressful because they are so much shorter than girls at that age
    c. boys and girls find it equally stressful
    d. neither boys nor girls experience as much stress as when they go directly from elementary school to high school

14. Of the following countries, which has the lowest percentage of high school graduates among adults age 25 to 34?
    a. Germany
    b. Japan
    c. Switzerland
    d. United States

15. Parents whose children do well in high school tend to be those who
    a. encourage children to look at both sides of an issue
    b. teach children not to argue with adults
    c. "ground" children who get low grades
    d. leave it up to children to do their homework

16. High school students with the lowest grades tend to have parents whose parenting style is
    a. authoritative
    b. authoritarian
    c. permissive
    d. inconsistent

17. Single parents tend to be
    a. authoritative
    b. authoritarian
    c. permissive
    d. inconsistent

18. Which of the following statements about the relationship between socioeconomic status and achievement in high school is true?
    a. Parents' educational and occupational levels are the most powerful factors in student achievement.
    b. Socioeconomic status is only weakly related to student achievement.
    c. Socioeconomic status indirectly affects student achievement through its influence on parenting styles.
    d. There is no significant relationship between socioeconomic status and student achievement.

19. A high school student who works more than 3 hours a day after school is more likely than a student who does not work part time to
    a. develop good work habits
    b. learn to handle money responsibly
    c. earn more money in later life
    d. drop out of school

20. Who of the following is most likely to drop out of high school?
    a. Ann, who lives with her divorced mother
    b. Brad, who lives with his divorced father
    c. Charles, who lives with his divorced father and stepmother
    d. Each of the above is equally likely to drop out.

21. Amy, who is 18, wants to be a teacher. She is applying to colleges with strong education programs and is working as a teaching aide at a local preschool. Which stage of vocational development does she appear to be in?
    a. fantasy
    b. tentative
    c. realistic
    d. active

22. Women who choose nontraditional careers tend to be
    a. only children
    b. eldest children
    c. middle children
    d. youngest children

True or False? In the blank following each item, write T (for *true*) or F (for *false*). In the space below each item, if the statement is false, rewrite it to make it true.

1. According to the Piagetian perspective, adolescents' idealism is a sign of cognitive immaturity. ____

2. Almost all adults reach cognitive maturity. ____

3. According to Elkind, adolescents exhibit egocentric thinking. ____

4. A high level of cognitive development produces an equally high level of moral development. ____

5. Kohlberg believed that morality results from internalizing the standards of parents and teachers. ___

6. A person at Kohlberg's postconventional level of morality can choose between two socially accepted moral standards. ___

7. According to Kohlberg, moral thinking is influenced by culture. ___

8. The Chinese system of morality is based on abstract principles of justice. ___

9. Colby and Damon's study of moral exemplars found that most of them scored at Kohlberg's highest level of moral reasoning. ___

10. Job performance is strongly correlated with IQ. ___

11. The transition to high school tends to be more stressful for youngsters who go to junior high school than for those who enter high school directly after 8 years of elementary school. ___

12. The average high school graduate today is better educated than an average graduate of 25 years ago. ___

13. Students who earn high grades tend to have parents who are highly involved and interested in their schooling. ___

14. Teenagers whose parents are experiencing marital conflict tend to have low grades. ___

15. Conflict with fathers seems to have more impact on teenagers' school performance than conflict with mothers. ___

16. Girls are more likely than boys to drop out of high school. ___

17. Students with poorly educated parents are more likely to drop out of high school than students whose parents are well educated. ___

18. Dropouts are more likely than high school graduates to lose their jobs. ___

19. A majority of dropouts later regret leaving high school. ___

20. Most high school seniors have a clear idea of how to reach their career goals. ___

21. Lack of vocational preparation tends to lead to crime. ___

22. A majority of high school students agree with their parents' educational expectations for them. ___

23. Boys generally have more mathematical ability than girls. ___

TOPICS FOR THOUGHT AND DISCUSSION

1. Do you agree with criticism (reported in your text) that Piaget's view of cognitive development is too narrow? Thinking back to the description of Piaget's background in Chapter 1, can you suggest possible reasons for the kinds of tasks he chose to assess cognitive maturity?

2. In research on Kohlberg's theory of moral development, why is the answer a child gives to a problem less important than the way the answer is arrived at?

3. Studies based on Kohlberg's theory of moral reasoning show that most adolescents are at a level where they have internalized standards of adult authorities, conform to social conventions, and define right conduct in terms of obedience to law. Yet, according to Elkind, teenagers take risks such as experimenting with illicit drugs because they believe they are not subject to the rules that govern the rest of the world. Can you suggest an explanation for this apparent contradiction?

4. Is criticism of Kohlberg's theory of moral development by Carol Gilligan and others similar to criticisms of intelligence testing for cultural bias? If these criticisms are valid, do they make both the theory and the tests useless? Can you suggest any ways to deal with these difficulties?

5. The authors of your text appear to espouse Gilligan's criticism of Kohlberg's "male-oriented" moral values of abstract justice, fairness, and rights. They suggest that we may need to "rethink our concept of morality" along the lines of "female-oriented" imperatives of compassion and caring. Do you agree that Kohlberg's system produces "black-and-white" thinking and omits concern for others? Do you see a danger in a moral system like the Chinese one, which is based on "intuitive and spontaneous feelings supported by society" rather than on analytical reasoning and individual choice?

6. How might a proponent of the view that intelligence is largely inborn respond to the information given in Chapter 15 about the influence of family relationships on adolescents' cognitive development and academic achievement?

7. Your text refers to the 6-3-3 pattern (6 years of elementary school, 3 years of junior high, and 3 years of high school) as typical. Years ago, the 8-4 pattern, in which youngsters went directly from eighth grade to high school, was the typical one. On the basis of the research discussed in Box 15-2, would you favor a return to this earlier pattern? Why or why not? Are there factors that should be considered besides those discussed in your text?

8. Socioeconomic status has been found to be an indirect rather than direct factor in school achievement. Does this finding suggest avenues that society could take to help parents at low socioeconomic levels improve their children's achievement?

9. Your text mentions one dropout prevention program, Upward Bound. However, that program appears to be aimed at a select group of students with potential for college success. Can you suggest any other approaches that might keep less able students from dropping out of high school?

10. Can you suggest ways to help adolescents make more realistic career plans?

CHAPTER 15 READING

INTRODUCTION

Rolland D. Lee, age 15, was president of his tenth grade class at Whitehorse High School in Montezuma Creek, Utah, when he wrote the following article, in which he talked about his art work, his Navajo heritage, and his future. His other interests ranged from singing and acting to playing basketball and editing the school yearbook. The article was originally published in the Summer 1989 issue of *Native Peoples* magazine; the excerpt below is from the Spring 1992 issue of *Teaching Tolerance*.

BECOMING NAVAJO

by Rolland D. Lee

My paintings tell what I'm like. They describe me in a way that fits my personality. My paintings tell what Navajo culture is like from my eyes. I am showing that we are deep thinkers.

Living here in Aneth, which is in the southeastern corner of Utah, is what you might call "OK." I live here with my mother, father, little brother and baby sister. We live in a Navajo housing community of 20 or so houses about 40 to 50 feet apart. It is quite boring to be living here. Most of the people here are not rich, but they work hard. My mother is a school teacher, and my father works in an oil field. They are both nice people and tell me to stay on top of my goals.

Almost every day my parents, my brother, baby sister and I go to my grandma's (shi'ma sani') house, which is on a mesa near Aneth. It takes us 10 minutes to get there. If there is no car, we just hike up the mesa in front of my house and walk a mile to grandma's house.

At my grandmother's house it is beautiful. To the south toward the San Juan River it is flat. To the east there is a mesa, and far away is the Sleeping Ute Mountain.

My grandmother's house makes me feel free. I can do anything up there. Run, play, bike, do chores, ride horseback and hike around. My grandmother watches out for me all the time and cares for my brother and sister. To me, she is a wise person who gives a lot of advice and listens to me. She is many persons to me. She's my teacher, guidance counselor and my friend. These things make the perfect grandmother.

While I paint, I think of my grandmother. She allows me to think. While I work on my art, I always put a part of her or her life into it. Although it doesn't come out clearly on my paintings, it shows after looking at it closely.

I noticed I use rug patterns, Navajo basket designs and Monument Valley landforms [in my paintings]. These are from my mother's side of the family. My aunts make rugs and baskets, and they live in Monument Valley. I also noticed I had things like Navajo jewelry and symbols of Navajo ceremonies such as feathers, tipis, waterbird pendants, drums and drumsticks. These things are from my father's family. So I know this is where my ideas for my paintings come from. All of these things are in my house.

When I look at my art I ask myself questions like, "What part of my life is in it?"

Like other artists, I think about growing up and what is in my future. To me, growing up is a struggle. I think of how I will be accepted in the world. I want to be known as Navajo by my family and on the reservation, but as a person out in the world. Being accepted as a person makes opportunities such as jobs and schooling.

Being a Navajo means different things to me. "Culture" is to believe in the traditions and the ways of your family. We keep our family together by doing lots of things. If somebody lets go, we bring them back in; make them feel like they belong. Culture also means a way to live. As a Navajo, I would prefer to live in a wide-open space and walk freely. If I moved to a city, I would have to give up these rights. I would live a "limit to what you can do" life. I know I would keep the ways of my family and still live regularly—get up, go to work, come home and spend time with family, but I would always remember where I came from.

QUESTIONS ABOUT THE READING

1. Your text stresses the influence of cultural factors on moral development. What values does Rolland Lee appear to hold most highly? Which, if any, of these values seem rooted in his Navajo culture? Is his pride in

his heritage and the symbols of his culture typical or atypical for a young person his age?

2. Throughout your text, the authors stress the influence of the family, particularly parents; in Chapter 15, they discuss parental influence on high school achievement and vocational planning. In comparing Rolland Lee's description of his parents and his grandmother, why do you think he gives so much more weight to his grandmother's influence? Are there things a grandparent can offer more easily than a parent to a child of that age? Or is the difference one of culture and lifestyle? What qualities does Lee say make his grandmother "perfect"? Do you think she would be as perfect for other high school students as she is for him?

3. Lee describes life in his community as merely "OK" and growing up as a "struggle." Yet he appears to be a superstar at school. How would you interpret his lack of enthusiasm about his social context?

4. Although Lee says that he would prefer to live in the wide-open spaces, he alludes to the possibility that he may someday move to a city. Do you think his values would be compatible with life in mainstream American society?

5. Lee refers to himself as an artist, and he speaks of his concerns about his future. From the clues given here, can you guess in which stage of vocational planning (discussed in Chapter 15 of your text) he appears to be?

ANSWER KEY FOR CHAPTER 15

Note: Numbers in parentheses refer to pages in the textbook where answers can be found.

CHAPTER 15 REVIEW

Important Terms for Section I
1. abstractly (page 589)
2. imaginary audience (594)
3. fable (594)
4. punishment (596)
5. internalized (596)
6. autonomous moral principles (596)
7. triarchic (605)

Learning Objectives for Section I
1. (pages 589-591)
2. (592)
3. (592-593)
4. (593-595)
5. (595-598)
6. (598-599)
7. (599-601)
8. (601-602)

9. (601-603)
10. (603)
11. (604)
12. (605-607)

Learning Objectives for Section II
1. (pages 607-609)
2. (609-610)
3. (611)
4. (611-615)
5. (615)
6. (616-618)

Learning Objectives for Section III
1. (pages 618-619)
2. (619-620)
3. (620-621)

CHAPTER 15 QUIZ

Matching-Numbers
1. 77 (page 610)

2. 3 (605)
3. 9 (616)
4. 80 (618)
5. 35 (616)
6. 75 (619)
7. 27 (618)
8. 14 (616)
9. 6 (597-598)

Multiple-Choice

1. d (page 589)
2. d (591)
3. a (592-593)
4. b (594-595)
5. c (596)
6. c (596)
7. d (597)
8. b (598)
9. a (599-600)
10. b (601)
11. b (602)
12. c (605)
13. a (608)
14. d (610)
15. a (613)
16. d (614)
17. c (614)
18. c (614)
19. d (615)
20. c (617)
21. c (619)
22. b (620)

True or False?

1. F—According to the Piagetian perspective, adolescents' idealism is a sign of attainment of cognitive maturity, the capacity for abstract thought. (pages 589-590)
2. F—Up to one-half of American adults apparently never reach cognitive maturity, as measured by formal operations tasks. (592)
3. T (594)
4. F—Factors other than cognition affect moral reasoning; advanced cognitive development is necessary for advanced moral development but does not guarantee it. (595, 598)
5. F—Kohlberg believed that morality is the result of reasoned judgments that people work out on their own. (596)
6. T (596, 597)
7. F—According to Kohlberg, moral thinking is universal—it transcends cultural boundaries. (601)
8. F—The Chinese system of morality is based on conciliation and harmony with community standards. (603)
9. F—Only half of the moral exemplars scored at Kohlberg's highest level of moral reasoning; the rest scored at the conventional level. (604)
10. F—Job performance is only weakly correlated with IQ but seems to be significantly correlated with aspects of tacit knowledge. (606)
11. T (607-608)
12. F—The average high school graduate today is not as well-educated as the average graduate in previous generations, when fewer people finished school. (610)
13. T (611-612)
14. F—According to one study, difficulties in parents' marital relationships do not seem to affect teenagers' grades. (612-613)
15. T (612-613)
16. F—Boys are more likely to drop out than girls. (616)
17. T (617)
18. T (618)
19. T (618)
20. F—Many high school seniors (about half in one study) do not plan on getting the appropriate amount of education to meet their career goals. (619)
21. T (620)
22. T (620)
23. F—There is little or no difference between boys and girls in tested mathematical ability. (620)

PERSONALITY AND SOCIAL DEVELOPMENT IN ADOLESCENCE

OVERVIEW

Chapter 16 focuses on the profound and sometimes disquieting personality developments that accompany the physical and cognitive changes of adolescence. In this chapter, the authors:

- Present theory and research on adolescent boys' and girls' search for identity

- Examine sexual attitudes and practices among adolescents

- Discuss teenagers' relationships with parents, siblings, and peers

- Explore causes, consequences, prevention, and treatment of teenage pregnancy and delinquency

- Examine findings on cohort differences in adolescents' attitudes and self-image

- Suggest further directions for research on how to help adolescents in high-risk environments

CHAPTER 16 REVIEW

Section I   The Search for Identity

FRAMEWORK FOR SECTION I

A.   Identity Versus Identity Confusion
B.   Research on Identity
 1.   Identity Statuses: Crisis and Commitment
 2.   Gender Differences in Identity Formation
  a.   Research on Female Identity Formation
  b.   Research on Female Self-Esteem
 3.   Ethnic Factors in Identity Formation
C.   Achieving Sexual Identity
 1.   Studying Adolescents' Sexuality
 2.   Sexual Attitudes and Behavior
  a.   Masturbation
  b.   Sexual Orientation
   (1)   What Determines Sexual Orientation?
   (2)   Homosexuality
   (3)   Attitudes, Behavior, and the "Sexual Evolution"
 3.   Communicating with Parents about Sex

IMPORTANT TERMS FOR SECTION I

Completion: Fill in the blanks to complete the definitions of key terms for this section of Chapter 16.

1.   **identity versus identity _____:** In Erikson's theory, the fifth crisis of psychosocial development, in which an adolescent must determine his or her own sense of self (identity), including the role she or he will play in society.

2.   **crisis:** Period of conscious decision making related to _____ formation.

3.   **commitment:** Personal investment in an occupation or a system of _____.

4.   **_____:** Identity status described by Marcia in which a person who has not spent time considering alternatives (that is, has not been in crisis) is committed to other people's plans for his or her life.

5.   **_____:** Identity status described by Marcia in which a person is currently considering alternatives (in crisis) and seems headed for commitment.

6.   **Identity _____:** Identity status described by Marcia, which is characterized by commitment to choices made following a crisis period, a period spent in thinking about alternatives.

7.   **Identity _____:** Identity status described by Marcia, which is characterized by absence of commitment and which may not follow a period of considering alternatives.

8.   **_____:** Sexual self-stimulation.

9.   **sexual _____:** Focus of sexuality, either heterosexual or homosexual.

10.   **heterosexual:** Sexually, romantically, and affectionately interested in members of the _____ sex.

11.   **homosexual:** Sexually, romantically, and affectionately interested in members of the _____ sex.

LEARNING OBJECTIVES FOR SECTION I

After reading and reviewing this section of Chapter 16, you should be able to do the following.

1.   Discuss how identity formation occurs in males and females and its relationship to the development of mature intimacy, according to Erikson.

2. Name the two elements that determine identity status, according to Erikson and James Marcia, and describe four categories of identity status identified by Marcia.

3. Summarize research findings on gender and ethnic differences in identity formation and self-esteem.

4. Name three difficulties of studying adolescents' sexuality.

5. Summarize research on the incidence of masturbation.

6. Summarize the present state of theory and research on origins of sexual orientation and give statistics on the incidence of homosexuality.

7. Discuss sexual behavior and attitudes among heterosexual adolescents today, reasons for early sexual activity, and the extent to which teenagers and parents communicate about sex.

Section II Social Aspects of Personality Development in Adolescence

FRAMEWORK FOR SECTION II

A. Relationships with Parents
   1. An Ambivalent Relationship
   2. Conflict with Parents
   3. What Adolescents Need from Their Parents
   4. How Adolescents are Affected by Their Parents' Life Situation
      a. Parents' Employment
      b. When Adolescents Care for Themselves
      c. Adolescents with Single Parents
B. Sibling Relationships
C. Relationships with Peers
   1. How Adolescents Spend Their Time—and with Whom
   2. Friendships in Adolescence
   3. Peer Pressure versus Parents' Influence
   4. Parents' Influence over Adolescents' Choice of Friends

IMPORTANT TERM FOR SECTION II

Completion: Fill in the blank to complete the definition of the key term for this section of Chapter 16.

1. **adolescent rebellion:** Pattern of tumult that may involve conflict with family, alienation from adult society, and hostility toward adults' _____.

LEARNING OBJECTIVES FOR SECTION II

After reading and reviewing this section of Chapter 16, you should be able to do the following.

1. Evaluate, on the basis of research, the concept of adolescent rebellion, and explain the ambivalent nature of adolescents' relationships with parents.

2. Describe the nature of most adolescent conflict with parents, and its course from early to late adolescence.

3. Identify the kind of parenting that seems to meet adolescents' needs best, and give at least three reasons.

4. Assess effects of maternal employment on adolescents.

5. Identify factors affecting the likelihood of antisocial behavior in "self-care" adolescents and those who live with single parents.

6. Describe changes in sibling relationships during adolescence and cite three factors that may influence these changes.

7. State how teenagers typically allocate their time among various activities and how much time they spend with family, friends, classmates, and others, and by themselves.

8. Describe the nature of friendship in adolescence and cite two factors affecting its quality.

9. Assess the relative influence of parents and peers.

Section III   Problems of Adolescence

FRAMEWORK FOR SECTION III

A. Teenage Pregnancy
    1. Understanding Teenage Pregnancy
        a. International Differences in Adolescent Pregnancy Rates
        b. Why Teenage Girls Do Not Use Contraception
        c. Who Is Likely to Get Pregnant?
    2. Consequences of Teenage Pregnancy
        a. The Mother
        b. The Children
    3. Preventing Teenage Pregnancy
    4. Helping Pregnant Teenagers and Teenage Parents
B. Adolescent Criminal Activity
    1. Personal Characteristics of Delinquents
    2. The Delinquent's Family
    3. The Delinquent's Neighborhood
    4. The Influence of the Peer Group
    5. Dealing with Delinquency

IMPORTANT TERM FOR SECTION III

Completion: Fill in the blank to complete the definition of the key term for this section of Chapter 16.

1. **status offender:** Juvenile charged with committing an act that is considered criminal only because the offender is a(n) _____ (for example, truancy, running away from home, or engaging in sexual intercourse).

LEARNING OBJECTIVES FOR SECTION III

After reading and reviewing this section of Chapter 16, you should be able to do the following.

1. Summarize current international trends in teenage pregnancy and policies for dealing with it.

2. Assess reasons teenagers give for failure to use contraceptives, and identify characteristics shared by teenagers who are likely to become pregnant and by the fathers of babies born to teenage mothers.

3. Cite consequences of teenage pregnancy for mothers and children.

4. List at least four guidelines for preventing teenage pregnancy, and identify ways of helping expectant teenagers and teenage parents.

5. Differentiate between two types of juvenile delinquency, and cite statistical trends in juvenile offenses by boys and girls.

6. Identify typical characteristics of juvenile delinquents, their families, and their neighborhoods, and cite two factors that increase the likelihood of falling in with antisocial peers.

7. Assess the impact of early childhood intervention in preventing delinquency, and discuss the difficulty of predicting how delinquents will turn out.

Section IV Adolescence: An Exciting Time of Life

LEARNING OBJECTIVE FOR SECTION IV

After reading and reviewing this section of Chapter 16, you should be able to do the following.

1. Discuss findings and implications of cohort studies of adolescents' attitudes and self-image.

2. List at least six possible directions for future research on how to help adolescents living in high-risk environments.

CHAPTER 16 QUIZ

Matching—Who's Who: Match each name in the left-hand column with the appropriate description in the right-hand column. (Note: Here, a description may be used to identify more than one name.)

1. G. Stanley Hall ___
2. Margaret Mead ___
3. Sigmund Freud ___
4. Anna Freud ___
5. Erik Erikson ___
6. James E. Marcia ___
7. Carol Gilligan ___
8. Laurence Steinberg ___

a. categorized identity statuses
b. studied peer pressure on self-care adolescents for antisocial behavior
c. held that parent-child friction comes from the adolescent's need for independence
d. formulated the first psychological theory of adolescence
e. held that the chief task of adolescence is to resolve the identity crisis
f. studied adolescence in cultures with minimal social change
g. studied female identity formation

Multiple-Choice: Circle the choice that best completes or answers each item.

1. According to Erikson, a major aspect of the adolescent's search for identity is the
    a. first sexual relationship
    b. changing relationship with parents
    c. career decision
    d. choice of a peer group

2. The virtue that arises from Erikson's fifth crisis is
    a. fidelity
    b. industry
    c. self-esteem
    d. independence

3. Erin has never experienced an identity crisis. She and her father have always been close. When he advised her to get an MBA and go into business, she took his advice. After getting her degree, she accepted a position with a large bank and made a down payment on a house. When she sees her friends agonizing over their career choices, Erin smiles with a trace of superiority. James Marcia would place Erin in the category of
    a. identity achievement
    b. foreclosure
    c. identity confusion
    d. moratorium

4. According to Gilligan, women achieve identity primarily through
    a. cooperation
    b. competition
    c. crisis
    d. careers

5. According to a survey by the American Association of University Women, which of the following girls would tend to show more self-esteem in high school?
    a. African American
    b. white
    c. Hispanic
    d. none of the above; no racial or ethnic differences in self-esteem were found

6. Research on sexual practices may be inaccurate because
    a. volunteers tend to be less sexually active than the population as a whole
    b. sexual mores are constantly changing
    c. subjects may not be truthful, and self-reports cannot be corroborated
    d. all of the above

7. Today, homosexuality is most widely attributed to
   a. mental illness
   b. seduction by a homosexual
   c. dominating mother and weak father
   d. a combination of biological, social, and psychological factors

8. The main reason teenagers give for early sexual activity is
   a. sexual desire
   b. curiosity
   c. social pressure
   d. media influence

9. The theorist who described adolescence as a time of "storm and stress" was
   a. G. Stanley Hall
   b. Sigmund Freud
   c. Anna Freud
   d. Erik Erikson

10. Margaret Mead's research on stress in adolescence highlights the importance of
    a. heredity
    b. culture
    c. sexuality
    d. maturation

11. The percentage of families in which serious conflict between adolescents and parents occurs is approximately
    a. 5 to 10
    b. 15 to 25
    c. 35 to 40
    d. 50 to 60

12. Which of the following usually is *not* an issue in arguments between adolescents and their parents?
    a. values
    b. schoolwork
    c. chores
    d. friends

13. Discord between adolescents and parents generally
    a. increases steadily during the teenage years
    b. increases during early adolescence, then decreases steadily during middle and late adolescence
    c. increases during early adolescence, then stabilizes during middle adolescence and decreases in late adolescence
    d. does not follow any particular pattern

14. Adolescents whose mothers are employed tend to
    a. show poorer social adjustment than other adolescents
    b. have more conflict with their families
    c. be more subject to peer pressure
    d. have lower self-esteem

15. The quality of sibling relationships in adolescence is most likely to be influenced by
    a. birth order
    b. spacing
    c. gender
    d. age

16. Adolescents tend to choose friends who are
    a. physically attractive
    b. outgoing
    c. athletic
    d. like themselves

17. Teenagers tend to rely more on the influence of parents than of peers in situations involving
    a. dress
    b. diet
    c. social activities
    d. job choices

18. The pregnancy rate in the United States for girls age 15 to 19 is about
    a. 5 percent
    b. 10 percent
    c. 25 percent
    d. 40 percent

19. What proportion of American adolescents use birth control during their first sexual experience?
    a. one-fourth
    b. one-third
    c. one-half
    d. two-thirds

20. *All but which* of the following are major factors in a teenage girl's likelihood of becoming pregnant?
    a. age
    b. sexual knowledge
    c. sexual practices
    d. amount of sexual experience

21. Which of the following is *not* a likely consequence of teenage pregnancy today?
    a. complications of pregnancy
    b. end or postponement of schooling
    c. low-birthweight baby
    d. quick adoption

22. According to one study, the single most important consideration cited by young teenagers in choosing a birth control clinic is
    a. location
    b. cost
    c. service
    d. confidentiality

23. *All but which* of the following are predictors of delinquency?
    a. record of imprisonment among family members
    b. low-income neighborhood
    c. strict parenting
    d. low IQ and poor educational achievement

24. Adolescents during which of the following decades seem to have had the most problems?
    a. 1960s
    b. 1970s
    c. 1980s
    d. none of the above; no significant differences were found

True or False? In the blank following each item, write T (for *true*) or F (for *false*). In the space below each item, if the statement is false, rewrite it to make it true.

1. According to Erikson, women cannot achieve mature intimacy until they have achieved identity. ___

2. According to Marcia, it may be just as healthy for women to achieve identity with or without going through a crisis. ___

3. High school girls tend to have higher self-esteem than high school boys. ___

4. The proportion of teenagers who say that they masturbate has increased since the early 1960s. ___

5. Homosexuals can change their sexual orientation with treatment. ___

6. Today's teenagers are more sexually active than those of the previous generation. ___

7. Most teenagers seem to become sexually active earlier than they say they should. ___

8. Teenagers who have talked with their parents about sex are more likely to use birth control consistently than teenagers who have not. ___

9. Recent research confirm's Freud's belief in the inevitability of adolescent rebellion. ___

10. Adolescents are more likely to have conflicts with their fathers than with their mothers. ___

11. Permissive parenting is the most effective style with adolescents because it gives them freedom consistent with their cognitive growth. ___

12. According to Steinberg's research, self-care makes adolescents vulnerable to peer pressure for antisocial behavior. ___

13. Adolescents who live with single mothers are less susceptible to peer pressure to get into trouble if the mother remarries. ___

14. Teenage siblings who are close in age tend to get along better than those who are spaced farther apart. ___

15. According to self-reports, adolescents spend about 5 percent of their time alone with their parents. ___

16. Adolescent friendships tend to be more intense than childhood or adult friendships. ___

17. Adolescent girls who feel guilty about premarital sex are more likely than other girls to use effective contraception. ___

18. Most fathers of babies born to teenage mothers are teenagers themselves. ___

19. A 15-year-old who robs a liquor store is considered a status offender. ___

20. Teenage boys are more likely than teenage girls to commit crimes. ___

21. Juvenile delinquents tend to commit crimes when they become adults. ___

TOPICS FOR THOUGHT AND DISCUSSION

1. According to your text, most psychologists today reject Freud's statement that "biology is destiny" in favor of the belief that "socialization is destiny." To what extent do the research findings cited throughout the text seem to support that position?

2. Erikson, who saw differences in the ways men and women achieve identity, has been criticized for taking the male pattern as the norm. To what extent is his theory consistent with the findings of Marcia and Gilligan concerning gender differences in identity achievement?

3. What similarities and differences do you see between Marcia's four categories of identity achievement and the three stages of career development described in Chapter 15? What factors are stressed by each?

4. Why does your text call the change in sexual behavior and attitudes since the 1920s a sexual "evolution" rather than a sexual "revolution"? What is the difference between the connotations of the two terms? Which do you consider more appropriate?

5. Freud agreed with Hall's view that storm and stress are inevitable in adolescence. But recent research shows that severe turmoil seems to occur only in a minority of adolescents. How might Freud explain this finding?

6. The Harris pollsters found very different results when they asked teenagers why other teenagers do not use birth control rather than why the respondents themselves do not use it. What other areas of research might benefit from this technique? Does it have any inherent flaws?

7. Sol Gordon, whose advice for preventing teenage pregnancy is included in Box 16-2 in your text, has said that teenage boys are "programmed to have sex" and that girls therefore must be taught to protect themselves. If so, would you hypothesize that such male "programming" comes from differences in socialization or differences in biological development? If boys had a more androgynous upbringing (as described in Chapter 10), would you expect the pressure for early sexual experience to diminish? Why or why not?

8. On the list of proposed new research approaches to help high-risk adolescents (on page 661 of your text), are there specific topics that would interest you as a prospective researcher? If so, how would you go about studying these topics? Would you like to add any topics to the list?

CHAPTER 16 READING

INTRODUCTION

Maya Angelou, born Marguerite Johnson, surmounted racial prejudice, the trauma of a rape at the age of 8, a teenage pregnancy, and a descent into prostitution to become a noted writer, dancer, and activist.

Marguerite, whose parents separated when she was 3 years old, was brought up by her strict, pious grandmother in a small, segregated town in Arkansas during the depression. For a brief period, she lived with her mother in the black ghetto of St. Louis, until she was raped by her mother's boyfriend.

Most of her sometimes unsettled teenage years were spent with her mother in San Francisco. The girl, who had always loved reading, got high grades in high school and took dance and drama classes at night on a scholarship.

This selection is from Maya Angelou's highly acclaimed autobiography, *I Know Why the Caged Bird Sings*, published in 1969. It is startlingly frank, remarkably objective, and impressively clear-sighted—qualities to be found in all of Angelou's work.

AN EXCERPT FROM "I KNOW WHY THE CAGED BIRD SINGS"

by Maya Angelou

A classmate of mine, whose mother had rooms for herself and her daughter in a ladies' residence, had stayed out beyond closing time. She telephoned me to ask if she could sleep at my house. Mother gave her permission, providing my friend telephoned her mother from our house.

When she arrived, I got out of bed and we went to the upstairs kitchen to make hot chocolate. In my room we shared mean gossip about our friends, giggled over boys, and whined about school and the tedium of life. The unusualness of having someone sleep in my bed (I'd never slept with anyone except my grandmothers) and the frivolous laughter in the middle of the night made me forget simple courtesies. My friend had to remind me that she had nothing to sleep in. I gave her one of my gowns, and without curiosity or interest I watched her pull off her clothes. At none of the early stages of undressing was I in the least conscious of her body. And then suddenly, for the briefest eye span, I saw her breasts. I was stunned.

They were shaped like light-brown falsies in the five-and-ten-cent store, but they were real. They made all the nude paintings I had seen in museums come to life. In a word, they were beautiful. A universe divided what she had from what I had. She was a woman.

My gown was too snug for her and much too long, and when she wanted to laugh at her ridiculous image I found that humor had left me without a promise to return.

Had I been older I might have thought that I was moved by both an esthetic sense of beauty and the pure emotion of envy. But those possibilities did not occur to me when I needed them. All I knew was that I had been moved by looking at a woman's breasts. So all the calm and casual words of Mother's explanation a few weeks earlier and the clinical terms of Noah Webster did not alter the fact that in a fundamental way there was something queer about me.

I somersaulted deeper into my snuggery of misery. After a thorough self-examination, in the light of all I had read and heard about dykes and bulldaggers, I reasoned that I had none of the obvious traits—I didn't wear trousers, or have big shoulders or go in for sports, or walk like a man or even want to touch a woman. I wanted to be a woman, but that seemed to me to be a world to which I was to be eternally refused entrance.

What I needed was a boyfriend. A boyfriend would clarify my position to the world and, even more important, to myself. A boyfriend's acceptance of me would guide me into that strange and exotic land of frills and femininity.

Among my associates, there were no takers. Understandably the boys of my age and social group were captivated by the yellow- or light-brown-skinned girls, with hairy legs and smooth little lips, whose hair "hung down like horses' manes." And even those sought-after girls were asked to "give it up or tell where it is." They were reminded in a popular song of the times, "If you can't smile and say yes, please don't cry and say no." If the pretties were expected to make the supreme sacrifice in order to "belong," what could the unattractive female do? She who had been skimming along on life's turning but never-changing periphery had to be ready to be a "buddy" by day and maybe by night. She was called upon to be generous only if the pretty girls were unavailable.

I believe most plain girls are virtuous because of the scarcity of opportunity to be otherwise. They shield themselves with an aura of unavailableness (for which after a time they begin to take credit) largely as a defense tactic.

In my particular case, I could not hide behind the curtain of voluntary goodness. I was being crushed by two unrelenting forces: the uneasy suspicion that I might not be a normal female and my newly awakening sexual appetite.

I decided to take matters into my own hands. (An unfortunate but apt phrase.)

Up the hill from our house, and on the same side of the street, lived two handsome brothers. They were easily the most eligible young men in the neighborhood. If I was going to venture into sex, I saw no reason why I shouldn't make my experiment with the best of the lot. I didn't really expect to capture either brother on a permanent basis, but I thought if I could hook one temporarily I might be able to work the relationship into something more lasting.

I planned a chart for seduction with surprise as my opening ploy. One evening as I walked up the hill suffering from youth's vague malaise (there was simply nothing to do), the brother I had chosen came walking directly into my trap.

"Hello, Marguerite." He nearly passed me.

I put the plan into action. "Hey," I plunged. "Would you like to have a sexual intercourse with me?" Things were going according to the chart. His mouth hung open like a garden gate. I had the advantage and so I pressed it.

"Take me somewhere."

His response lacked dignity, but in fairness to him I admit that I had left him little chance to be suave.

He asked, "You mean, you're going to give me some trim?"

I assured him that that was exactly what I was about to give him. Even as the scene was being enacted, I realized the imbalance in his values. He thought I was giving him something, and the fact of the matter was that it was my intention to take something from him. His good looks and popularity had made him so inordinately conceited that they blinded him to that possibility.

We went to a furnished room occupied by one of his friends, who understood the situation immediately and got his coat and left us alone. The seductee quickly turned off the lights. I would have preferred them left on, but didn't want to appear more aggressive than I had been already—if that was possible.

I was excited rather than nervous, and hopeful instead of frightened. I had not considered how physical an act of seduction would be. I had anticipated long soulful tongued kisses and gentle caresses. But there was no romance in the knee which forced my legs, nor in the rub of hairy skin on my chest.

Unredeemed by shared tenderness, the time was spent in laborious gropings, pullings, yankings and jerkings.

Not one word was spoken.

My partner showed that our experience had reached its climax by getting up abruptly, and my main concern was how to get home quickly. He may have sensed that he had been used, or his lack of interest may have been an indication that I was less than gratifying. Neither possibility bothered me.

Outside on the street we left each other with little more than "Okay, see you around."

Thanks to Mr. Freeman nine years before, I had had no pain of entry to endure, and because of the absence of romantic involvement neither of us felt much had happened.

At home I reviewed the failure and tried to evaluate my new position. I had had a man. I had been had. Not only didn't I enjoy it, but my normality was still a question.

What happened to the moonlight-on-the-prairie feeling? Was there something so wrong with me that I couldn't share a sensation that made poets gush out rhyme after rhyme, that made Richard Arlen brave the Arctic wastes and Veronica Lake betray the entire free world?

There seemed to be no explanation for my private infirmity, but being a product (is "victim" a better word?) of the southern Negro upbringing, I decided that I "would understand it all better by and by." I went to sleep.

Three weeks later, having thought very little of the strange and strangely empty night, I found myself pregnant.

QUESTIONS ABOUT THE READING

1. What motivated Angelou's sexual encounter? How does her motivation compare with those found by researchers on early sexual activity cited in your text? As far as you can tell, which, if any, of the factors cited in Table 16-6 seem to apply to Angelou?

2. In what ways did Angelou fit the pattern, described in your text, of adolescent girls who are likely to become pregnant? In what ways did she not fit the pattern?

3. Angelou appears to have given no thought to the possibility that she might become pregnant. Does her behavior demonstrate any of the adolescent thought processes discussed in Chapter 15 of your text?

4. This passage was written years after the incident it recounts. What indications can you find that this is the case? If Angelou had been writing in a diary at the time of the event, what (if anything) do you imagine might have been different about the narrative? What (if anything) might be much the same?

ANSWER KEY FOR CHAPTER 16

Note: Numbers in parentheses refer to pages in the textbook where answers can be found.

CHAPTER 16 REVIEW

Important Terms for Section I

1. confusion (page 627)
2. identity (630)
3. beliefs (630)
4. foreclosure (630)
5. moratorium (632)
6. achievement (632)
7. confusion (632)
8. masturbation (635)
9. orientation (635)
10. other (635)
11. same (635)

Learning Objectives for Section I

1. (pages 627-629)
2. (630-632)
3. (632-634)
4. (635)
5. (635)
6. (635-636)
7. (637-639)

Important Term for Section II

1. values (page 640)

Learning Objectives for Section II

1. (pages 640-642)
2. (642)
3. (643)
4. (643-644)
5. (644-645)
6. (645-646)
7. (646-648)
8. (648-649)
9. (649-650)

Important Term for Section III

1. minor (page 656)

Learning Objectives for Section III

1. (pages 650-651)
2. (651-653)
3. (653-654)
4. (654-656)
5. (656)
6. (656-658)
7. (658-659)

Learning Objectives for Section IV

1. (pages 659-660)
2. (660-661)

CHAPTER 16 QUIZ

Matching—Who's Who

1. d (page 641)
2. f (641)
3. c (641)
4. c (641)
5. e (627-629)
6. a (630)
7. g (632)
8. b (644)

Multiple-Choice

1. c (page 628)
2. a (629)
3. b (630-632)
4. a (632)
5. a (634)
6. c (635)
7. d (636)
8. c (638-639)
9. a (641)
10. b (641)
11. b (642)
12. a (642)
13. c (642)
14. c (643)
15. d (646)
16. d (649)
17. d (649)
18. b (650)
19. d (651)

20. c (652)
21. d (654)
22. d (655)
23. c (656-657)
24. b (660)

True or False?

1. F—According to Erikson, men cannot achieve mature intimacy until they have achieved identity, but women achieve both intimacy and identity at the same time. (page 629)
2. T (632-633)
3. F—According to a survey by the American Association of University Women, high school boys' self-esteem exceeds that of girls and drops less precipitously during adolescence. (634)
4. T (635)
5. F—There is no good evidence that treatment can change sexual orientation, and many mental health providers question the ethics of trying to do so. (637)
6. T (637)
7. T (638)
8. T (640)
9. F—Recent research suggests that rebellion is not a necessary hallmark of adolescence. (641)
10. F—Adolescents are more likely to have conflicts with their mothers than with their fathers. (642)
11. F—Authoritative parenting is the most effective style with adolescents; it takes their cognitive growth into account by explaining reasons behind the stands parents take. (643)
12. F—According to Steinberg's research, self-care does not, in itself, create vulnerability; the nature and environment of the self-care and the degree of indirect parental supervision are important factors. (644)
13. F—The presence of a stepfather does not reduce susceptibility to negative peer pressure except among the oldest adolescents, and then only slightly. (645)
14. F—Teenage siblings who are farther apart in years tend to get along better than those who are closer in age. (646)
15. T (647)
16. T (648)
17. F—Adolescent girls who feel guilty about premarital sex are less likely than other girls to use effective contraception. (652)
18. F—Most fathers of babies born to teenage mothers are beyond their teens. (653)
19. F—Robbery is an adult crime; status offenses involve violations of laws regulating minors only. (656)
20. T (656)
21. F—Except for a small group of "hard-core" offenders, it is almost impossible to predict which teenagers will commit crimes as adults. (658)